THE SUBTERFUGE OF ART

❈ THE SUBTERFUGE OF ART

Language and the Romantic Tradition

❈ Michael Ragussis

THE JOHNS HOPKINS UNIVERSITY PRESS

BALTIMORE AND LONDON

This book has been brought to publication with the generous assistance of the Andrew W. Mellon Foundation.

Manufactured in the United States of America

The Johns Hopkins University Press, Baltimore, Maryland 21218
The Johns Hopkins Press Ltd., London

Library of Congress Catalog Card Number 78-5845
ISBN 0-8018-2059-6

Library of Congress Cataloging in Publication data will be found on the last printed page of this book.

To Daniel

CONTENTS

ACKNOWLEDGMENTS

Garrett Stewart did more than anyone else, particularly at the beginning stages of this project (when we were colleagues together, and good friends, at Boston University), to encourage me to complete this book. His enthusiasm and subtle criticism led me to see this project whole, and to finish it.

J. Hillis Miller and Avrom Fleishman read large portions of this book when it was a completed manuscript; their advice was a great help to me and their generosity was, and still is, warmly appreciated.

By permission of the Oxford University Press, I have quoted from William Blake, *The Complete Writings of William Blake,* ed. Geoffrey Keynes (1966); Samuel Taylor Coleridge, *Coleridge: Poetical Works,* ed. Ernest Hartley Coleridge (1912); John Keats, *The Poetical Works of John Keats,* ed. H. W. Garrod (1956); Percy Bysshe Shelley, *The Complete Poetical Works of Percy Bysshe Shelley,* ed. Thomas Hutchinson (1905); William Wordsworth, *The Prelude,* ed. Ernest de Selincourt, 2d ed. rev. Helen Darbishire (1959); and William Wordsworth, *The Prose Works of William Wordsworth,* ed. W. J. B. Owen and Jane Worthington Smyser, 3 vols. (1974).

By permission of the Macmillan Publishing Co., Inc., I have quoted from the following works by W. B. Yeats: *Autobiography* (copyright 1916, 1935 by Macmillan Publishing Co., Inc., renewed 1944, 1963 by Bertha Georgie Yeats); *Collected Plays* (copyright 1934, 1952 by Macmillan Publishing Co., Inc.); *Collected Poems* (copyright 1906 by Macmillan Publishing Co., Inc., renewed 1934 by William Butler Yeats; copyright 1928 by Macmillan Publishing Co., Inc., renewed 1956 by Georgie Yeats; copyright 1933 by Macmillan Publishing Co., Inc., renewed 1961 by Bertha Georgie Yeats); *Essays and Introductions* (© Mrs. W. B. Yeats, 1961); *Explorations* (copyright © Mrs. W. B. Yeats, 1962); *The Letters of W. B. Yeats,* ed. Allan Wade (copyright 1953, 1954 by Anne Butler Yeats); *Mythologies* (© Mrs. W. B. Yeats, 1959); and *A Vision* (copyright 1937 by W. B. Yeats, renewed 1965 by Bertha Georgie Yeats and Anne Butler Yeats).

By permission of Harcourt Brace Jovanovich, Inc., I have quoted from the following works by E. M. Forster: *Aspects of the Novel* (1955); *A Passage to India* (1952); and *Two Cheers for Democracy* (1951).

By permission of the Viking Press, Inc., I have quoted from the following works by D. H. Lawrence: *Apocalypse* (copyright 1931 by the estate of David Herbert Lawrence); *Sex, Literature, and Censorship* (copyright © 1953, 1959 by Harry T. Moore); *Studies in Classic American Literature* (copyright 1923, 1950 by Frieda Lawrence, copyright © 1961 by the estate of the late Mrs. Frieda Lawrence); and *Women in Love* (copyright 1920, 1922 by David Herbert Lawrence, copyright 1948, 1950 by Frieda Lawrence).

LIST OF ABBREVIATIONS

A   W. B. Yeats, *Autobiographies* (London: Macmillan and Co., 1966)

AE   E. M. Forster, *Albergo Empedocle and other Writings* (New York: Liveright, 1971)

AN   E. M. Forster, *Aspects of the Novel* (New York: Harcourt, Brace and World, 1955)

Ap   D. H. Lawrence, *Apocalypse* (New York: Viking Press, 1960)

C   D. H. Lawrence, *The Complete Poems of D. H. Lawrence*, ed. Vivian de Sola Pinto and Warren Roberts, 2 vols. (London: Heinemann, 1967)

CAL   D. H. Lawrence, *Studies in Classic American Literature* (New York: Viking Press, 1961)

CL   D. H. Lawrence, *The Collected Letters of D. H. Lawrence*, ed. Harry T. Moore, 2 vols. (New York: Viking Press, 1962)

CP   W. B. Yeats, *The Collected Plays of W. B. Yeats* (London: Macmillan and Co., 1966)

CPY   W. B. Yeats, *Collected Poems of W. B. Yeats* (New York: Macmillan Co., 1966)

E   W. B. Yeats, *Explorations* (London: Macmillan and Co., 1962)

EI   W. B. Yeats, *Essays and Introductions* (London: Macmillan and Co., 1961)

HE   E. M. Forster, *Howards End* (New York: Random House, 1921)

L   John Keats, *The Letters of John Keats*, ed. Hyder Edward Rollins, 2 vols. (Cambridge, Mass.: Harvard University Press, 1958)

LY   W. B. Yeats, *The Letters of W. B. Yeats*, ed. Allan Wade (New York: Macmillan Co., 1955)

M   W. B. Yeats, *Mythologies* (London: Macmillan and Co., 1962)

P   William Wordsworth, *The Prelude*, ed. Ernest de Selincourt, 2d ed. rev. Helen Darbishire (Oxford: Oxford University Press, 1959)

PI   E. M. Forster, *A Passage to India* (New York: Harcourt, Brace and World, 1952)

PP   D. H. Lawrence, *Phoenix: The Posthumous Papers of D. H. Lawrence*, ed. Edward D. McDonald (London: Heinemann, 1967)

PW   John Keats, *Keats: Poetical Works*, ed. H. W. Garrod (London: Oxford University Press, 1966)

PWW   William Wordsworth, *The Prose Works of William Wordsworth*, ed. W. J. B. Owen and Jane Worthington Smyser, 3 vols. (Oxford: Oxford University Press, 1974)

R   D. H. Lawrence, *Reflections on the Death of a Porcupine and Other Essays* (Bloomington: Indiana University Press, 1963)

SLC   D. H. Lawrence, *Sex, Literature, and Censorship*, ed. Harry T. Moore (New York: Viking Press, 1968)

SPP   William Wordsworth, *William Wordsworth: Selected Poems and Prefaces*, ed. Jack Stillinger (Boston: Houghton Mifflin Co., 1965)

1

✻ THE SUBTERFUGE OF ART

LAWRENCE, FREUD, AND "VERBAL CONSCIOUSNESS"

D. H. Lawrence's position on the artist may at first seem mystifying. His charge that the artist is usually "a damned liar" is well-known, and my book takes its title from his general indictment: "Truly art is a sort of subterfuge" (*CAL*, 2). What may seem puzzling at the outset is the way Lawrence's practical criticism is aimed at a double target; it is directed against a list of famous writers (including Tolstoy, Hardy, Hawthorne, and Poe) at the same time that it is directed against Freud. After all, Freud is the twentieth century's most famous interpreter of subterfuge (whether it be in dreams, neurotic symptoms, parapraxes, or even art), and Lawrence's criticism of his fellow writers, it must be admitted, is distinctly Freudian. To make Freud a party to the tradition of subterfuge, and not the great author of a science that exposes and unmasks it, seems like a confusion on Lawrence's part.

Lawrence defines the problem by using a model of interpretation that has become the classic hermeneutical example for the nineteenth and twentieth centuries, namely, the idea of exegesis in Scripture (here it is the Book of Revelation). He even uses the archeological example (he wants to "dig the actual truth out of" the American texts, *CAL*, 2) seen in other writers of this tradition and made most famous in Freud's archaisms: "It is one book, in several layers: like layers of civilisation as you dig deeper and deeper to excavate an old city. Down at the bottom is a pagan substratum, probably one of the ancient books of the Aegean civilisation: some sort of book of a pagan Mystery. This has been written over by Jewish apocalyptists, then extended, and then finally written over by the Jewish-Christian apocalyptist John: and then, after his day, expurgated and corrected and pruned down and added to by Christian editors who wanted to make of it a Christian work" (*Ap*, 54). The example is important because it suggests how, in the literary texts Lawrence examines (*Anna Karenina* or *The Scarlet Letter*), a cosmetic morality exists at the surface of the work. The terminology Lawrence uses, even here in this scriptural example, is close to Freud's, with the substratum being pagan and obviously passional or unconscious, and with the Freudian censor expurgating and distorting the original text (the pruning down is a particularly vivid image of expurgation as castration). The moralizing that Lawrence detects in novels makes them immoral (in a play on words he learned from Nietzsche), by upsetting the natural balance between theory and praxis, or philosophy and life: the novelist becomes didactic, and the novel's superficial purpose depends on some moral principle (or what Nietzsche calls "interest").

Lawrence's analysis typically explains the author's purpose, then moves deeper into the passion that is being censored and masked. Lawrence uses his analyses not only to revise a tradition (or to unearth it), but also to remind himself that "the danger is, that a man shall make himself a metaphysic to excuse or cover his own faults or failure. Indeed, a sense of fault or failure is the usual cause of a man's making himself a metaphysic, to justify himself." Tolstoy is a central example: "Probably because of profligacy in his youth, because he had disgusted himself in his own flesh, by excess or by prostitution, therefore Tolstoi in his metaphysic, renounced the flesh altogether, later on, when he had tried and tried and had failed to achieve complete marriage in the flesh" (*PP*, 479). The example of Tolstoy here is a crucial one because it so clearly bears the earmarks of both Nietzsche and Freud: the general notion of art as compensation is finally pinpointed by an emphasis on sexual repression. Moreover, it shows the failure of ideas in the novel. It is an example of the central danger of the novelist, namely, that "having made himself a metaphysic of self-justification, or a metaphysic of self-denial, the novelist proceeds to apply the world to this, instead of applying this to the world" (479).

The argument takes a crucial turn, however, when we find that this is not a danger that only the artist faces. Freud is not exempt from the problematic relationship between theory and life that Lawrence sees in the novelist. In fact, Lawrence turns the tables (or couch) on Freud. If Freud sees in art only a particular form of wish fulfillment whose strategies of distortion, projection, and displacement it shares with dreams, myth, fairy tales, and slips of the tongue and pen, Lawrence sees in psychoanalysis the same kind of theorizing he detects in art. Freud can thus take his place beside Tolstoy or Hawthorne or Poe on the patient's couch:

> Theory as theory is all right. But the moment you apply it to *life*, especially to the subjective life, the theory becomes mechanistic, a substitute·for life, a factor in the vicious unconscious. . . .
> In short, the analyst is just as much fixed in his vicious unconscious as is his neurotic patient, and the will to apply a mechanical

incest-theory to every neurotic experience is just as sure an evidence of neurosis, in Freud or in the practitioner, as any psychologist
could ask. (*PP,* 378)

This is a call to the physician to heal himself. Psychoanalysis is no
longer the universal science that unravels all puzzles, but just one more
theory, itself a neurotic puzzle. It is no different from the artist's own
theorizing because it is an attempt to apply one's metaphysic to the
world. This attack on Freud is a somewhat familiar tactic that the writers
in this tradition use, placing art's greatest critics in an embarrassing position next to the artist himself. For example, Yeats makes Plato's law-
givers the co-conspirators of the artist in "Nineteen Hundred and Nineteen" the way Lawrence makes Freud's psychoanalysts similar conspira-
tors. It is true that Lawrence's approach to the American classics sounds
psychoanalytic in its attempt to bring to light the hidden, or latent,
instinctual impulse behind a collection of classic American stories,
novels, and poems. Contemporary moral codes that become internalized
in the writer mask the often erotic impulses of a work, and Lawrence's
reading of the American writers is justifiably often psychoanalytic: these
American writers "always put up a sort of double meaning," they "revel
in subterfuge," they "prefer their truth safely swaddled in an ark of bul-
rushes . . . until some friendly Egyptian princess comes to rescue the
babe" (*CAL,* viii). The princess turns out to be, however, no bearded
psychoanalyst, but (as if in a fairy tale of its own) the reader himself,
art's only true apologist. The reader is able to save the tale from the
artist, if not the artist from the neurosis.

Actually, the artist can save himself from neurosis, we discover. But
first Lawrence makes it clear that, typically, both the tale and the artist
are prisoners to a philosophy, or metaphysic: the tale is imprisoned by
the philosophy of the author, and the artist himself is prisoner to a moral
philosophy that in turn distorts his tale. The artist's passions go underground, and the work of art seems to declare a didactic philosophy.

The turning point in Lawrence's criticism occurs when he imagines
quite another kind of text: "The degree to which the system of morality,
or the metaphysic, of any work of art is submitted to criticism within the
work of art makes the lasting value of that work" (*PP,* 476). At first this
notion of self-criticism may seem no more than Lawrence's claim, in his
study of the American classics, that while the artist is a liar, the tale always tells the truth. Even the declaration that "the author may have a
didactic 'purpose' up his sleeve. . . . But even a didactic purpose so wicked
as Tolstoi's or Flaubert's cannot put to death the novel" (*R,* 104) keeps
the artist prisoner, if not the tale. I suggest, however, that Lawrence conceives of the greatest artists as internalizing that mechanism of self-

criticism that he mysteriously bestows on the tale: rather than remaining a liar till the end and never learning the true meaning of his tale, the great artist deliberately sets out to turn a self-critical eye on his work. Lawrence envisions art, and particularly the art of the novel, as a special kind of reflection that can in fact criticize its own systems and theories.

This leads Lawrence to the famous and often misunderstood claim, "One sheds one's sicknesses in books, repeats and presents again one's emotions to be master of them" (*CL*, 234). Lawrence takes the Aristotelian view of art as catharsis, then turns it around by making not the audience (at least at first) but the writer the one who benefits from the catharsis. Shedding one's sicknesses in books does not mean simply an unbridled rehearsal of one's emotions or even a simple cathartic release. There is a sophisticated discrimination, in Lawrence's view, between the artist whose art is his cure and the artist whose art is merely his symptom (like Tolstoy, for example). To use the terms of Lawrence's foreword to *Women in Love,* to shed these sicknesses requires the presentation of one's emotions or the recording of the profoundest experiences of the self. Lawrence in fact imagines this curative process to be like the "talking cure" of psychoanalysis, which posits as a cure the coming into full consciousness, and thereby a freedom to direct one's own destiny, through the articulation, to the analyst and to oneself, of one's deepest emotions and thoughts. Freud and Lawrence even use the same term— "verbal consciousness"—to describe this process. Freud explains that "the process of becoming conscious," at least "as regards memories," "consists for the most part in the appropriate *verbal* consciousness." He draws the conclusion that "an increase in the uninhibited processes to the point of their alone being in possession of the path to verbal consciousness produces *psychoses.*"[1] The corollary is clear, and is of course at the center of the recent interpretations of Freud, most obviously by Jacques Lacan and Paul Ricoeur, where the psychoanalytic venture becomes the adventure into language. Lawrence similarly sees in the "record of the writer's own desires, aspirations, struggles" the shedding of his sicknesses: to make "a record of the profoundest experiences in the self" is to engage, Lawrence tells us, in "verbal consciousness," that is, in "the passionate struggle into conscious being" (*WL*, viii).

Freud and Lawrence, however, part company even here, not because of any overt disagreement, but over a step Lawrence takes in his esthetics that Freud, never giving us a complete esthetic theory, neglects. While Lacan can talk about the subject's becoming the exegete of his own dream,[2] there is, of course, still the dependency on the analyst: Lacanian psychoanalysis depends on intersubjectivity, on the dialectic between the subject and the analyst. Lawrence attempts to describe a similar dialectic (which I will describe fully in my chapter on *Women in Love*) without recourse to the psychoanalyst. He manages this because of the special nature of verbal consciousness as he defines it: if language is the royal road to consciousness for Freud (to alter one of his most famous apothegms), he neglects the fact that the writer may develop a special language through which he sheds his sicknesses. The dialectic between patient and analyst becomes replaced in Lawrence by another kind of dialectic: it is not the work of art (like the dream-work) submitted to the analyst (though this is something like the cure for literary texts Lawrence finds governed by repression), but the artist's discovering a special language that analyzes and tests itself (what Freud was able to do in some of his most interesting essays; in fact Freud the writer, as opposed to Freud the practising analyst, even uses the writer's dialectical strategy when he invents, in *The Question of Lay Analysis* and *The Future of an Illusion,* an imaginary interlocutor). This language is capable of a subtle overhearing of itself. In this sense it becomes "art-speech" (*CAL,* 1-2), and is like Yeats's choice of poetry ("a quarrel with ourselves") over rhetoric ("a quarrel with others") (*M,* 331). It is to be conceived not simply as the script of a writer, but as a kind of writing that attains the dialectic of speech, really of dialogue. This special language avoids, then, the pitfalls of free association (psychoanalysis) and algebraic symbolization (logic). It is not the repressed and distorted language of the neurotic, dependent on the trained psychoanalyst for unravelling, sometimes about to lapse into the language of madness, or even into complete silence; neither is it what Lawrence mocks as "the algebraical tack: Let X stand for sheep and Y for goats" (*PP,* 520), a symbolic language that, to avoid ambiguity, has so diminished itself that its relation to life is insignificant. It is a language that enables heart and mind to join in an interrogation of each other.

LITERATURE AND REGRESSION

Lawrence's position on the artist as liar and on the language the writer uses is a late one. Literary criticism has assiduously claimed the impossibility of finding the roots of Lawrence's thought. This is a result, I think, of literary criticism's own romantic myth of genius, which steadfastly holds on to a rather naïve idea of originality to allow Lawrence's greatness. I take the opposite view; I think that Lawrence's debt to European thought (particularly to Hegel, Nietzsche, Marx, and Freud) is as clear as it is profound; and my prime interest in this book is to define a literary tradition of which Lawrence is perhaps the climax, namely, the tradition of English Romantic and post-Romantic literature. If Lawrence, in my reading, is this tradition's omega, Wordsworth is its progenitor, its alpha (for me the first and last letters that articulate the language of Romanticism). By reopening the argument over Nature and Art, Wordsworth begins for the writers I analyze the reinvestigation of language and its relationship to art, which still remains something of a terra incognita in our understanding of this tradition.

My chapter on Wordsworth shows his meditation on this problem in the well-known Arab dream episode from *The Prelude,* a passage not often thought crucial in this regard. The dream begins with an apparently irreconcilable distinction—Nature is everlasting, while Art is temporary— but by slowly disclosing similarities, it eventually reveals that both have their origins in language, even the same language. The common language of humanity, true and universal, is Wordsworth's answer to the argument over Nature and Art—a language of nature is what art speaks. I end this chapter on Wordsworth by considering his fears about language: it can be a set of tricks and hieroglyphics, to subvert and derange. Ironically, it is these fears, more than any hope, that the subsequent writers inherit: if the main thrust of Wordsworth's thought at the beginning of the nine- teenth century is to reinterpret the language of poetry and to distinguish and save it from the false rhetoric of the previous century, his legacy to the writers who follow is not the natural language he invents (or redis- covers). Instead, the new standards for verse—particularly its truth to experience—become increasingly an end that eludes these writers. In short, Wordsworth's solution looms less grand on the horizon of this tra- dition than the fears that underlie it.

The Arab dream provides my study with a dominant theme, and even with a topography: each writer in his turn takes up the same landscape of the dream (a setting so universal that its source goes beyond Wordsworth, beyond Milton, to Ovid and Plato and the Old Testament)—the desert void, and the Word able to transform it—but in succeeding writers the Word's efficacy dwindles. This may at first seem to contradict what I have said about Lawrence's hopes for language. Suffice it to say at this point, first, that the language each writer develops is not necessarily based strictly on the Word (and may in fact even be defined as its anti- thesis) and, second, that the language each writer develops is open to its own further criticism—a special form of verbal irony that is as crucial to this tradition as is its hopeful new language.

Again a Freudian model is useful to illustrate the coherence of the tradition (beyond the more obvious thematic and technical similarities I have already mentioned) and to articulate the problem of art's subterfuge in its most well-known twentieth-century formulation. I do not have in mind my own criticism, or even analysis, of Freud's esthetics (if there even is such a thing). I wish simply to take Freud's description of three kinds of regression to show how the writers in this literary tradition define art not only as opposed to, but even as a cure for, regression. This is counter to the popular suggestion that art, because so often seen as analogous to dreams and neurotic symptoms, is regressive.[3] "Three kinds of regression are thus to be distinguished: (a) *topographical* regression, in the sense of the schematic picture of the ψ-systems which we have explained above; (b) *temporal* regression, in so far as what is in question is a harking back to older psychical structures; and (c) *formal* regression, where primitive methods of expression and representation take the place of the usual ones. All these three kinds of regression are, however, one at bottom and occur together as a rule; for what is older in time is more primitive in form and in psychical topography lies nearer to the perceptual end."[4] Happily this model of triple regression is rather consistently either anticipated by the writers before Freud or answered by his contemporaries.

Each chapter of my book studies the devising of a strategy against subterfuge in a particular poem or novel. Perhaps the clearest contradiction of the Freudian model in these writers is the deliberate short-circuiting of the basic association between dreams and art: it is of course an association older than Freud, which such writers as Keats and Yeats turn around so profoundly that the nightmare becomes a clearer model for the literary work. In Keats the dream is either abruptly interrupted or turned to nightmare and in Yeats the dream gives way to the Vision of Evil, a special form of the nightmare. In Forster the vision of evil, lest it become too grandiose and itself a concocted artistic sublimity, comes not to poetry at all, but to the everyday world of fiction. (Freud's later work with the recurring nightmare has the status in his work of a correction similar to that found in these writers, where the earlier association, dream-art, is replaced, or at least deepened, by nightmare-art. Because it prepares the subject to meet the shocks of reality, the recurring nightmare Freud describes seems a better model for the work of art than the ego-gratifying daydream he used earlier.) In all cases this means a resistance to consolation: art, we discover, well knows the folly of being comforted. The writer's desire is redefined as the desire for whatever happens (Yeats), and the Nietzschean Eternal Return (based on the classical *amor fati*) and the Freudian Ananke (Necessity) are its analogues.

This dissociation between art and dreams quintessentially defines writer and reader not as children, but as adults; the work of art criticizes the dream state, and educates one to discriminate between illusion and reality. In this way the work of art criticizes what Freud calls "temporal regression," or the return to infancy. In fact, as work, it becomes the burden of the adult, not the play of the child. Despite the modern view of play as a form of work (Freud's notion of play as mastery, the language games of Saussure and Wittgenstein, and Nietzsche's view of the philosopher as the one who plays the dangerous game), such writers as Keats and Yeats see the work of art as the antithesis to the idleness or play of fantasy where wishes are easily fulfilled. (Freud, with his insistence on such terms as the dream-work or the work of mourning or the *durcharbeiten*, suggests the labor of all mental processes.) The work of art is the labor of self-education, pictured most famously in the labor imposed on the poet in "The Fall of Hyperion." This labor in fact is seen as the deed of life.

These writers begin, like Freud himself, to impress upon us the word's power by reiterating, even while they subtly devalue, the ancient discrimination between word and deed (or work). Freud explains, for example, that "Nothing takes place between [the analyst and the patient] except that they talk to each other. . . . Do not let us despise the *word*. After all it is a powerful instrument; it is the means by which we convey our feelings to one another, our method of influencing other people. Words can do unspeakable good and cause terrible wounds. No doubt 'in the beginning was the deed' and the word came later; in some circumstances it meant an advance in civilization when deeds were softened into words. But originally the word was magic—a magical act; and it has retained much of its ancient power."[5] Freud is somewhat equivocal, and while in the end he chooses Goethe's formulation over that in the Fourth Gospel, still he makes clear the power of the word. Keats sounds a similar note when he explains, "fine writing is next to fine doing the top thing in the world" (*L*, 2, 146). Kierkegaard explains what eventually all these writers try to remind us (and themselves) of, namely, "It seems to be quite forgotten that to be an author is action."[6] Wittgenstein brings to a close the long development of nineteenth- and twentieth-century thought about the language act: "Words are also deeds."[7] While the regressive character of dreams allows merely the hallucinatory fulfillment of desire (we know that the nocturnal nature of the dream suspends motor activity, and thereby the potential external consequences of the dream), the literary *work*, as the deed of language, directs an idea not backward to the perceptual end of the psychical apparatus where it becomes a hallucinatory image (Freud's "topographical regression"), but forward to language and action (here one must acknowledge the conjunction of word and deed). Some may even claim the word prior, in time and value, to the deed: Lacan turns the Goethe text around, for example, to make his version of Freudian psychoanalysis put the word once again in the beginning.[8] Even Freud's explanation that nothing takes place between analyst and patient except talk may suggest the primacy of the word, either by showing the word as work (the work of analysis is the "talking cure") or by showing talk as the necessary preparation for action ("In the beginning was the word").

Sexuality, perhaps even more than labor, signals the awakening from the childish dream state because, quite naturally, it is the mark of adulthood; and by a pun labor manages to represent at once not only work but also the childbirth that is the result of sexuality. The dream is an expression of infantile fantasy, and as such, imagines love too easily, with no view to its consequences and the responsibilities it involves, even picturing love as a sleepy state of womblike gratification in which the subject has yet to separate from its love object. This kind of regression, for example, is seen in Madeline's dream wish to be a bud again, despite the evidence of the (sexual) stain of rose-bloom all about her ("St. Agnes"); or in a modern culture's dream wish to intoxicate itself with its toys (defined by Yeats as its art and politics), even though these toys "un-man" it, reducing it to a childish state of impotence ("Nineteen Hundred and Nineteen"); or in Gudrun and Gerald's desire, in *Women in Love,* to gain from sexual desire a sleep that is a return to the womb—a sleep like Madeline's, or even like that of Hyperion, who rests in the cradle of a womblike heaven he nostalgically sees disappearing.

Art criticizes infantile wishes and seeks a goal similar to that of psychoanalysis—to make us renounce archaic practices. In fact, in what Freud calls *"the education to reality,"*[9] can be found that great theme of English Romanticism, the development from innocence to experience, or what the German tradition has called the Bildungsgeschichte and the Bildungsroman. The education to reality is made possible only by art's refusal to indulge these childish wishes, so that rather than providing a comfortable environment in which the reader can enjoy, without the anxiety of reproach, his daydreams (what Freud claims art does),[10] the artist develops strategies to awaken the reader from the dream. The willing suspension of disbelief becomes a suspension of all critical faculties that is criticized as a naïve and sometimes dangerous practice. Moreover, the work of art has the power to engage us in the magic of illusion, and thereby use its power of subterfuge, only to turn on itself critically and in this moment to show how it is one step ahead of us. It shows how we as readers are its dupe, in need of art to teach us the consequences of daydreaming: art contains within itself a warning against some of its most potent powers. The work of art, then, exposes, not hides, the gap between illusion and reality (often placing writer and reader on unexpected sides of this gap), particularly in its closing words, where it can best dramatize the silent void always about to swallow up the word. The fragmented work is a result of the most radical form self-criticism takes, and is the clearest illustration of the writer's refusal to close the charmed circle of art around himself and his audience.

Formal regression, for Freud, is the regression from word-presenta-tion to thing-presentation. If Freud sees "verbal consciousness" as the act that makes possible the process of becoming conscious, without which there is no cure for mental illness, I see the literary work as a similar language act. It heals the modern illness that T. S. Eliot diagnosed as the dissociation of sensibility, and its product is the kind of sanity Keats describes after the writing of a poem: language becomes an inquiry into the emotions, and produces sanity. When he protests, "I am ever afraid that your anxiety for me will lead you to fear for the violence of my temperament continually smothered down," Keats attempts to dispel this anxiety not simply with a poem, but with a summary of the poem's effect: "Sane I went to bed and sane I arose." Keats imagines the poet as physician to all men (poet-physician and dreamer are sheer antipodes), even to himself evidently, and if sometimes in his earliest work poetry seems to bring madness (in this he follows Plato), here it brings sanity. Poetry becomes the unbottling of the emotions (notice that language is associated with a release from being "smothered down," a talking cure that saves the writer from the suffocation of dumb insanity) and teaches the knowledge of the emotions. Keats seeks a language of heart and mind, and concludes about the poem, "it was written . . . with no thirst of anything but knowledge when pushed to the point though the first steps to it were throug[h] my human passions—they went away, and I wrote with my Mind—and perhaps I must confess a little bit of my heart" (L, 2, 81). Romantic and post-Romantic literature, for me, is not simply the product of the dissociation of sensibility, as Eliot claimed; it is the etiology of this illness, and sometimes its cure. For Freud, psychoanalysis provides just such a function—the reintegration of the ego and the instincts—and he defines psychoanalyst and patient as representing, respectively, the critical faculties and the passions: he speaks of the "struggle between the doctor and the patient, between intellect and instinctual life, between understanding and seeking to act."[11]

The writer sees in language this same power of reintegration. Wordsworth's poetry, at the beginning of the nineteenth century, reiterates the problem in its most characteristic form by showing the struggle of the child to become the man (the opposite of regression). His most hopeful vision sees the "glad animal movements" of his "thoughtless youth" (WPW, 164), while past, memorialized, and even developed into maturity, through language. The continuity Wordsworth imagines between Nature and Art depends on the integration of child and man, of instincts and mind, where emotion is recollected in tranquillity, and where the animal experiences of youth develop into the philosophic mind of man. Freud writes of the process of becoming conscious and makes his goal no loss of knowledge about youth and infantile wishes: it is what Wordsworth hopes for (and Yeats, a century later, sometimes despairs of), that is, knowledge without the loss of power.

Wordsworth's Boy of Winander stands at the heart of this tradition. The reader is presented with a double picture: the boy's mimicry of the owls leads naturally to his death (his copying of nature's language requires his subsumption into the natural world), and the child's death silences, at least temporarily, the mature Wordsworth, who stands mutely at the boy's grave (the gap between child and man is a linguistic one, a silence). Here the Child is father to the Man, but the Man is born only in the Child's death. To put it more hopefully, the Child is reborn in the Man's memory and language. There seems to be a subtle discrimination that is rarely, if ever, made explicit between the two languages Wordsworth tries to believe are the same, namely, the language of nature and the language of humanity. In fact, the silence at the grave is the silence that separates these two languages.

The child in Wordsworth's poetry and the savage in Keats's poetry suggest a grand march of intellect, to use Keats's phrase. There is first of all the march backward to rediscover lost dreams and wishes. This is a regression for the simple dreamer, but an archeology for the writer who uncovers what Freud calls the primeval period, the child and the savage in us. The march forward is the articulation of these other selves, saving them from being "smothered down." Child and savage are spoken for by the poet. This is the word-presentation that opposes, according to Freud, formal regression. The dead child is the potential adult silenced; that is, the child of nature dies because he is unable to speak the language of humanity. Like Keats's savages who are unable to tell their dreams, or like Wordsworth's Boy of Winander and Lucy Gray, the instinctive life dies a silent death. The prologue to "The Fall of Hyperion" explains that "Poesy alone can tell her dreams" and thereby "save Imagination."

Keats adds to the essentially Wordsworthian idea of the child of nature his own view of the fallen Titans. Dead child and fallen god are perhaps the most extreme parameters marking the compass of man's fate; in fact, child and god express perfectly the dissociation of sensibility, and we begin to see how these writers, even in the act of writing itself, try to locate man in the middle. We find, in a tradition that so often has been associated with both primitivism *and* transcendentalism, the criticism of both. This tradition refuses the myths of the child and of the god as models for the man; it even ironically fuses them, making Hyperion's habitation, for example, a cradle of rest, and describing Gudrun, Gerald, and Loerke at once as godlike and infantile. Demystifying both models, this tradition sees the child as the mischievous magpie (Lawrence's term for the boyish Loerke, also appropriate to the Boy's mimic hootings) and the god as an abstraction, drained of all lifeblood. The latter demystification results in a depopulation of heaven, to use Hegel's phrase, that explains more fully the connection between child and god: we remember

Freud's claim that in the relinquishment of God the Father lies the child's access to adulthood and reality.

These writers, then, seek a language that, unlike Milton's, deliberately charts a middle course. It defines itself by finding either the natural child swallowed up by nature or, instead of the traditional heaven, the depopulated or what Yeats calls the "desolate heaven" (*CPY,* 206), that is, heaven become the desert waste the Word should order, the void itself. Keats's savages are mute like Wordsworth's children (the Boy and Lucy), and the abstract gods become bestial in Keats's poetry—in other words, regressive to the extreme—because of their loss of verbal power. God and nature are confused, and nowhere is man, the creature of language, to be found.

Freud, in his own metaphoric language, shows the fusion of child and god by comparing the Titans to infantile wishes smothered down, not allowed to escape into language: "These wishes in our unconscious . . . remind one of the legendary Titans, weighed down since primaeval ages by the massive bulk of the mountains which were once hurled upon them by the victorious gods and which are still shaken from time to time by the convulsion of their limbs. But these wishes, held under repression, are themselves of infantile origin."[12] Keats's Hyperion poems become, in this light, an imaginative archeology. The poet tells his dreams by giving voice to the Titans, and the telling is his own cure. The cure, however, is not the hallucinatory fulfillment of these dreams, or even an escape from suffering, but precisely suffering borne, even reborn. Speech, the muscular activity that articulates the language of the body, cures the convulsion the Titans suffer from, and bears the child (or child-god) reborn as the man: the Child is father to the Man now, whether we look to Wordsworth, Keats, or Freud. It is in this sense that the narrator in "The Fall of Hyperion" calls the poet a physician to all men. The work of art unearths the child (or god) through language, and thereby matures him into the man. This is the labor of language.

Acknowledging Nietzsche (especially because of his reference to dreams) and neglecting to acknowledge Hegel, Freud sees the individual's development as a microcosm of the race's or species' development: "Behind this childhood of the individual we are promised a picture of a phylogenetic childhood—a picture of the development of the human race, of which the individual's development is in fact an abbreviated recapitulation influenced by the chance circumstances of life. We can guess how much to the point is Nietzsche's assertion that in dreams 'some primaeval relic of humanity is at work which we can now scarcely reach any longer by a direct path.'"[13] Dreams and neuroses seem to have preserved more mental antiquities than we could have imagined possible, so that psychoanalysis may claim a high place among those human sciences concerned with the reconstruction of the earliest and most obscure moments of our past. But so may literature; it should be clear that the work of art, as these writers see it, is a preservation, but with a difference. In dreams and neurosis the archaic state is master of the subject. Freud consistently uses the Hegelian notions of master-slave and domination, and Paul Ricoeur in fact suggestively describes psychoanalysis in these Hegelian terms: "the patient likewise has his truth at first in the other, before becoming the master through a work comparable to the work of the slave, the work of the analysis."[14] I press for a third kind of therapeutic work, the work of art, which according to Lawrence (using the same Hegelian terminology) allows the artist to "master" his emotions, and thereby shed his sicknesses. Art preserves the archaic for the artist's eye to judge and evaluate. The writers in this tradition see in our archaic past not simply an individual's childhood, but mankind's. In this light, the dead child can be a prognostication of the extinct species. The alternative to perishing "with the new life strangled unborn within" is, according to Lawrence, to "speak out to one another" (WL, viii).

Each literary work I will examine, then, can be viewed as an archeology, a cultural archeology that discovers the beginnings of man. Keats's "Eve of St. Agnes" and Hyperion poems are archeologies in their views of infantile wishes, whether shown through the young woman, Madeline, or through the fallen gods. The Hyperion poems especially give the cultural aspect of this problem, where the poet's view of the giant-gods is the unearthing of the ancient classical world. The Muse Memory allows Keats a glimpse of the earliest stages of Western culture, with its simpler wishes. In "Nineteen Hundred and Nineteen," the archeology takes the form of the poet's seeing, ironically enough, a survival in the present day of these same naïve classical simplicities, where the ivories of ancient Greece are matched by the pretty toys of humane laws, but where an older, still more primitive force whirls us back to an almost prehistoric evil. In "Her Vision in the Wood" there is a return to the pre-Olympian form of myth, to an ur-myth that is essentially antimythic, to an individualized interpretation of myth that is anticommunal, prior to myth's social function, and therefore prehistoric, if you will. In A Passage to India Forster attempts to describe primitive evil by going outside the western tradition altogether, and outside the romanticizations of verse (two steps beyond Yeats's Vision of Evil), to the prehistoric caves of India and what he calls the way the planet looked before man arrived with his itch for the seemly. In Women in Love man's fate seems about to lead him to extinction, or what amounts to the same thing, back to the primal swamp (the dark river of dissolution Birkin describes) out of which he came. In fact Lawrence's swampy marsh is infested with something like Freud's death wish to return to a prior inorganic state of matter. The death wish clashes

with, and sometimes becomes confused with, the human passions in
Lawrence's archeological view of a self deeper than what convention has
defined as personality or "the old stable ego" (CL, 282). Lawrence most
fully articulates a cultural regression by refashioning Darwinism into a
linguistic selection of the fittest. The failure of creative evolution depends,
for Lawrence, on a failure at utterance, at expression. The Bohemians'
studied primitivism (pictured best in Minette's babyish lisp, a linguistic
representation that captures her regression), or even the genuine primitivism of the African races, is inauthentic for modern man. Lawrence
sees as our great danger the break "between the senses and the outspoken
mind" (WL, 245), a version of the dissociation of sensibility that caused
the death of the African culture (we remember Keats's dumb savages).
Even Wordsworth pictures, in the Boy of Winander episode, the infantile
wish to be part of the natural world whence man came—to be an indistinct
thing, the way Lucy becomes one with rocks and stones and trees, rather
than the exiled human consciousness filled with pain and suffering, pictured memorably in such figures as the discharged soldier, the Arab
Quixote, the drowned man, and the blind beggar in London. The first
type is historyless (Hegel, we remember, insists that nature, unlike consciousness, has no history), while the second is our history, even if, when
we try to write it, it appears as impoverished as the few facts scratched
on the blind beggar's placard ("to explain / His story, when he came, and
who he was")—"an apt type / This label seemed of the utmost we can
know, / Both of ourselves and of the universe" (P, 7.641–42, 7.644–46).

As archeologies, these works reveal a past that, outside of art, is
glimpsed only in dreams and madness, in the secret words of repression
(or in no words at all, but in pictures), where it cannot be fully understood. They make us visit the "internal foreign territory"[15] that Freud
claims inhabits us; this is the passage to India, generalized. Language
opens this foreign territory, makes us know ourselves and our fellow
man. While the language of dreams is private, the language of literature
is public: history is the public record of man's dreams and their clash
with reality. Hegel, for instance, describes the itinerary of consciousness
as the way of doubt because it meets continually with the error of its
beliefs, only to reconstitute itself, and thereby make history, out of its
errors.

These archeologies require translation: this in fact is the connection
between archeology and hermeneutics, and is suggested by the fact that
Keats's Hyperion poems are literally conceived as the Muse's translation
of a dead language. Freud spoke of "the translation of what is unconscious into what is conscious," and explained that "the interpretations
made by psychoanalysis are first and foremost translations from an alien
method of expression into the one which is familiar to us."[16] So are the

interpretations of literature: these works in fact write, in plainer terms
at least than the dream, not a private case history, but every man's
history. One might say that what characterizes the movement of thought
from Wordsworth, Hegel, and Keats, to Nietzsche, Freud, and Lawrence
is a coherent search to appropriate a portion of the life history that has
been lost. In such translations, however, there must always be gaps,
lacunae, ellipses. These literary works so often apparently exhibit the
symptoms of the dream or the neurosis precisely because they attempt
to write human history, even prehistory. Here the gaps in the text are
not symptoms of repression, but of something far larger; they tell, even
in their silences, something of the uninterpretable nature of history. If in
neuroses such gaps are the subject's attempt to deceive himself about himself, in these literary works they are just the opposite—they are the
writer's refusal to protect himself in a closed and private world, to take
cover in defense mechanisms that shield him from reality. They are the
clear signs that each literary work is in fact a translation, and as such, an
incomplete or imperfect text. They are translations because they attempt
to go beyond the domain of language as it is traditionally defined; they
attempt to write the language of the body, the language of evil, even the
language of silence. As my last example suggests, there is something impossible in this venture. We meet again and again in these texts the uninterpretable or the overdetermined meaning or the Other that refuses to
recognize us: the ancient earth of India whose message is impossibly confused; the passions that, while in need of articulation according to Lawrence, always remain partially beyond language and thought; or the giant-
gods who, themselves without the power of language, are spoken for by
Moneta in a dead language that is never fully recoverable but yet is more
accessible than the ancient hieroglyphics that could reveal an even earlier
culture than the Greek if the key to translation had not been lost for all
time.

In all these cases the writer is also an interpreter or translator of a
text whose language resists being completely deciphered. Wordsworth,
seeking the common language of humanity, feared that words might become hieroglyphics (SPP, 466), and Freud of course saw the psychoanalytic goal as the decipherment of the hieroglyphic writing of repression.[17] Both writer and psychoanalyst, then, attempt to bring to light
our prehistory, and the literary equivalent to psychoanalysis interminable[18] is the incomplete style. In the words of Kierkegaard, "he only has
a style who never has anything finished":[19] such a style and its consequences can be seen in Keats's fragmented poems, in Yeats's distrust of
complete ideas, in Forster's elliptical style, and in Lawrence's novelistic
version of the blanks left on the canvas by Cézanne. In every case the
Logos clashes with chaos, with primitive passion, with evil, with every-

thing that lies outside reason. Now I can restate the topographical basis of all these works: each is the same archeology because each unearths, through words, the abysmal desert before the Word made order. We can say with Freud, "Our god, Λόγος, will fulfill whichever of those wishes nature outside us allows, but he will do it very gradually, only in the unforeseeable future, and for a new generation of men. He promises no compensation for us, who suffer grievously from life."[20] Only we must, as this book hopes to do, redefine Logos in terms broader than Freud imagined.

2
WORDSWORTH

THE ARAB DREAM: THE LANGUAGE BEHIND NATURE AND ART

Music . . . is in the highest degree a universal language. . . . In this respect it resembles geometrical figures and numbers, which are the universal forms of all possible objects of experience.

Nietzsche

Critics have followed Wordsworth's lead in neglecting books when considering the growth of the poet's mind. Wordsworth wonders at his neglect of books, chastises himself for playing "an ingrate's part" (*P*, 5.173),[1] and sets his fifth book aside "in memory of all books which lay / Their sure foundations in the heart of man" (5.198-99). He speaks of having been long detained by nature, and disclaims that his memorial to books is a mere afterthought. If he calls books "the best of other guides" (5.168), "only less . . . / Than Nature's self" (5.219-21), he wishes for children that "books and Nature be their early joy!" (5.423) in the first of a series of couplings that tries to maintain the delicate balance between these two powers. Clearly it is in the section entitled "Books" that the reader must seek, in *The Prelude* at least, a resolution of the argument over Nature and Art that Wordsworth revives for the whole romantic tradition. Still, "Books" is often paid little regard, and is usually approached by critics with some hesitation. Overshadowed by *The Prelude*'s dominant theme of nature, "Books" also seems to contain more glaring problems for the critic of Wordsworth than any other book of *The Prelude,* and R. D. Havens's judgment that it is "not unified or homogenous"[2] seems almost as true today as it did three decades ago. This integration of books into a poem so obviously "dedicate to Nature's self" is at once a problem for Wordsworth and for his critics, but Wordsworth is quick to add, in book 5, that this verse is "dedicate to Nature's self, / And things that teach as

This chapter first appeared in *Modern Language Quarterly* 36, no. 2 (June 1975): 145-65.

Nature teaches" (5.230–31). In book 5 we find, even if somewhat delayed, a central moment in the romantic poet's rapprochement between
Nature and Art.

While Havens's remark stimulated several critics to come to the
defense of "Books," each attacked the problem from a different angle;
in search of the key to the book's unity critics have read it, for example,
in the light of eighteenth- and early-nineteenth-century educational
theory or with a psychological eye to Wordsworth's relation to his
parents.[3] As helpful as such studies are in identifying important strands
of the argument of book 5, I still feel a certain inadequacy about some
of its major episodes. In fact, I wish to reverse the usual approach by ad-
mitting that one of the reasons there is so much difficulty with the problem of unity in book 5 is that the reader does not always understand its
individual parts. Granted that book 5 contains a marked dissociation
between subject and incident, an episode like the Arab dream in and of
itself provides the reader with one of the most puzzling moments in all
of Wordsworth's poetry. The very form it takes—that of a dream—while
typical perhaps of Keats or Coleridge, is unusual for Wordsworth and
seems by its very nature to elude our grasp.

Jane Smyser, over two decades ago, made us feel somewhat more
comfortable with the episode by providing it with a clear biographical
background.[4] She showed that Wordsworth's dream resembled one of
the three dreams that Descartes had on 10 November 1619, in which he
saw two volumes containing all of poetry and all the sciences. She also
argued that it was probably from Coleridge that Wordsworth learned of
Descartes's dream, and thus explained Wordsworth's attributing the
dream in the 1805 version not to himself but to a friend. This information, interesting as it is, provides only a background for the dream; it has
not, to my knowledge, been used in an interpretation of the episode
simply because it does not reflect the dream's complex substance. Yet
by looking beyond *The Prelude* itself for a clue to this difficult passage,
Smyser was, it seems to me, on the right track. Indeed, in what other
section of *The Prelude* than this, dedicated to books, would it be more
appropriate for Wordsworth to send the reader to "that delicious world
of poesy" (*P*, 5.581), "that golden store of books" (5.479)?

A crucial clue to the Arab dream is contained in one of the first
books that introduced the young boy to "the shining streams / Of
faery land, the forest of romance" (*P*, 5.454–55). Wordsworth's debt
to all those "tales," "romances," "legends," and "adventures" (5.469–
500) that sparked his youthful imagination is illustrated subtly, but
importantly, in his transposition of some of the details of a well-known
episode of Ovid's *Metamorphoses* into the Arab dream. The arbitrariness
critics have felt about the episode's symbols—Helen Darbishire remarks,

for example, that in altering Descartes's dream, Wordsworth "with poetic license calls the first book a Stone, and the second a Shell"[5]—is due to the failure to recognize that these symbols play a significant part in the deluge described by Ovid in the story of Deucalion and Pyrrha.

While modern scholarship has, in passing, documented Wordsworth's reading of the *Metamorphoses,* the most direct statement of Ovid's influence on Wordsworth is in the poet's own words. In his prefatory note to the "Ode to Lycoris" he writes, "But surely one who has written so much in verse as I have done may be allowed to retrace his steps in the regions of fancy which delighted him in his boyhood, when he first became acquainted with the Greek and Roman Poets. Before I read Virgil I was so strongly attached to Ovid, whose Metamorphoses I read at school, that I was quite in a passion whenever I found him, in books of criticism, placed below Virgil."

The connections between the Arab dream and the *Metamorphoses* can be fully grasped only after reviewing in some detail Ovid's story of the flood. Jupiter, upon discovering that the human race has given itself up to infamous crimes, decides to destroy it. With the help of Neptune he sends a great deluge that makes sea and earth indistinguishable, and thereby destroys mankind. A single mountain, however, rises high enough to escape the flood, and it is here on Parnassus that Deucalion and Pyrrha are saved. Jupiter sees that the couple is entirely guiltless and reverent; they offer prayers to Themis, the goddess who foretells the future from Parnassus's oracular shrine, and Jupiter saves them. The sea god Triton blows his echoing shell and recalls the destructive waters by this signal. The shell's notes reach the farthest expanses of the earth, check the flood, and restore order to the world. Deucalion wishes, however, that he could create the nations of the earth anew, that he could mould the earth and give it breath. The couple seeks the aid of the holy oracle, which responds with the following enigmatic answer: they are to throw behind them the bones of their great mother. Finally realizing that their great mother is the earth and that her bones must be the stones in the earth, Deucalion and Pyrrha follow the oracle's directions; the stones grow soft and begin to develop a likeness to human form, and the human race is thereby restored. This is, then, a deluge like the one Wordsworth describes, and a stone and a shell are the instruments of the restoration of order to the earth and to mankind. It is also interesting that Parnassus, the mountain holy to Apollo and poetry, is the salvation of Deucalion and Pyrrha, and that it contains (like Wordsworth's shell) the power of prophecy. With these details before us, the meaning of the Arab dream becomes significantly clearer.

It is generally assumed, I think, that the Arab dream is a restatement of the philosophical opening about the perishability of books. Havens, for example, explains the relationship between the beginning of book 5 and the subsequent dream in the following way: "The first forty-nine lines deal with the perishability of books; these are followed by the dream of the Arab with the stone and shell, which serves as a second and longer introduction (115 lines) to the theme of V."[6] If we look closely at the beginning of book 5, however, we will see that Wordsworth's emphasis on his reflective mood is already an indication that this prologuelike opening and the dream itself are vastly different in method, and perhaps in intent. Book 5 opens in the sternest manner possible, in a manner, I would suggest, sharply different from the wild romantic dream that follows. Wordsworth's subject is a dirge, and, lest we misrepresent his feelings and think that he is simply the prey of melancholia, he emphasizes the calm and quiet tone of his reflections:

> When Contemplation, like the night-calm felt
> Through earth and sky, spreads widely, and sends deep
> Into the soul its tranquillizing power,
> Even then I sometimes grieve for thee, O Man,
> Earth's paramount Creature!
>
> (P, 5.1–5)

In the opening line of the 1805 text Wordsworth explains, in other words, that "Even in the steadiest mood of reason" such grief comes upon him. This grief takes the quiet form of philosophical inquiry. The opening of book 5 is a carefully reasoned inquiry into the perishability of books by natural cataclysm; it is slow paced and categorical as it develops a tentative intellectual argument. And really, in many ways, its subject is traditional enough for philosophy's reasoned consideration. Book 3 of Plato's *Laws*, for example, opens with a discussion of natural cataclysm and turns immediately to the loss of the arts, and of all wisdom and culture, as a consequence of deluge and pestilence. The *Timaeus*'s well-known account of Atlantis begins with an aged priest admonishing Solon for the Greeks' failure to safeguard their books against the deluge; indeed, Solon is ignorant of Atlantis precisely because, as the priest tells him, "with you and others, writing and the other necessities of civilization have only just been developed when the periodic scourge of the deluge descends, and spares none but the unlettered and uncultured, so that you have to begin again like children, in complete ignorance of what happened in our part of the world or in yours in early times."[7]

The story of the deluge, then, and its effects on the products of human civilization (and particularly on books) is a fit subject for Wordsworth's contemplation. And if Wordsworth's mood is one of steadiest reason, he emphasizes that his grief likewise stems from an intellectual source:

> Even then I sometimes grieve for thee, O Man,
> Earth's paramount Creature! not so much for woes
> That thou endurest; heavy though that weight be,
> Cloud-like it mounts, or touched with light divine
> Doth melt away; but for those palms achieved,
> Through length of time, by patient exercise
> Of study and hard thought.

> (*P*, 5.4-10)

Wordsworth's mind is carefully turned, then, toward the products of the mind, toward

> all the meditations of mankind,
> Yea, all the adamantine holds of truth
> By reason built, or passion, which itself
> Is highest reason in a soul sublime;
> The consecrated works of Bard and Sage.

> (5.38-42)

That the poet's grief stems from his contemplation of the mind's best achievements is explained in the ensuing argument. The crux of that argument is a comparison that immediately leads Wordsworth to a significant distinction: both "the sovereign Intellect" and man have wrought "Things that aspire to unconquerable life," but whereas nature has diffused through it "a deathless spirit" (*P*, 5.15-20), man's things—books—are perishable. This is the central distinction of the prologue, and threatens to open up a rift between Nature and Art that can have darker consequences. It is elaborated upon in terms we will need for a reading of the Arab dream:

> Should the whole frame of earth by inward throes
> Be wrenched, or fire come down from far to scorch
> Her pleasant habitations, and dry up
> Old Ocean, in his bed left singed and bare,
> Yet would the living Presence still subsist
> Victorious, and composure would ensue,
> And kindlings like the morning—presage sure
> Of day returning and of life revived.

> (5.30-37)

Against this faith stands the certain understanding that books, unlike nature, are perishable. The section ends with a series of questions asking why books do not have a similar power: in such a cataclysm,

"where would they be?" (*P,* 5.45). These questions imply a dismal fate
for books, but the very fact that they are questions leaves the problem
partially open. It is here that the poet's grief is important; it sets up a
subtle but growing tension between what Wordsworth's best sense tells
him, namely, that books are perishable, and the emotional underthought
of the passage, namely, the desire, unsupported by reason, that books,
like nature, be immortal. The final questions, prodded by the poet's
grief, end the section by reaching beyond it for their answers.

The meditative tone of the prologuelike opening of book 5 is significant, as I suggested before, because it leads the reader to contrast this section with the subsequent dream. I raise this question of the relationship of
parts first because it throws light on the dream itself, and second because
it is a perennial stumbling block in interpretations of *The Prelude.* Book
5 epitomizes this problem. It seems a congeries of unrelated episodes,
and in it we search in vain for that "dark / Inscrutable workmanship that
reconciles / Discordant elements, makes them cling together / In one
society" (*P,* 1.341–44). Wordsworth himself declares at one point, "My
drift I fear / Is scarcely obvious" (5.293–94). It appears as if I am making
matters worse by criticizing the simple relationship, which has been taken
for granted for so long, between the prologue and the Arab dream—that
they are restatements of each other. Yet it seems to me that one of the
reasons there is so much difficulty with the relationship between episodes
in book 5 is that they have not been allowed a vital, organic relationship.

The book's major sections seem to mirror, technically, either the
prologue or the Arab dream; one could say that book 5 largely modulates
between discursive argument (the prologue on the perishability of books,
the denunciation of modern education) and symbolic narrative (the Arab
dream, the Boy of Winander, the drowned man). Some of these episodes,
to be more precise, are even combinations of argument and narrative;
the symbolic episode of the drowned man, for example, ends with an
argument for youthful reading. The point is that in book 5 discursive
and symbolic modes do not meet easily. In the case of the drowned man,
for example, I have always felt that the few lines of argument that conclude it are not adequate to its meaning. Likewise, the symbolic episode
of the Boy of Winander certainly seems to transcend its rather easy introduction about modern education. And so it is with the two sections in
question: if the philosophical prologue suggests "steadiest reason's" view
of the perishability of books, the dream, with its fantastic landscape,
unusual symbols, and intricate doublings (stone and shell as books, Arab
as Quixote, Arab as Wordsworth), seems to transcend the terms of the
sober prologue. At least the technical differences between the two sections are as significant as their thematic similarity.

Actually, the kind of formal distinction I am suggesting between these two sections (and the other sections of this book) is part of their theme; the prologue discusses those works of men "by reason built, or passion, which itself / Is highest reason in a soul sublime" (*P,* 5.40–41). And while granting the dream's unreasonable surface, one could say about it what Wordsworth says about the Arab: "In the blind and awful lair / Of such a madness, reason did lie couched" (5.151–52)—highest reason, perhaps. The prologue's terms receive further elaboration in the dream when we realize that geometry is founded upon "reason" (5.105) and poetry upon "passion" (5.96). The terms I have used, discursive and symbolic, are similar to Wordsworth's description (following Milton) of the two great kinds of intellect, "discursive or intuitive" (14.120). In the dream's suggestion that, despite geometry's power, we will find in poetry "something of more worth" (5.89), may be a clue to the dream's importance not as a simple restatement of the prologue but as a solution to the problem it presents. Indeed, in its imaginative answer to the question of the perishability of books, I would argue, the dream presents us with one of the best illustrations of Wordsworth's ultimate faith that "Imagination . . . in truth, / Is but another name for absolute power / And clearest insight, amplitude of mind, / And Reason in her most exalted mood" (14.189–92).

That the dream is in fact such an answer becomes clear, however, only when we recognize the Ovidean source for the stone and shell. At first the dream seems at least as tentative as the prologue; if the prologue ends with a series of questions, the dream is dramatically cut short, interrupted. As from a nightmare, Wordsworth awakens in terror before the dream has come to a conclusion. The reader is left with the poet's terror, the approaching deluge, and the disappearing Arab. The center of the dream's concern, the fate of the books, does not seem resolved. Its actual resolution eludes us precisely because of the form of the episode: the dream is resolved not in the way a philosophical inquiry might be, but in a way appropriate to a dream, that is, through the use of symbols. It is from the significance of the stone and shell that the meaning of the dream flows. From Ovid we know that the stone and shell not only do not perish but are the instruments of the world's and of man's revival.

There is a direct connection between nature and books, then, that eludes Wordsworth's reason. While he can perceive a "living Presence" that revives nature after the deluge, he does not see books as having such a presence, let alone as being its sacred vessel. And it is the dream's apparent confusion that suggests this connection. By this I mean that the confusing doubling of stone and shell with books, once we recognize the real connection between nature and books, is indeed "highest reason." Actually, such doublings throughout the dream make it a special kind of language: "I plainly saw / The one to be a stone, the other a shell; / Nor doubted once but that they both were books" (*P*, 5.111-13). Wordsworth continually reminds his reader that when he speaks of the stone and shell, he is also speaking of something else. Far from being merely a language of confusion, "the language of the dream" (5.87) is highly successful and complex. It is, in fact, poetic language, precisely because its doublings allow it to say at least two things at once. The dream, then, is symbolic language extrapolated. In its dissolution of reason's earlier distinction and in its revelation that nature and books share an everlasting life, we see how such language works, and realize its power.

The frame of the dream—the symbolic landscape in which its central drama occurs—helps define the relationship between "the living Presence" that revives all nature and a similar spirit contained by books. While there has been a general tendency to read the desert and deluge strictly in such Wordsworthian terms as Nature and Imagination, I again suggest that we consider a literary model (actually, several) that Wordsworth may have had in mind. Wordsworth finds himself in a desert that is an "illimitable waste" (*P*, 5.136), "a boundless plain / Of sandy wilderness, all black and void" (5.71-72), which is about to be drowned by the deluge. This is remarkably close, in image and idea, to Milton's description of chaos before creation, that "vast immeasurable Abyss / Outrageous as a Sea, dark, wasteful, wild."[8] Moreover, creation in Milton significantly involves the orderly division of sea and land. In Wordsworth, then, the natural world seems about to fall back into this primal chaos in which sea and land once again are at war. Of course, there are sources for this myth of creation well before Milton, sources that Milton himself echoes. Wordsworth may have in mind, in addition to Milton, the beginning of Genesis, or the *Metamorphoses* again, or the *Timaeus*. Each of these describes a primal void, a dark waste that is transformed into order, and the separation of water and earth as part of this metamorphosis: in short, all describe creation.

The creator and sustainer of harmony in these myths of creation is the Logos or the Word—classical and Christian versions of Wordsworth's "highest reason."[9] Milton, for example, explains that "th' Omnific Word" (*Paradise Lost*, 7.217) announces and effects the end of discord. If the dream suggests that books are like nature in their capacity for revival, this concept of the Word suggests that both books and nature are based upon language, perhaps upon the undying Word. For example, the prologue of book 5 describes nature as "the *speaking* face of earth and heaven" (*P*, 5.13, emphasis added). At first this seems a casual metaphor, but it is really part of a well-developed idea running throughout the poem, namely, that nature is quintessentially a language. In book 1, Wordsworth describes nature in precisely the same way: "the earth / And common

face of Nature spake to me / Rememberable things" (1.586-88). Elsewhere he directly compares one's perception of nature to the reading of
a book: "With such a book / Before our eyes, we could not choose but
read" (6.542-43). This idea of nature's language dramatically qualifies,
then, an important point made in the philosophical opening of book 5:
while the prologue makes an initial comparison that is immediately
turned into a distinction between nature (the product of "the sovereign
Intellect") and books (the product of man), we have just seen that nature
and books are related through language.

Wordsworth introduces the Christian concept of the Word in book
5 not simply through the associations his dream has with the Miltonic
idea and imagery of creation. In what has been traditionally seen as one
of the pietisms of the 1850 text, Wordsworth directly refers to the concept when he explains that books are "only less, / For what we are and
what we may become, / Than Nature's self, which is the breath of God, /
Or His pure Word by miracle revealed" (P, 5.219-22). The direct introduction of this concept is appropriate in this section on books for two
reasons. First, it suggests the traditional trope, developed throughout
The Prelude, that Nature is God's book.[10] While critics have briefly connected nature and books in book 5 through this idea, no one, it seems
to me, has seen its full implications for the dream.[11] If Wordsworth sees
nature as a language, he sees it as a sacred language that most men have
lost the power to read and understand; men gaze upon nature "as doth
a man / Upon a volume whose contents he knows / Are memorable, but
from him locked up, / Being written in a tongue he cannot read" (10.58-
61).

The poet, then, reveals the sacred mysteries of creation at the same
time that he insists that these meanings are there to be read by all. And
he explains that these mysteries, whether revealed by nature or by man
himself, are expressed by God through a sacred language: Wordsworth
experiences "conformity as just as that of old / To the end and written
spirit of God's works, / Whether held forth in Nature or in Man" (P,
4.350-52). The poet's relationship to nature, then, is that of a reader to
a sacred text. Like Daniel, who reads the mysterious writing on the wall,
or like the prophet in Revelation who sees a sacred book, closed to
others and opened to him, Wordsworth is granted the ability to read the
sacred text of nature—"characters of the great Apocalypse, / The types
and symbols of Eternity, / Of first, and last, and midst, and without end"
(6.638-40). The poet's "visionary power" depends on his ability to read
and hear the "ghostly language of the ancient earth" (2.309-11).

This idea of a sacred language brings me to the second reason behind
Wordsworth's introduction of the concept of the Word in book 5; it
provides him with the basis for the central idea of the dream, namely,

that books possess an undying language. The description in the *Timaeus* of the safeguarding of books in a temple is significantly altered by the Christian belief that the Word of God, of its own power, survives any cataclysm. St. Augustine (recalling Matt. 24:35 and Is. 40:8), for example, addresses God in the following manner: *"Though heaven and earth should pass away, your words will stand.* The scroll shall be folded and the mortal things over which it was spread shall fade away, as grass withers . . . *but your Word stands forever."*[12] Crucial to the Christian tradition, then, is a significant distinction between the immaterial Word and the matter that it creates and sustains. Wordsworth uses in book 5, in his description of both nature and books, the Christian concept of body and spirit to suggest this distinction:

> Hitherto,
> In progress through this Verse, my mind hath looked
> Upon the speaking face of earth and heaven
> As her prime teacher, intercourse with man
> Established by the sovereign Intellect,
> Who through that bodily image hath diffused,
> As might appear to the eye of fleeting time,
> A deathless spirit.
>
> (*P*, 5.11–18)

Nature, then, is a "bodily image" of a "deathless spirit." Its speech, an expression of that bodily image, becomes a finite transcription of the deathless Word. Books are seen through this same distinction between body and spirit; after the dream, when Wordsworth calls books "Poor earthly casket[s] of immortal verse" (5.164), he means that while books themselves are perishable (as is nature, that "bodily image"), they contain an "immortal" spirit—more precisely, the immortal language of verse—that is capable of its own revival. Thus, books contain a language that attains to the qualities of the Word. Here, then, is that subtle likeness between nature and books for which the image of Nature as God's book provides the background: both are based upon a sacred, undying language.

While it is true that the prologue's distinction between "bodily image" and "deathless spirit" can help us describe nature and books generally, we must remember that the dream singles out only two books that share in nature's capacity for revival. We must now ask, why poetry and geometry? A partial answer to the question is given in a short preamble to the dream. Wordsworth describes how, when reading by the sea one day, he began to muse on the perishability of books. He describes an important superiority that poetry and geometry have over other books, and even more significantly, over nature itself: "On poetry and geometric truth, / And their high privilege of lasting life, / From all internal injury exempt, / I mused" (*P*, 5.65–68). The meaning here becomes clear only if we return to the opening lines of book 5, for once again the reader is presented with variations on a theme that is presented, but not fully developed, in the prologue. Wordsworth explains that nature is destructible both through "fire come down from far" (5.31) and "inward throes" (5.30). We therefore can conclude that poetry and geometry are exempt from an injury that nature suffers (variously defined as "inward throes" and "internal injury"). Another way of putting this is to say that nature is built upon inner strife; while its laws are perfect and unchanging, one of its first laws is the law of change. The dream, whatever it says about books, makes this plain. In the imagery of desert and deluge we see nature's primal elements once again separate and at war.

The dream, then, admits of the hypothesis of the prologue: in the language of the dream, nature is capable at any time of degenerating into the primal war of elements out of which it arose; in the language of the prologue, nature is vulnerable to "inward throes," to its own inner discord. Poetry and geometry, on the other hand, are worlds of unalterable order. Unlike nature, and unlike other books, they are built on the very premise that they perfectly and harmoniously fulfill their own inner demands: it is for this reason that they are exempt from internal injury.

The dream's answer to the further question of the vulnerability of books to external injury (in this case, the deluge) takes it a significant step beyond the preamble. In manuscript W in a rejected version of his discursive description of nature and books, Wordsworth reveals the true meaning of what is to follow in the dream by stating that books are also "exempt from external injury" (*P*, 5.42). But this is rejected; the idea disappears from the earlier section only to surface again through the symbols of stone and shell. While the dream, as we have seen, clearly represents poetry and geometry's survival of the flood, we still must discover the qualities they possess (above all other books) that give them such power. Wordsworth's description of nature's survival of the deluge through the mysterious power of the "living Presence" becomes for book 5, and for *The Prelude* as a whole, the model whereby books in general, and his poem in particular, are measured.

In other words, it is because poetry and geometry are created "worlds" that they attain to nature's everlasting life. Indeed, poetry and geometry are often seen as created worlds of perfect order that rival, not simply copy or reveal, the divine order in nature. It is through their creative spirit that they attain to the power of the Word. Geometry, for example, is seen as "an independent world, / Created out of pure intelligence" (*P*, 6.166–67). And the great labor that is the elaborate process of the

fourteen books of *The Prelude* is the labor of divine creation: Wordsworth hopes to become, like Shakespeare and Milton, one of these
"labourers divine" (5.165). While he doubts his power at significant
points in the poem, by the time we reach book 14 his success is fully
revealed. In a final divine gesture, Wordsworth looks down upon his
world, at the conclusion of its making, and sees that it is good:

> Anon I rose
> As if on wings, and saw beneath me stretched
> Vast prospect of the world which I had been
> And was; and hence this Song, which like a lark
> I have protracted, in the unwearied heavens
> Singing, and often with more plaintive voice
> To earth attempered and her deep-drawn sighs,
> Yet centring all in love, and in the end
> All gratulant, if rightly understood.
>
> (14.379-87)

It is a subtle point. Poetry, geometry, his life as it is recreated
through his poem—all are seen as "worlds" because Wordsworth's most
original faith is in nature's "living Presence," nature's eternal life. And
yet, by transferring this faith to books, Wordsworth is granting man's
worlds the same power. His hope throughout *The Prelude,* then, is that
his poetry will become a created and orderly world like nature: he
hopes to be granted that "privilege whereby a work of his, / Proceeding
from a source of untaught things / Creative and enduring, may become /
A power like one of Nature's" (*P,* 13.309-12). He hopes to be "capable /
Of building up a Work that shall endure" (14.310-11). The "living
Presence," which the prologue says is able to "subsist" eternally, becomes in book 14 the power of love (a traditional transcription of the
Word) that is the power at once behind nature and Wordsworth's own
work (his song "centring all in love"). It is precisely through this immaterial love that all things—nature, his life and work—live eternally:
"By love *subsists* / All lasting grandeur, by pervading love; / That gone,
we are as dust" (14.168-70, emphasis added). The "subsisting" power
of nature's "living Presence," then, is also the power behind Wordsworth's
life and work: it is found at the same time in nature and in books.[13]

The everlasting power of the stone and shell belongs to geometry and
poetry, and only those other books with the same particular qualities of
geometry and poetry share in this eternal life. Critics should not be
troubled, then, that in this section on "Books" Wordsworth spends so
much time on the denunciation of the books used in modern education.
It is precisely the goal of book 5 to distinguish between books, and to
establish which books are eternally valuable and why.

This brings me to the final quality that poetry and geometry share
with each other and with no other books: they are universal languages.
Geometry, quite simply, is a system of signs and symbols that is universally understood. In their search for the universal language, philoso-
phers of the Renaissance and the Enlightenment inevitably used mathe-
matics as their model precisely for this reason.[14] Because geometry was
traditionally seen as a kind of language it was not uncommon for philos-
ophers of science, for example, to vary the trope of Nature as God's book
by seeing that book written in mathematical signs.[15] Wordsworth himself
sees the importance of geometry in this light. In geometry's figures he
recognizes

> A type, for finite natures, of the one
> Supreme Existence, the surpassing life
> Which—to the boundaries of space and time,
> Of melancholy space and doleful time,
> Superior, and incapable of change,
> Nor touched by welterings of passion—is,
> And hath the name of, God.
>
> (*P*, 6.133-39)

The dream itself likewise insists on geometry's freedom from the restric-
tions of time and space: it "held acquaintance with the stars, / And
wedded soul to soul in purest bond / Of reason, undisturbed by space
or time" (5.103-5).

At first the dream seems to suggest something quite different about
poetry; the shell speaks to Wordsworth "in an unknown tongue" (*P*,
5.93). What is significant, however, is that Wordsworth immediately
adds that it is a language "which yet I understood" (5.94). The shell
speaks "articulate sounds, / A loud prophetic blast of harmony" (5.94-
95): it speaks a primal language understood by all people. Its "harmony"
is a universally understood order like music: "the Poet, singing a song in
which all human beings join with him, rejoices in the presence of truth
as our visible friend and hourly companion" (*WPW*, 738).[16] Wordsworth
is told in the dream that the shell "was a god, yea many gods, / Had
voices more than all the winds, with power / To exhilarate the spirit,
and to soothe, / Through every clime, the heart of human kind" (*P*, 5.106-
9). Poetry, then, transcends the bounds that separate men, the Babel
of languages. While Wordsworth is aware of how languages become obsolete—he speaks, for example, of the dead languages "that want the living
voice / To carry meaning to the natural heart" (6.111-12)—for him
poetry transforms language into an eternally and universally understood
form. Poetry is in fact the living voice that carries meaning to all men.
In the preface to the second edition of *Lyrical Ballads,* Wordsworth

cautiously tells how "the affecting parts of Chaucer are almost always expressed in language pure and universally intelligible even to this day" (*WPW*, 735). He goes on to express his deepest faith, namely that "the Poet binds together by passion and knowledge the vast empire of human society, as it is spread over the whole earth, and over all time" (738). Here is poetry's supreme power to recreate and sustain civilization and culture.

While it is clearly beyond the bounds of this chapter to consider the other episodes of book 5 in any detail, I hope in these concluding remarks to suggest briefly how the meaning of the Arab dream significantly colors the other aspects of the book, and particularly the episode of the drowned man. The Arab dream, it seems to me, is the source of the book's complex progress from the grief of the opening prologue to the exultant praise of words and books that concludes book 5. One way of putting the problem of the book's unity is to say that there is a continual and marked dissociation of emotion and incident in book 5. By this I mean that all three symbolic narratives—the Arab dream, the Boy of Winander, and the drowned man—are reasonable subjects for the poet's grief because all contemplate, in one form or another, death; and yet, all three episodes are used by Wordsworth to affirm a vision that looks beyond death, and therefore beyond grief.

Geoffrey Hartman's excellent reading of the Boy of Winander has shown how that episode turns from a vision of death to one of immortality.[17] While the scene is a contemplation of the death of the body (to use the terms of my reading), its real meaning arises out of its enactment of the growth and development of the mind. One could even show how the scene's subtle enactment of the metamorphosis of the child into the poet hinges on the interruption of the simple uses the child makes of language. The child's "mimic hootings" (*P*, 5.373), which are his wondrous acknowledgment of nature's language, and their silencing are stages in the development of the poet's finer and more complex vision of language.[18] In any case, it is clear that the prologue and the Arab dream are models for the pattern of this episode: a primary sense of grief at death is elided through an ultimate affirmation of the everlastingness of spirit.

The encounter with the drowned man is book 5's final, and in many ways clearest, expression of this pattern. The episode is linked to the Arab dream first through the image of the drowned man: the mythic hypothesis of the prologue and the dream—a deluge come to drown the entire world—here becomes a chance encounter, "a plain tale" (*P*, 5.443) the child experiences in one of his many ambles. The episode is more subtly linked to the opening of book 5 through the image of the garments.

In the prologue Wordsworth refers to books as the "garments" (5.24) of our immortal being; here, later in the book, the man's garments, curiously enough, have the power of books—"Those unclaimed garments telling a plain tale" (5.443). This chance occurence slowly assumes the formal proportions of a fiction: first it is perceived as "a plain tale" and then it is further embroidered upon by the child nurtured on books until it has for him a "decoration of ideal grace" (5.457). This decoration is the garment of poetry. The encounter is compared to sights the boy has seen "among the shining streams / Of faery land, the forest of romance;" it assumes "A dignity, a smoothness, like the works / Of Grecian art, and purest poesy" (5.454-59). The crucial meaning of the episode is, of course, this imaginative power of transformation, and actually the idea of metamorphosis is the key to every aspect of the episode. "Twilight was coming on" (5.435), and the whole day seems involved in a mysterious transformation: "the calm lake / Grew dark with all the shadows on its *breast*" (5.439-40), and the open field the child enters is "shaped like *ears*" (5.433, emphasis added to both lines).

Read in this light, the central action of the episode—the drowned man's sudden bolt upright out of the water—suggests the kind of Ovidean transformation of the body into many forms that the young Wordsworth did indeed encounter in his reading of the *Metamorphoses.* In any case, the most significant metamorphosis occurs in the child's mind: the child's imaginative strengths prevent him from being "possessed" (*P,* 5.453) by a soul-debasing fear, and even distinguish him from the "passive" (5.445) crowd of onlookers. The grotesque body of the dead man, "with his ghastly face, a spectre shape / Of terror" (5.450-51), is implicitly and significantly contrasted with the undying "spirit" (5.456) of books that hallows the sad spectacle and makes of it a scene of mythic transformations. In this episode, then, there is the same essential distinction between body and spirit that was defined in the prologue and dramatized in the Arab dream. The episode reveals once again the mind's ability to face (here through the intercession of books) the corruption and death of the body, and not grieve.

The power of the word to transform is once again the crux of the episode, and leads to the book's final vision of the "endless changes" words work, transforming a world of shadowy darkness into one circumfused with divine light:

> Visionary power
> Attends the motions of the viewless winds,
> Embodied in the mystery of words:
> There, darkness makes abode, and all the host
> Of shadowy things work endless changes,—there,

As in a mansion like their proper home,
Even forms and substances are circumfused
By that transparent veil with light divine,
And, through the turnings intricate of verse,
Present themselves as objects recognised,
In flashes, and with glory not their own.

(P, 5.595-605)

Wordsworth has taken Ovid's prayer at the opening of the *Metamorphoses*—that the spinning of his tale be inspired by the same gods responsible for the transformations he is to relate—and has turned it into a fact about all poetry: "the intricate turnings of verse" embody the godly powers of metamorphosis and creation. This is why, in one of the book's subtlest ambiguities, Wordsworth calls books "the best of other guides" (5.168), second only to nature. In his dream Wordsworth imagines the Arab as a "guide" (5.80) for himself as well as for books (the Arab's mission is to lead the precious volumes of poetry and geometry to safety). Yet we finally learn that, far from needing such a guide, books are themselves the child's and the man's best guide through a drowning world.

I have presented in this chapter what might be called, to use Geoffrey Hartman's phrase in a somewhat different context, Wordsworth's dream of communication.[19] It is a belief, both in the common nature of humanity and in the poet's ability to speak "the general language of humanity" (*PWW*, 2:57), that is predicated upon the poet's discovery of the kind of language imagined in the Arab dream and described in such famous prose works as the preface to the second edition of *Lyrical Ballads,* the appendix to the preface, and *Essays upon Epitaphs.* The dream of communication has a nightmarish edge: its special nature is to couple every man's fear of death, picturing our quixotic and frenzied attempt to save our works from the approaching deluge, with the knowledge that words are weak and that by twisting and turning they can lead our minds and hearts astray. The dream of communication, then, faces the double danger that words can die and that, even without such a death, words can be blankly uncommunicative and even self-deceptive.

I have been describing a characteristic turn in Wordsworth's mind from nightmare to dream, from near despair to hope, from thoughts of the grave, and of the deluge that buries our words with us, to intimations of the immortality of spirit and word. Wordsworth responds to his fears, then, with an answer that stands at the head of a century and a half of English literature: "Poetry is the first and last of all knowledge—it is as immortal as the heart of man" (*SPP*, 456). The essays, like the Arab dream, step over into the land of salvation. They revive the problem of Nature versus Art, and solve it: a language of nature is what the greatest art speaks. Hence Wordsworth's search for a "natural language," for "the real language of nature," for a poetry "in which the language closely resembles that of life and nature" (468, 457, 462). He sketches in the history of poetic taste, but it seems a sacred history that tells of a mortal fall and foretells eventual salvation. It shows how, while poetry originated from "the language of men" and was "the genuine language of passion," it became a "distorted language," but one that nevertheless was "received with admiration." This history of poetry shows what factors "separated the genuine language of Poetry still further from common life," so that "the true and the false were inseparably interwoven until, the taste of men becoming gradually perverted, this [unusual, distorted] language was received as a natural language" (465-66). The task of the true poet is to recover the natural language. It is a task Wordsworth thinks of immediately: when he asks, "What is a Poet?" he is led to ask, "What language is expected from him?" (453). The answer is of course among the most famous in poetic theory. The language the poet speaks defines what the poet is, and vice versa: he is a man speaking to men, and he therefore must of necessity speak the general language of humanity.

Wordsworth's history of poetic language is, like most histories, diachronic: it exists in time, reaching back to an Edenic origin in the distant past, describing a present of emptiness and obfuscation in which true and false are confused, and seeking a future that depends on the poet. Wordsworth's notion of language, however, is synchronic as well. By this I mean that language always maintains a dangerous duplicity, and at every moment inherent in it is a double capacity for true and false, for good and evil (Wordsworth deliberately gives his terms a religious cast).

> Words are too awful an instrument for good and evil to be trifled with: they hold above all other external powers a dominion over thoughts. If words be not (recurring to a metaphor before used) an incarnation of the thought but only a clothing for it, then surely they will prove an ill gift; such a one as those prisoned vestments, read of in the stories of superstitious times, which had power to consume and to alienate from his right mind the victim who put them on. Language, if it do not uphold, and feed, and leave in quiet, like the power of gravitation or the air we breathe, is a counter-spirit, unremittingly and noiselessly at work to derange, to subvert, to lay waste, to vitiate, and to dissolve. (*PWW*, 2:84-85)

These two alternatives face the writers who follow Wordsworth. One is a genuine language that, for Wordsworth at least, is judged by natural qualities: words should be as simple and direct as gravitation itself (perhaps a subtle suggestion that all things do subsist in words and find their ground of meaning in language) and as fresh as the air we breathe. The other produces the subterfuge of art, interrupting the sacred marriage Wordsworth imagines between Nature and Art: it is a language of subversion, with a rhetoric that is nothing but a "trick of words;" the universal language of men lapses until it becomes "a motley masquerade of tricks, quaintnesses, hieroglyphics [a suggestion that language, or a certain kind of language, does in fact die], and enigmas" (SPP, 466). The dream of communication, of a language open and comprehensible to all men, can become a nightmarish Babel.

Each writer after Wordsworth wages a war against the subterfuge of art, often on the battlefield of language and rhetoric, and always with the same landscape on the horizon: in Keats, Yeats, Forster, and Lawrence we find the desert void and the brightness of the creative Word hovering above. Equally often, however, we find the dream of communication turned into nightmare, the Word's powers less efficacious than Wordsworth imagined. The suspicions about the duplicity of language become insurmountable obstacles in the writer's purview. Wordsworth's strategy, as he stands at the end of the century of Pope (the end, for Wordsworth, of the long decline and fall of the Word), is to invent a new language, or more precisely, to return the language of poetry to its origins, both historic and personal—from the earliest times poetry naturally originated in the heart of man. It is Wordsworth's genius to have reconciled the experience of nature with that of books, to make nature and books the twin lodestars directing the child's, and the man's, courses through a world threatened by deluge.

3

KEATS

THE LANGUAGE OF GODS AND MEN: THE FRAGMENTED WORLD OF THE HYPERION POEMS

This one
Seems, by the action of his throat, alive.
Underlined by Keats in his copy of *The Inferno*

The idea of the long narrative poem, and of completing it, haunted Keats's imagination. In the simplest terms, the long poem was for him the hallmark of the great poets: "a long Poem is a test of Invention. . . . Did our great Poets ever write short Pieces? I mean in the shape of Tales—This same invention seems indeed of late Years to have been forgotten as a Poetical excellence" (*L,* 1, 169). "Endymion," "Hyperion," and "The Fall of Hyperion" are all marked by a profound sense that the long poem is the supreme challenge of the poet. "Endymion," for example, "will be a test, a trial of my Powers of Imagination and chiefly of my Invention" (1, 169). Believing that completion is always the greatest part of the challenge, Keats chides himself for talking about the poem before it has been completed: "I have no right to talk until Endymion is finished;" "But enough of this, I put on no Laurels till I shall have finished Endymion" (1, 170). He changes an old adage, making it fit his own peculiar compulsion: "There is an old saying 'well begun is half done'—'tis a bad one. I would use instead—'Not begun at all till half done' so according to that I have not begun my Poem and consequently (a priori) can say nothing about it" (1, 141). The completion of the long poem seems to authenticate the poet: it gives him his rights and dresses him in symbolic laurel.

When "Endymion" was finally completed, the critics judged it poor. Keats was half-satisfied, for at least the task had been completed. Of course, he never had even that satisfaction from the Hyperions. If Keats looked upon fine phrases like a lover (as he says), the Hyperions inveigled him into an affair that was to end as tragically as that with Fanny Brawne.

Or rather, both affairs were fated not to conclude at all, but to be cut short, interrupted. The long poem appealed to Keats not simply because it was a link to the past and to the great poets. It seemed (like the affair with Fanny) a brazen stare in the face of destiny, a desperately bold adventure: it was a commitment to, really a leap into, the future. To the poet short on time, the long poem is the final trial, and everything depends on it. Completed, it seems to dangle a double guarantee of life before Keats: it assures him of fame (that is, life after death, a place among the English poets) and of longevity here and now.

Keats's understanding of the archetypal space of blankness he inherits from Milton and Wordsworth is, at first, entirely personal: the desert waste that the Word can transform is a personal challenge. The metaphor of the Book of Nature becomes for him a personal Book of Life: he worries over "the leaves of his Life's book" (L, 2, 104); he would like "to tear from the book of Life all blank leaves" (1, 140). Finally, the long poem is a matter of stature in more ways than one: "Mister John Keats five feet hight" (1, 342) is always eager, and anxious, "to show you how tall I stand by the giant." He sees in Wordsworth's poetry a sizeable achievement by which his accomplishments seem to shrink.

In this light, the blank page is for Keats a terrible emptiness, and the fragmentary poem a specter out of this deep, its life cut short and unfulfilled, unfinished. His eye is even caught by the blank space on a letter to Reynolds: "Forgive me for not filling up the whole sheet" (L, 2, 147). To say that Keats is haunted by the long poem is to suggest two different kinds of spirits. First, there is (as he often hoped) "a good genius presiding over you," a Shakespeare or Chaucer, the triumphant poet. Second, there are what Keats calls "strange stories of the death of Poets—some have died before they were conceived" (1, 140). It is no accident that the poem of 4,000 lines is dedicated to the memory of Chatterton, the poet cheated by time: its length seems to contravene, symbolically, the shortness of Chatterton's life. Keats mentions Abbey reading extracts from Byron to him, and he hears Byron's flippancy: "What is the end of Fame? 'tis but to fill / A certain portion of uncertain paper . . ." (2, 192). But for Keats the words fill the page with the promise of life. Part of that "feud / 'Twixt Nothing and Creation" (PW, "Endymion," 3.40–41) about which the poet speaks is the feud between the blank page (or the metaphysical void) and the word (or the Word). In terms similar to Byron's (but with a meaning that resounds profoundly throughout his work), Keats declares that in "Endymion," "I must make 4000 Lines of one bare circumstance and fill them with Poetry" (L, 1, 169–70). These terms—a bareness that rapidly grows into a barrenness for Keats, and a poetic invention that fills a bare space the way God fills the void with the creation—frame Keats's efforts at the long poem.

In the prologuelike opening of "Endymion," for example, this necessity to fill in the bare circumstance with words becomes part of the very subject of the poem:

> so I will begin
>
> . . . .
> Now while the early budders are just new,
> And run in mazes of the youngest hue
>
> . . . .
> . . . . And, as the year
> Grows lush in juicy stalks, I'll smoothly steer
> My little boat, for many quiet hours,
> With streams that deepen freshly into bowers.
> Many and many a verse I hope to write,
> Before the daisies, vermeil rimm'd and white,
> Hide in deep herbage; and ere yet the bees
> Hum about globes of clover and sweet peas,
> I must be near the middle of my story.
> O may no wintry season, bare and hoary,
> See it half finish'd: but let Autumn bold,
> With universal tinge of sober gold,
> Be all about me when I make an end.
>
> $\qquad\qquad\qquad\qquad\qquad\qquad$ (*PW*, 1.39-57)

Many and many a verse, and a plea for completeness!

The poet's writing is consistently linked to the earth's growth. Indeed, a timetable that deliberately associates the seasons with his writing is the ground plan of the entire poem. Filling the page is like filling the universe, and this excess of ontological energy evidently pours over into Keats's life and reassures him of well-being.

> And now at once, adventuresome, I send
> My herald thought into a wilderness:
> There let its trumpet blow, and quickly dress
> My uncertain path with green, that I may speed
> Easily onward, thorough flowers and weed.
>
> $\qquad\qquad\qquad\qquad\qquad\qquad$ (*PW*, 1.58-62)

That "bare" season (winter) always threatens interruption and incompleteness; it is like the "bare" circumstance, the bare page glaring its challenge at the poet, the barren imagination unable to invent. But the poet's wish is granted: "Endymion" ends in and with the completeness of autumn. In fact, the poem obsessively creates an autumnal fruitfulness that contradicts the orderly timetable proposed in the prologue. If the poet begins the poem in early spring ("the early budders are just new"), already in the initial descriptive passage after the prologue we are lunged into a world that almost threatens to be overgrown: "Upon the sides of Latmos was outspread / A mighty forest; for the moist earth fed / So plenteously all weed-hidden roots / Into o'er hanging boughs, and precious fruits" (1.63–66).

One rarely loses sight of the fact that this poem is a self-appointed test: the lushness is proof of the poet's invention and signals the kind of poetry we expect of the young poet. The 4000 lines are rich with fruit; indeed, the poetry tends to "overteem / With mellow utterance" (PW, 1.575–76). It is a description of "earth too ripe" (1.142) and an example of poetry become prolix. "Many and many" in this case becomes too many. From the start it is a world "fully blown" (1.169), "over brimm'd" (1.137), and "o'erflowing" (1.143). It is a world full to the point of suffocation, as health and well-being almost become sickness: the mushrooms are "swollen" (1.215), the parsley is "smothering" (1.230).

The same kind of parallel between narrator and protagonist that I will explain in "The Eve of St. Agnes" operates in "Endymion": if the nagging fear of Endymion is that he has loved nothing—"I have clung / To nothing, lov'd a nothing, nothing seen / Or felt" (PW, 4.636–38)—his nothing turns out to be everything. Cynthia is "that completed form of all completeness" (1.606), and as such she is as much the bride of the narrator as of Endymion. In this sense "the path of love and poesy" (2.38) is the same. Endymion wins a complete love, and the narrator a complete poem.

These remarks on Keats's obsession with completeness are not meant to cast the harsh glare of irony on the fragmentary Hyperions or to make their place in Keats's life and poetic career more poignant than it already is. The relation between "Endymion" and the Hyperion poems is crucial; these three poems are, after all, Keats's major attempts at the long narrative poem. In what remains the same and in what alters, between "Endymion" on the one hand and the Hyperions on the other, I find the best key to understanding his efforts at the long poem. There is, first of all, the same insistence on completeness as in "Endymion." Keats refuses to show any of the Hyperions until they are completed, or nearly completed: "I will not give you any extracts because I wish the whole to make an impression" (L, 2, 12); "I will not give any extracts from my large poem which is scarce begun" (2, 18). Moreover, the same kind of metaphor describes the act of poetry, and there is an exacting attention to the words on the bare page: when Keats finally does show some of the lines of "Hyperion" to Woodhouse (a sign that he has given up all hopes of finishing?), he writes, "My poetry will never be fit for any thing; it doesn't cover its ground well" (2, 172). Keats is talking specifically about

how unevenly the words fill the empty space on the page, and he uses
once again a metaphor of vegetation. Poetry as groundcover, to hide an
unsightly and otherwise barren, or at least large and hard-to-grow, area!

Keats's long poems also employ the analogous image of garments hiding another kind of bareness, the poet's nakedness. In "Endymion," the
poet's "herald thought" must "quickly dress" the wilderness, and his
path "thorough flowers and weed" suggests not simply a passage through
a dressed and fruitful universe, but a poet dressed in appropriate Shake-
spearean weeds. In "The Fall of Hyperion," the robes of the gods are
equally suggestive—those

> large draperies,
> Which needs had been of dyed asbestos wove,
> Or in that place the moth could not corrupt,
> So white the linen, so, in some distinct
> Ran imageries from a sombre loom.
>
> *(PW*, 1.73-77)

The "imageries" from the somber loom are connected subtly with the
description in the prologue of the imaginative faculty: "Fanatics have
their dreams, wherewith they *weave* / A paradise for a sect; the savage
too / From forth the loftiest *fashion* of his sleep / Guesses at Heaven."
Poetry is a garment, as it is in Wordsworth, and "*bare* of laurel they live,
dream, and die" (1.1-7, emphasis added in both passages) who cannot
transform their dreams into the garb of poetry. Finally, the whole idea
of the long poem seems to offer Keats a kind of protection: "No sooner
am I alone than shapes of epic greatness are stationed around me, and
serve my Spirit the office which is equivalent to a king's body guard"
(*L*, 1, 403). The long poem does indeed haunt Keats, and just as poetry
dresses the world and the poet, so its heroic figures people his empty
solitude with familiar shapes.

There is an implicit distinction for Keats between "Endymion" and
"Hyperion": both are long narrative poems, but whereas the first was a
poetic romance, "Hyperion" was to be an epic. For that reason the
Hyperions were an even greater challenge, the *ne plus ultra:* the "epic
was of all the king, / Round, vast, and spanning all like Saturn's ring"
(*L*, 1, 111). If the epic is the ultimate challenge, it also presents the ultimate reward: it is round and vast, like plenitude itself; and if it is vast,
it is not empty, indeed it spans or circumscribes a created world. But
this is a difference in degree, not kind. A crucial change does occur,
however, in the metaphor that Keats uses to describe poetry, and it is
associated with the greater task of the Hyperions. First let us look at
one more example (and it may be the central one) of the kind of metaphor Keats associates with "Endymion" and his defense of the long

poem: "Do not the Lovers of Poetry like to have a little Region to wander in where they may pick and choose, and in which the images are so numerous that many are forgotten and found new in a second Reading: which may be food for a Week's stroll in the Summer" (1, 170). The long poem is a luxurious Eden where one is free to wander and stroll; it is a laborless garden where one finds at hand all the fruits of summer. The long poem suggests a leisureliness, an unhurriedness, that Keats was always drawn to yet was never allowed to experience.

After "Endymion," the poem is still a kind of divine nourishment, but with a significant change. In hindsight, "Endymion" appeared more and more a failure to Keats. Like the overgrown landscape it describes, it seemed the work of an unbridled and undisciplined author, a poem of perverse emptiness (despite, or perhaps because of, Keats's attempt to the contrary), short on meaning if long on lines. Keats's deliberate and steady movement toward what he called philosophy always seems sparked by the failure of "Endymion": "I hope I am a little more of a Philosopher than I was, consequently a little less of a versifying Pet-lamb" (L, 2, 116), a statement ironically associating himself with the "baaing" poets he criticized in "Endymion" (PW, 3.3). The kind of self-corrective criticism at the heart of so much of romanticism, then, begins to take shape in Keats's mind as he formulates a balance between imagination or invention (the central motives in "Endymion") and a more philosophical judgment. He knows "we must temper the Imagination, as the Critics say, with Judgment" (L, 2, 97), to "make use of my Judgment more deliberately than I yet have done" (2, 128). About "Endymion," he says, "Had I been nervous about its being a perfect piece, & with that view asked advice, and trembled over every page, it would not have been written" (1, 374). He hopes, "I may write independently & *with judgment* hereafter" (1, 374). It is in fact just toward the completion of the fourth book of "Endymion" that he begins to contemplate this balanced and complex mind—"one that is imaginative and at the same time careful of its fruits" (1, 186). After "Endymion," Keats emphasizes the labors of the poet and his hard-won fruit over and against the leisurely Eden he once pictured. In "The Eve of St. Agnes" the romancer suddenly starts up to a poison fruit he must pluck and eat. If Keats's poetry more and more is constructed to enable him to see the balance of good and evil, the Hyperions require that he leave behind the simple Eden of his youthful poetry.

The Hyperion poems replace private compulsion with universal necessity. If the drive behind "Endymion" is (as it finally seemed to Keats) directed toward too simple a wish fulfillment, too vapid a daydream, Keats was on his guard against these faults in the Hyperions. While "Endymion" seems written out of a personal necessity and its fruitful-

ness a compensation too readily evident—the work of a Keats whom
Yeats characterizes "with face and nose pressed to a sweet-shop window"
(*CPY*, 159)—the Hyperions, like much of Yeats's own poetry, attempt
to convince us that they are written out of a necessity that is far beyond
the personal, a necessity that is in fact historical and finally universal. In
both Hyperions Keats refers to the poet as a scribe, and in "The Fall" it
becomes particularly clear that the poet is being dictated to by a transcendent power connected to the necessity that drives the Titans down.
As scribe, the poet copies and teaches the sacred history of a people;
Keats's job is even more magisterial, telling the fall of a race of gods.
From the domineering potion he drinks to the steps he is commanded to
ascend, everywhere an element of necessary labor is evident. The dream
of the paradisaical garden of plenty (reminiscent of "Endymion") is lost
for a dream-within-a-dream that turns out to be more a nightmare of
suffering. Keats's final vision in these poems seems constructed as an
antidote to the daydream or wish fulfillment: it is a prolonged look, almost against his will, at what Keats most feared; a deliberate attempt at
short-circuiting the pleasure principle and an invitation to nightmare.

   Ultimately, the poems reveal a kind of language that does not simply
and romantically dress the void, but strips it of all embroidery. Poetry
as a mere jack-o'-lantern looking out of the dark void with light and with
the hint of life and animation is a child's game at counterfeiting life. The
center of the Hyperions is an avoidance of the subterfuge of art, and
what Keats asked of Reynolds—to distinguish in them between "the
false beauty proceeding from art" and "the true voice of feeling" (*L*, 2,
167)—is the kind of self-critical faculty Keats himself exercised in the
writing of these poems.

Fallen Saturn in the shady vale is the primal scene of the Hyperion fragments: it is literally the starting point of "Hyperion" and is placed centrally, at the heart of the poet's vision, in "The Fall of Hyperion." It is
in every way the germ of the poems and from it everything else seems
to evolve by way of elaboration and addition or, far less frequently, by
way of contrast. Even its near sonnetlike structure suggests its special
status as not simply part of an introduction but as a poem itself, which,
like certain primitive organisms, through division reproduces itself again
and again.

> Deep in the shady sadness of a vale
> Far sunken from the healthy breath of morn,
> Far from the fiery noon, and eve's one star,
> Sat gray-hair'd Saturn, quiet as a stone,
> Still as the silence round about his lair;

Forest on forest hung about his head
Like cloud on cloud. No stir of air was there,
Not so much life as on a summer's day
Robs not one light seed from the feather'd grass,
But where the dead leaf fell, there did it rest.
A stream went voiceless by, still deadened more
By reason of his fallen divinity
Spreading a shade: the Naiad 'mid her reeds
Press'd her cold finger closer to her lips.

                                        (*PW*, 1.1–14)

This description of general lifelessness is sharpened by two crucial
ideas that dominate the succeeding scenes of the poems: first, and perhaps most important, the idea of silence; second, the idea of motionless-
ness. These two ideas are deliberately confused. The central image of
Saturn "quiet as a stone" economically captures both the silence of the
god and a stony immobility that is so great that he is later seen
"postured motionless, / Like natural sculpture in cathedral cavern"
(*PW*, 1.85–86). "Quiet as a stone" is elaborated upon by "Still as the
silence round about his lair," in which "Still" provides both its meanings, silent and immobile. The surrounding landscape shares Saturn's
fate and finalizes the dominant association the passage is building. The
absence of any "stir of air," for example, reiterates how far the landscape has fallen from "the healthy breath of morn" and anticipates the
poem's consistent association of air with both motion and sound (for
example, the epic simile that describes Thea's words as a gust of wind
in 1.72–79 or "the Zephyr breathes the loudest song" in 3.26). Likewise,
the stream's voicelessness (like Saturn's) seems to extend into an interruption of its activity. While the stream at first appears to go by undisturbed, its action seems halted by the modifier "still deadened more,"
with "still" not only beginning an adverbial description stating that the
stream is additionally deadened, but also adjectively answering how.
That is, "still" repeats its earlier double association in the description of
Saturn, and "still deadened" describes a stream whose voicelessness at
once becomes its immobility. It is like Keats's use of the adjectival "dead
still" in "Endymion," 1.405. If we are told that the stream goes by, in a
curious way its voicelessness seems to contradict this: with the absence
of its familiar murmurs we fail to conceive of its moving at all. In fact,
Keats uses the adjective "voiceless" for the adverb "voicelessly" as if the
adverb would be a contradiction in terms; while the stream itself can be
voiceless, its activity can not. The positioning of "deadened" between
"still more" repeats the more obvious interruption of "went by" with
"voiceless." Tmesis describes Saturn's world: the unusual interruption

of the normal speech pattern suggests at once a world whose movement and speech have been interrupted. The activity of both the air and the stream, or rather their lack of activity, is described with an insistently negative syntax and diction. The triple negative—"No stir of air," "Not so much life," and "Robs not one light seed"—trips the reader by making him anxiously hesitate over the syntactic brink of an erroneous double negative, and, by slowing down his progress through the passage, postpones his reaching the actual activity (it turns out to be the end of activity) being described—"But where the dead leaf fell, there did it rest." In fact, in the opening lines there is a postponement of the verb until line 4, and the verb itself turns out to signal no activity at all—"Sat gray-hair'd Saturn," where the name "Saturn," in its echo of "sat," seems to name Saturn's essential nature. (Similarly in "The Fall," 1.301, we read, "So Saturn sat. . . .)

In these different ways the reader experiences the central conjunction of impeded speech and movement that is the ruling idea of the passage. The negatives that describe how the air did not act are like the description of the stream by a quality it lacks rather than possesses: it is "voiceless" the way Saturn, in the following lines, is "nerveless," "listless" (without list or desire or choice), and "realmless." The final image of the passage, the Naiad's pose, anticipates the entranced posturings of Saturn and Thea. She seems frozen into a characteristic pose, awed into a fixed silence by the god's fall. Her finger is about to press her lip's closer in a hush (like the "hushing finger" of Saturn in PW, 2.119) that symbolizes the silence of the whole scene. The pile up of sibilants—"reeds," "Press'd," "closer," and finally "lips" (the s's in "reeds" and "lips" are particularly emphasized; these two monosyllables almost make a concluding couplet)—suggests the hushing sound.

From start to finish, the passage has about it a sense of the inexorable. In fact, there seems to be no start or finish in the passage at all as it circles round and round its central association. The repetitions in diction and syntax describe something inescapable. In a passage of fourteen lines there is an oppressive sense of repetition: the repetition of "Far" at the beginning of lines 2 and 3; the almost redundant use of three clauses that reiterate how far Saturn has fallen from the light (like the triple negative to follow); the description, "Forest on forest hung about his head / Like cloud on cloud," with its doubled doublings; the double use of "there" in the sentence about "No stir of air," with the circuitous and repetitive phrases always seeking a way out of their own imprisonment and finally settling on the localized place beyond which the seed and the syntax seem unable to travel. The air is so still it can cast no single seed to the wind to implant it in a fertile soil: like the immobile Saturn and like the stream that apparently goes nowhere, the seed seems destined, through the absence of any wind, not to escape this barren landscape of death. There is an unalterable and inescapable rhythm sounded in the double prepositional phrases, "Where the dead leaf fell, there did it rest." Saturn, so far sunken from the healthy breath of morning, the fiery noon, and evening's one star, appears to miss the passage of time altogether: he exists not in an eternal heaven but in a time-less world that is stagnant, static, and so insistently repetitive that genuine change seems not to exist at all.

But the reader is moved to a subtle discrimination, perhaps a way out. The description of "No stir of air," with its triple negatives, suggests that life is grading down to an inestimable minimum, almost beyond words themselves, or any method of quantification for that matter. The whole scene has a kind of inexpressible lifelessness that seems to resist, and stand in opposition to, the poet's own activity of articulation. If at first the passage appears mesmerized by the lack of activity it describes and seems simply to travel in circles unable to progress beyond its original association, ultimately it becomes a brilliant and untiring utterance. The poet and his words work overtime, tirelessly laboring at the dominant association that stands in direct opposition to his activity. He makes his words reach out toward what all words seem to resist, namely a lack of activity, a silence, a nothingness. Indeed, the only sign of life here is not in the scene but of it: it is the activity of the words themselves, interact-ing and exchanging meanings, doubling in unexpected ways their syntactic and thematic functions. The language is pregnant with meaning, in a de-scription of a silent and forlorn god and a barren landscape. If the scene (not to mention the whole of the poem) seems actionless, so much so that Keats's critics are bothered by its lack of epic action, it starts to become clear that the subject of the poem is a very special kind of action and its lack: Keats began to see that "fine writing is next to fine doing the top thing in the world" (L, 2, 146), and in the Hyperion poems (this becomes even clearer in the prologue to "The Fall") the activities of language—speech and writing—stand in opposition to the stillness of the fallen gods.

The primal scene of Saturn's fall is generalized, by Saturn himself, into a description of the universe, of "all space": "space starr'd, and lorn of light; / Space region'd with life-air; and barren void; / Spaces of fire, and all the yawn of hell" (PW, 1.118–20). These are familiar terms because half of them have been used in the opening scene of the poem: the first set of terms describes the world the Titans have fallen from, and the second the world they now inhabit. I say the Titans because the catalogue of fallen gods in book 2 of "Hyperion" enlarges upon the opening scene and is in fact "the yawn of hell" Saturn describes. Like the opening scene it is certainly "lorn of light": "It was a den [like Saturn's "lair"] where no insulting light / Could glimmer on their tears" (2.5–6). It is in fact a

place in which many of the senses appear deadened: sight is impossible
because of the darkness—"No shape distinguishable, more than when /
Thick night confounds the pine-tops with the clouds" (2.79-80)—and
hearing is also partially prevented in what at first appears to be a comfort to the gods. There is not the silence here of the opening scene, but
a noise that has a similar effect: "where their own groans / They felt, but
heard not, for the solid roar / Of thunderous waterfalls and torrents
hoarse" (2.6-8). Speechless like Saturn, they are able only to groan, and
deafened by the noise, it is as if they are silent to each other: "Each one
kept shroud, nor to his neighbor gave / Or word, or look, or action of
despair" (2.39-40). The deafening sounds may seem like a protection
against hearing their own groans, but the noise they hear in fact ironically broadcasts their defeat in every direction. The "thunderous waterfalls" cruelly remind them of Saturn's lost power—what Thea calls "Thy
thunder, conscious of the new command" (1.60)—and the "hoarse" torrents echo their own sick inarticulateness.

The gods are, like Saturn, surrounded by a landscape that pictures
their own defeat: "Crag jutting forth to crag, and rocks that seem'd /
Ever as if just rising from a sleep, / Forehead to forehead held their
monstrous horns" (PW, 2.10-12). If the rocks curiously seem to contradict their own insentience by rising from a sleep, these gods seem always
on the verge of becoming the barren stones that surround them. They
are "like a dismal cirque / Of Druid stones" (2.34-35). The crags and
rocks are personified into foreheads and horns, adding to the implicit
logic of the whole passage: once again the stones are more like the giants
than the giants themselves, anticipating the question of identity—the gods
continually ask, Lear-like, who they are—that is asked about the gods
throughout the poems. The rocks certainly seem transformed into "the
whole mammoth-brood" (1.164), with large "forehead to forehead"
(like Thea's "large forehead" in 1.80) and "monstrous horns." In any
case, the activity is so emphatically potential—"Seem'd / Ever as if just
rising"—that it suggests an impossible, or at least improbable, hypothesis
about action that applies equally to the rocks and to the gods.

This question of the gods' activity is crucial and, like their inability
to hear each other's groans, is based upon a cruelly deceptive comfort.
The Titans are divided according to two activities that seem opposite but
are ironically alike—"Some chain'd in torture, and some wandering"
(PW, 2.18). The narrator elaborates upon "some wandering": "Mnemosyne
was straying in the world; / Far from her moon had Phoebe wandered; /
And many else were free to roam abroad, / But for the main, here found
they covert drear" (2.29-32). The two activities turn out to be versions
of each other: whether abroad or in the covert drear, the Titans' loss of
power is signalled by their lack of purposeful activity. Abroad, they dis-

cover an ironic freedom that reveals only their superannuation. Phoebe wanders far from her moon (the phrase repeats Saturn's position "Far from the fiery noon"), no longer able to direct it (like Hyperion, in book 1, unable to direct the dawn). Generally, the "free" gods stray, wander, and roam, all verbs describing directionless activities, like the description later of "Many a fallen old Divinity / Wandering in vain about bewildered shores" (3.8-9). Our initial view of Saturn becomes extended here both by the "free" and "chained" gods.

Saturn's rest—an idea that can be fully grasped only when compared to the "rest divine" (PW, 1.192) the gods have lost—is a crucial indication of his loss of power: Saturn's stillness was implicitly compared to the landscape in which "where the dead leaf fell, there did it rest." If the "free" gods repeat Saturn's rest—both are free from purposeful activity, what he calls the "influence benign on planets pale" (1.108)—the chained gods are allowed no activity at all:

> Coeus, and Gyges, and Briareüs,
> Typhon, and Dolor, and Porphyrion,
> With many more, the brawniest in assault,
> Were pent in regions of laborious breath;
> Dungeon'd in opaque element, to keep
> Their clenched teeth still clench'd, and all their limbs
> Lock'd up like veins of metal, crampt and screw'd;
> Without a motion, save of their big hearts
> Heaving in pain, and horribly convuls'd
> With sanguine feverous boiling gurge of pulse.
>
> (2.19-28)

The gods are punished by an ironic inversion of Saturn's rest. Unable to move at all, their rest becomes exhausting labor: they are "pent in regions of laborious breath." It is a world so exhausting and so suffocatingly empty of "life-air" or "stir of air" that to breathe is a labor, which they perform neither well nor easily. Labor becomes defined, again and again in the catalogue of the gods, as the senseless pain the gods undergo: Cottus, for example, "ground severe his skull, with open mouth / And eyes at horrid working" (2.51-52, emphasis added).

Even the labor of childbirth, given the fate of the gods, becomes a description of a fatal activity. We find "nearest him / Asia, born of most enormous Caf, / Who cost her mother Tellus keener pangs, / Though feminine, than any of her sons" (PW, 2.52-55). What Tellus purchases with her labor is death, a cost Yeats eloquently speaks of in his famous question, "What youthful mother . . . / Would think her son, did she but see that shape / With sixty or more winters on its head, / A compensation for the pang of his birth, / Or the uncertainty of his setting forth?"

(*CPY*, 214). This idea reaches its most poignant moment with Clymene: "Neighbour'd close / Oceanus, and Tethys, in whose lap / Sobb'd Clymene among her tangled hair" (2.74–76). Clymene, daughter of Oceanus and Tethys, is positioned in Tethys's lap, a grim reminder of the labor she cost her mother, with sobs and tangled hair the unmistakable signs of the daughter's doom. It is a picture of what Keats calls in "The Fall of Hyperion" "the families of grief" (1.461), and it makes pathetic "this nest of woe" (2.14), "this nest of pain" (2.90). Keats is indebted here to what he termed "the sublime pathetic" in Milton, a technique he consistently associates with Milton and the parent-child relationship. In Milton, as an example of the sublime pathetic, he points to the passage "where Satan's progeny is called his '*daughter dear*,'" and in choosing Milton over "the brief pathos of Dante," he gives two similar examples: he praises the lines, "which cost Ceres all that pain" (obviously the model for the passage on Tethys's cost) and "Nor could the Muse defend her son."[1] In any case, the senseless labor of Keats's Titans, whether hard and purposeless work or what is here the fatal labor of childbirth, can be summed up, ironically enough, with an image originally used to describe Thea's power: she "would have . . . with a finger stay'd Ixion's wheel" (1.30).

The immobility of the Titans—they are "cramp't and screw'd" and they lay "prone" and "prostrate" (*PW*, 2.49 and 85)—is of course the most direct sign of their loss of power. Coelus, in his speech to Hyperion, for example, associates godly power with movement: "as thou art capable, / As thou canst move about, an evident God" (1.337–38). But I am concerned here with the association in the opening scene of the poem between immobility and silence. It is stated almost emblematically in the midst of the catalogue of the gods in the description of Iapetus's serpent, "With its barbed tongue / Squeez'd from the gorge, and all its uncurl'd length / Dead" (2.45–47). Saturn's stillness is repeated in the image of the Titans' "clenched teeth still clench'd," in which "still" has similar associations. Adverbially, it extends the agony of the gods into an indefinite future, but adjectively it suggests that the teeth are clenched still and silent. After all, it is clearly a description of a kind of enforced silence; lack of movement again means lack of speech. In fact, in "Hyperion" speech becomes the supreme activity, and there are upwards of a dozen references to an organ of speech, often characterized by some malady, or at least disuse. By metonymy, lips, teeth, tongue, throat, even head and neck, suggest the ability or inability to speak, and we encounter, for example, a "palsied tongue" (1.93), a "convuls'd head and neck" (1.262), a "barbed tongue" (2.45), a "feeble tongue" (1.49), a "too indulged tongue" (2.298), and "hollow throats" (2.391).

Images of restraint are used throughout the Hyperions but they

usually suggest the particular restraint of speech—strangling, stifling, suffocating, or smothering—as when the poet asks in "The Fall" why death
comes not "to choke my utterance" (PW, 1.140). An example of a brilliantly associative passage in this vein in "Hyperion" is Saturn's speech
to the gods:

> Who had power
> To make me desolate? Whence came the strength?
> How was it nurtur'd to such bursting forth,
> While Fate seem'd strangled in my nervous grasp?
> But it is so; and I am smother'd up,
> And buried from all godlike exercise,
> Of influence benign on planets pale,
> Of admonitions to the winds and seas,
> Of peaceful sway above man's harvesting,
> And all those acts which Deity supreme
> Doth ease its heart of love in.

(1.102–12)

It is interesting that Saturn applies to his enemy, Fate, the same kind of
torture that is used on him. He thought he had strangled Fate, but instead
he discovers that it is he who is smothered up. Both these images are intimately connected with the failure of "godlike exercise," a phrase that
suggests how the capability for simple movement merges with the ultimate activity of power. "I am smother'd up" seems equated with the
fact that I am "buried from all godlike exercise." An image that re-
emphasizes how the loss of power is signalled by smothering, it conjures
up a deadly suffocation, the god buried alive. The failure of activity is
also signified by the gods' loss of "influence benign on planets pale"
(like Diana's failure to direct the moon or Hyperion's the sun). Finally,
the loss of powerful activity is related to "man's harvesting": man's
labor is productive of the harvest, while the gods either wander in vain
or labor in vain, in a landscape that can never hope to produce a harvest.
There is a subtle irony in the fact that Saturn sees his loss of power as a
loss of the gods' ability to "ease" their hearts in love, an ease that is
distinguished from the productive labor of the harvest and perhaps leads
to the enforced rest (really labor) of Saturn and the Titans.

The picture "Hyperion" gives us of its title character is significantly
located between the opening images of Saturn and Thea, and the catalogue of the fallen gods that begins book 2. Comprising the second half
of the first book, it is meant to be an epic contrast in the manner of
Milton's brilliant juxtaposition, as when (according to Keats) "we see
the Great God and our first parent, and that same satan all brought in
one's vision." Lines 1–157 of book 1 describe fallen Saturn and Thea,

then seven lines of transition look forward to the covert of the fallen
gods, and then lines 164–357 describe Hyperion. The introduction of
Hyperion at this point is meant to convey the "Magnitude of Contrast"[2]
that Keats so admired in Milton:

> But one of the whole mammoth brood still kept
> His sovereignty, and rule, and majesty;—
> Blazing Hyperion on his orbed fire
> Still sat, still snuff'd the incense, teeming up
> From man to the sun's God.
>
> (*PW*, 1.164–68)

Once again "still" insistently (it is used three times) describes a god and,
while here it suggests a continuity of powerful repose, as the description of Hyperion continues we learn that such stillness has been lost by
Hyperion, and will soon turn into the unhealthy stillness of the fallen
Titans.

> And so, when harbour'd in the sleepy west,
> After the full completion of fair day,—
> For rest divine upon exalted couch
> And slumber in the arms of melody,
> He pac'd away the pleasant hours of ease.
>
> (1.190–94)

Hyperion's slumber is no longer allowed. He is racked by dreams
(really nightmares) whose "busy" shapes refuse him any rest by describing the torturous and purposeless labor of his fallen brothers: "O
dreams of day and night! / O monstrous forms! O effigies of pain! / O
spectres busy in a cold, cold gloom!" (*PW*, 1.227–29). Significantly,
heaven was a place of rest apparently quite different from the region of
these busy specters, a heaven-haven of shelter:

> Am I to leave this haven of my rest,
> This cradle of my glory, this soft clime,
> This calm luxuriance of blissful light,
> These crystalline pavilions, and pure fanes,
> Of all my lucent empire?
>
> (1.235–39)

Keats locates these descriptions of the unfallen god and heaven strategically before the catalogue of the gods. The covert of the gods that at
first appears only as a place of punishment (and it certainly is that) is
also a description of the symptom of the disease of heaven. Heaven's
divine rest can lapse, as the poem makes clear, into the "rest" of Saturn
—that is, a kind of sleepy death—and finally into the fallen gods' agonizing restraint on activity. It is a version of the subtle study in contrasts

and similitudes that Keats noticed in *Paradise Lost:* "Heaven moves on like Music throughout—Hell is also peopled with angels it also moves on like music not grating and harsh but like a grand accompaniment in the Base to Heaven—".[3] Keats's heaven turns out to have far more in common with hell than Milton's does. Hyperion is connected with Clymene and Asia the way heaven is connected with hell. While we are moved by these children who suddenly find their doom, heaven is seen as a childish place, all infantile slumber and no activity: it is a "cradle," and the fall from it necessarily is at once the child's fate and doom. Saturn's earlier description of the "barren void" as "the yawn of hell" is now doubly significant: "yawn" suggests the luxuriant restfulness and slumber that the infantile gods once enjoyed and the result of hard and exhausting labor. The "yawn of hell" collapses heaven and hell, and with its own metaphoric logic points to the connection between the two.

Hyperion's questions about his haven of rest turn out to be rhetorical. He follows them with the correct answers: "It is left / Deserted, void, nor any haunt of mine" (*PW*, 1.239-40). Heaven has become the void that hell is, and Hyperion already seems like the phantoms and specters he describes, his empire no "haunt" of his. He begins to show all the signs of his fallen brothers: the shady visions, he complains, "Insult, and blind, and stifle up my pomp" (1.245). The image of the stifled god is elaborated upon in a series of images that describe (as they do for the other Titans) a loss of the power of speech:

> He spake, and ceas'd, the while a heavier threat
> Held struggle with his throat but came not forth;
> For as in theatres of crowded men
> Hubbub increases more they call out "Hush!"
> So at Hyperion's words the Phantoms pale
> Bestirr'd themselves, thrice horrible and cold.
>
> (1.251-56)

If Hyperion wants to silence these phantoms, ironically enough he himself is visited with a deadly silence as the phantoms wax in power; his failure to speak is ironically matched by their hubbub.

Upon his failure to quiet these specters, a proleptic vision arises, which foretells Hyperion's fate by looking forward to the catalogue of gods in book 2.

> And from the mirror'd level where he stood
> A mist arose, as from a scummy marsh.
> At this, through all his bulk an agony
> Crept gradual, from the feet into the crown,
> Like a lithe serpent vast and muscular

Making slow way, with head and neck convuls'd
From over-strained might.

(*PW*, 1.257-63)

This is modeled after Satan's entrance into the serpent in the ninth book
of *Paradise Lost*, a passage that fascinated Keats: "Whose spirit does not
ache at the smothering and confinement—the unwilling stillness—the
'waiting close'? Whose head is not dizzy at the possibly [sic] speculations
of satan in the serpent prison—no passage of poetry ever can give a greater pain of suffocation."[4] The serpent prison Keats uses in "Lamia," of
course, and in the final description of Saturn in "The Fall of Hyperion."
His sense of the "pain of suffocation" makes it particularly relevant to
this description of Hyperion, the stifled god, and his phrase "the unwilling stillness" has all the associations we would expect. Not only does
Hyperion see visions of his fallen brothers, then, he seems, in a horrid
metamorphosis, to be transformed into their agony. Worse, the image
proleptically declares in the midst of heaven a hell, and in the midst of
paradise the serpent. He is become the serpent in his own Eden, another
sign of the self-destruction of the Titans. Hyperion seems transformed
into Iapetus's serpent, whose suffocation, because of his inability to spit
out his poison, links him to the powerless, speechless, convulsed god.
Hyperion's "overstrained might," a labor the god is unused to, vainly attempts to stifle the hubbub of his visions, but instead the god himself
is seen convulsed because of his own impotent speechlessness.

While the reader has seen and understood all the signs of Hyperion's
fall, the act that makes the god himself realize his loss of power is his
failure at activity.

Fain would he have commanded, fain took throne
And bid the day begin, if but for change.
He might not:—No, though a primeval God:
The sacred seasons might not be disturb'd.
Therefore the operations of the dawn
Stay'd in their birth, even as here 'tis told.

(*PW*, 1.290-95)

It is a stillbirth, labor gone awry: the failure of his labor points to the
enforced rest that is the worst labor of all. "And all along a dismal rack
of clouds, / Upon the boundaries of day and night, / He stretch'd himself in gulf and radiance faint" (1.302-4). In a grotesque parody of the
birth process—of "the operations of the dawn"—Hyperion stretches his
body, where "faint" seems to characterize not only the radiance but
also the agony of the fainting god whose labor is no birth. Keats adds
poignance to the scene at this moment, with another example of "the
sublime pathetic." The son (Hyperion) is unable to give birth to another

son (or at least the sun) and the father (Coelus) fondly remembers the son's birth:

> There as he lay, the Heaven with its stars
> Look'd down on him with pity, and the voice
> Of Coelus, from the universal space,
> Thus whisper'd low and solemn in his ear.
> "O brightest of my children dear, earth-born,
> And sky-engendered, Son of Mysteries
> All unrevealed even to the powers
> Which met at thy creating; at whose joys
> And palpitations sweet, and pleasures soft,
> I, Coelus, wonder, how they came and whence;
> And at the fruits thereof. . . ."

(1.305-15)

The two labors are distinct, sheer antipodes: one produces nothing, the other "the fruits" that are the opposite of the nothing, of "the barren void." Coelus's speech, while it attempts to comfort, just makes plainer Hyperion's powerlessness.

The incomplete third book of Hyperion, with its description of Apollo, is a breath of fresh air (quite literally) in the otherwise oppressive atmosphere of the poem. It is a single sustained moment (sustained, that is, through 140 lines or so and then cut off) of optimistic romance, and as such it reminds one of "Endymion." In fact, it seems a deliberate attempt at contradicting the mood of what has gone before. The poet enters the poem, and asks the Muse, "Meantime touch piously the Delphic harp, / And not a wind of heaven but will breathe / In aid of soft warble from the Dorian flute; / For lo! 'tis for the Father of all verse" (PW, 3.10-14). Life enters the poem with a breath from heaven, and in the person of Apollo, who as sun god and the god of poetry, fathers the fruition that is at once vegetable and linguistic. The imagery of this book consistently associates air with both breathing and singing, in contrast to the labored breathing and absence of any stir of air in the first two books: "Rejoice, O Delos, with thine olives green, / And poplars, and lawn-shading palms, and beech, / In which the Zephyr breathes the loudest song" (3.24-26). The "voiceless" stream of the opening scene is replaced by a melodious body of water that seems to fill with its sound anything resembling a void or barren place: "Throughout all the isle / There was no covert, no retired cave / Unhaunted by the murmurous noise of waves" (3.38-40).

To say that the third book of "Hyperion" is earmarked by its return to the earlier mode of "Endymion" is to declare the sudden failure of the poem. Like "Endymion," the third book seems directed too simply by wish fulfillment, and the poet's directing presence is obtrusive and singularly out of place. He simply asks for a wind of heaven, and it is granted, as if he were suddenly in the world of happy romance. In fact, the narrator's romancelike commands—"Let the rose glow intense and warm the air" (PW, 3.15)—do not sit well with his consistent and what now seem to be his merely conventional epic reminders of his own sad powers of speech and the gods' divine tongue. He usurps, suddenly, this divine tongue, in the series of summoning imperatives that begin book 3: "Let the rose glow," "let the clouds . . . ," "Let the red wine . . . ," "let faint-lipp'd shells . . . ," and so forth. The poet's words seem to function the way they do in "Endymion": they enact his wishes, fill the page with his desires fulfilled and with a dream landscape. Rather than being a subtle contrast to what has gone before, book 3 grows into an obvious escape from the mode of the first two books. "Hyperion" then can be said to break off not simply in the midst of the third book, but to be thematically and stylistically fragmented by the unmanageable differences between the first two and the third books. The literal fragmentariness of "Hyperion" seems a sign of this sudden divergence of mode and intention, and the poem is constructed anew in "The Fall of Hyperion" to solve this problem.

The meetings with the muse (Apollo and Mnemosyne in "Hyperion" and the poet and Moneta in "The Fall of Hyperion") are the clearest bridge between the two poems. Both meetings enact a transfer of power. Apollo asks, "Where is power?" (PW, 3.103), and his question is answered as knowledge pours into his brain to deify him. Moneta tells the poet, "My power, which to me is still a curse, / Shall be to thee a wonder" (1.243-44), and the poet similarly experiences "A power within me of enormous ken / To see as a god sees" (1.303-4). But what is implicit in the scene with Apollo—the transfer of power at least partially involves a linguistic power—becomes in the scene with the poet the overriding theme, and the transfer of power is dramatically defined wholly as a transfer of linguistic power. There is even a striking difference between the silence of the scene in "Hyperion" and the actual speech in "The Fall." Here is the deification of Apollo:

Mute thou remainest—mute! yet I can read
A wondrous lesson in thy silent face:
Knowledge enormous makes a God of me.
Names, deeds, grey legends, dire events, rebellions,
Majesties, sovran voices, agonies,
Creations and destroyings, all at once

Pour into the wide hollows of my brain,
And deify me.

(3.111–18)

Keats emphasizes Mnemosyne's muteness twice, and then a third time
through her "silent face." Her silence may immediately link her to
Saturn's quiet, but of course it is filled with meaning and power. Apollo
"reads" a lesson in her face, and here the matter becomes triply complicated. First, a silent language, that is, words that exist as written (as in a
lesson book), may be read by Apollo. Second, this silent language may
contain, paradoxically, a vocal quality: certainly "sovran voices" has this
sense, as opposed, for example, to the "names" he may read. Finally,
much of his knowledge may be present to him simply as unworded
images that he "reads."

All this seems equivocal when compared to the undeviating focus of
the scene in "The Fall." Moneta is anything but mute, being at first no
more (and no less) than speech itself—"From whose white fragrant curtains thus I heard / Language pronounc'd" (PW, 1.106–7). The point at
which the poet is deified (to make the comparison precise) is clearly
marked once again not by silence but by the power of Moneta's voice:

Then Moneta's voice
Came brief upon mine ear—"So Saturn sat
When he had lost his Realms—" whereon there grew
A power within me of enormous ken
To see as a god sees.

(1.300–304)

Even a string of a few words, an incomplete sentence, turns the poet into a godhead. If in "Hyperion" the Muse seems an embodied silence, an
unspoken language, in "The Fall" she seems a disembodied voice. This
sense of voice makes a sharper and richer contrast with the failure of
speech on the part of the fallen Titans. In fact, this transfer of linguistic
power structures "The Fall of Hyperion": it connects such things as the
narrator's epic intrusions about his "feeble tongue" with the poem's
central action, and conversely deepens the story of the fall of the gods
by framing it with the poet's own activity.

The brief prologue of the poem acts as an introduction to the idea
of speech and begins to suggest the contrast that will eventually differentiate between power and the state of the fallen gods:

Fanatics have their dreams, wherewith they weave
A paradise for a sect; the savage too
From forth the loftiest fashion of his sleep
Guesses at Heaven; pity these have not

Trac'd upon vellum or wild Indian leaf
The shadows of melodious utterance.
But bare of laurel they live, dream, and die;
For Poesy alone can tell her dreams,
With the fine spell of words alone can save
Imagination from the sable charm
And dumb enchantment. Who alive can say,
"Thou art no Poet—may'st not tell thy dreams?"
Since every man whose soul is not a clod
Hath visions, and would speak, if he had loved,
And been well nurtured in his mother tongue.
Whether the dream now purpos'd to rehearse
Be poet's or fanatic's will be known
When this warm scribe my hand is in the grave.

$$(PW, 1.1-18)$$

Poetry is insistently seen as speech; it is "melodious utterance." Twice
we hear that poetry can "tell" its dreams, and finally, that it can "speak"
them. There is, however, the added sense that the poet writes as well as
speaks, a difference important to consider. Suffice it to say now that
while there is a difference between speaking and writing, both the
metonymies Keats uses ("tongue" and "hand") emphasize the activity
involved in the making of words. Once again language is associated with
a part of the body, and if speech is the more obvious activity (given the
kinds of muscular examples we have been noticing), still Keats would
have it that the writer also is a laborer, a manual laborer in fact, not unlike the weaver or harvester. There is, in this notion of activity, a curious
distinction between "the fine spell of words" and "the sable charm /
And dumb enchantment." Imagination seems vulnerable to a deadly
sleep (the sable charm, the dumb enchantment), and the fine spell of
words alone can save it. Salvation is the theme of the poem, salvation
through spelling. The pun joins magical vision (like charms and enchant-
ments) with its being spelled out, spoken and told. In fact, "weave,"
"save," and "grave" are the articulate voiced sounds out of which the
melody of the passage grows. The dreamer's weaving of beautiful
fashions can be saved only through the further labor of words; without
that labor all is destined for the grave. The saving power of words literally stands at the center of the passage (line 9 in a passage of 18 lines), so
this prologue becomes a case in which Keats's verse covers its ground
suggestively.

The effect of Thea's address to Saturn can be compared to the
hypothesis of the prologue, namely, that words save:

As when upon a tranced summer-night

Forests, branch-charmed by the earnest stars,
Dream, and so dream all night without a noise,
Save from one gradual solitary gust,
Swelling upon the silence; dying off;
As if the ebbing air had but one wave;
So came these words, and went.

(PW, 1.372-78)

The epic simile compares Saturn to the branch-charmed forests and
Thea's words to a noise that is at the same time a solitary gust of air.
Keats reminds us of the notion of the saving power of words by making
the landscape without a noise "save from one gradual solitary gust."
Thea's words, then, are at once the exception that alone can save. But
words seem unable to save Saturn here. The rhythm of the passage—the
gust swells and dies off, the words come and go—reminds one of the unalterable and deadly rhythm of the primal scene of Saturn's fall in which
"where the dead leaf fell, there did it rest."

It is clear that the hypothesis of the prologue does not work: Saturn
seems entranced so deeply that he can not be awakened, and his charm is
a kind that is inaccessible to words, not the kind that can be spelled. The
passage is not meant to deny the hypothesis but rather to suggest that some
words are weak and some charms (here it is in perfect agreement with the
prologue) are absolutely dumb. It is a scene that dominated Keats's imagination, and it appears in "Endymion" with different characters. Here the
words are able to awaken the entranced sleeper: "But in the self-same
fixed trance he kept, / Like one who on the earth had never slept. / Aye,
even as dead still as a marble man, / Frozen in that old tale Arabian"
(PW, 1.403-6). This picture of Endymion is an early study of Saturn's
dead stillness. All around Endymion are men who "out-told / Their fond
imaginations" (1.392-93) and are thereby saved from his trance. Peona
attempts (like Thea) and succeeds (unlike Thea) in awakening the sleeper
with speech: "Her eloquence did breathe away the curse" (1.412).

In the passage in "The Fall," if we have the full meaning of the prologue in mind, we can see that an implicit distinction is being made between the poet and Saturn: the poet is rehearsing a dream, we remember,
and Saturn here is in a deep sleep, dreaming the whole night through (to
use the terms of the simile). While Saturn's dream remains dumb, the very
descriptions of Thea's words and their inability to awaken Saturn are the
articulations, the "melodious utterance," of the poet's dream rehearsal.
The epic intrusion about the narrator's feeble tongue that was used con-
ventionally and sometimes inconsistently in "Hyperion" here becomes deliberately ironic. Thea's speech is in fact introduced with the convention:

> some words she spake
> In solemn tenor and deep organ tune;
> Some mourning words, which in our feeble tongue
> Would come in this-like accenting; how frail
> To that large utterance of the early gods!
>
> (*PW*, 1.349-53)

If the poet seems to want us to believe (an example of epic humility) that the gods' language is superior to his own, we discover that what is being dramatized is the exact opposite. Given the failure of the effect of Thea's words and the salvation that the poet is enacting for himself through words, the epic convention begins to play an integral, if ironic, role in the poem. First, it points to language as a sign of power, and second, it begins to suggest the slow transfer of power to the poet through words that shapes the poem's development.

Saturn's speech is the most elaborate example of the gods' loss of power pictured in terms of their speech. In "Hyperion," Saturn's power, like that of most gods, depended on his ability to speak: he longs for the days "when all the fair Existences of heaven / Came open-eyed to guess what we would speak" (a fine example of Keats's marriage of vision and speech, *PW*, 2.337-38). Continually, in both Hyperions, the fallen gods await his words. At the appearance of Hyperion in the first poem, all the gods "gave from their hollow throats the name of 'Saturn!'" (2.391). Similarly in "The Fall," the fallen gods are "listening in their doom for Saturn's voice" (2.12). While Thea's speech is summarized by an epic simile about language, Saturn's is introduced by one:

> As the moist scent of flowers, and grass, and leaves,
> Fills forest dells with a pervading air,
> Known to the woodland nostril, so the words
> Of Saturn fill'd the mossy glooms around,
> Even to the hollows of the time-eaten oaks,
> And to the windings of the foxes' hole,
> With sad low tones, while thus he spake, and sent
> Strange musings to the solitary Pan.
>
> (1.404-11)

It is an impressive beginning, and what we would expect of a god. In fact, it is clearly modelled on Keats's obsessive wish at the beginning of his career that language fill a bare world. Saturn's words have the productive power of "the healthy breath of morn," and are an analogous production to nature's "flowers, and grass, and leaves." As we listen attentively to the words he speaks, however, we discover something else:

"Moan, brethren, moan; for we are swallow'd up / And buried from all Godlike exercise / Of influence benign on planets pale, / And peaceful sway above man's harvesting" (1.412–15). This speech also appears in "Hyperion," but here in "The Fall" it has a different introduction (the epic simile above) and an extended and more meaningful conclusion. Saturn's words are the encouragement not to more godly speech but to moans, and if the epic simile led us to believe his words were fruitful even as the earth is, here he admits that he is divorced from the "peaceful sway above man's harvesting." Saturn connects his loss of power with a loss of linguistic power when he characterizes himself as "weak as the reed—weak—feeble as my voice—" (1.428). (In "Hyperion," Saturn makes no such admission; a similar line—"I am but a voice" (1.340)—belongs to Coelus.)

At this point Saturn's speech takes a desperate turn in an attempt at power. If Saturn represents a loss of identity, and Hyperion is on the brink of such a loss, it is fitting that their speech fluctuates between agonizing and unashamed questions on the one hand and vain commands on the other. In "Hyperion," for example, Saturn ends this very speech with "I will give command: / Thea! Thea! Thea! where is Saturn?" (PW, 1.133–34). The exclamations amount less to commands than to desperate cries, and the question in which he shows he is unable even to associate his name with himself is the ultimate dissociation of language and the power of self-identity.

> Moan, moan, for still I thaw—or give me help;
> Throw down those imps, and give me victory.
> Let me hear other groans, and trumpets blown
> Of triumph calm, and hymns of festival,
> From the gold peaks of Heaven's high-piled clouds;
> Voices of soft proclaim, and silver stir
> Of strings in hollow shells; and let there be
> Beautiful things made new.
>
> (1.430–37)

Saturn expects to will their "moans" into "Voices of soft proclaim," as his own voice takes on the godlike tones of power. The two clauses that begin with "let" suggest this growing power: if the first has more the sense of "allow me to hear," the second is unmistakably the divine commandment, "let there be."

At this point Keats adds a description of Saturn's speech (there is no such summary-evaluation by the narrator in "Hyperion"), making clear that, rather than the divine speech that will fill the world, it is itself hollow, merely the empty rhetoric of an old man: "So he feebly ceas'd, / With such a poor and sickly sounding pause, / Me thought I heard some old man of the earth / Bewailing earthly loss" (*PW*, 1.438–41). It is the final undercutting of the epic intrusion about the immortal tongue of the gods. The next time this epic trope is sounded it is about Moneta, not Saturn or Thea, and is not even spoken by the narrator but by Moneta herself, whose words evidence their immortal quality.

The narrator continues his description of Saturn:

> nor could my eyes
> And ears act with that pleasant unison of sense
> Which marries sweet sound with the grace of form,
> And dolourous accent from a tragic harp
> With large-limbed visions.—More I scrutinized:
> Still fix'd he sat beneath the sable trees,
> Whose arms spread straggling in wild serpent forms,
> With leaves all hush'd: his awful presence there
> (Now all was silent) gave a deadly lie
> To what I erewhile heard—only his lips
> Trembled amid the white curls of his beard.
> They told the truth, though, round, the snowy locks
> Hung nobly, as upon the face of heaven
> A mid-day fleece of clouds.
>
> (*PW*, 1.441–54)

Saturn is "still fix'd" once again, now beneath "the sable trees" that recall the "sable charm." His words evidently are not sufficient protection against this sable charm; indeed their falseness seems to have delivered him over to "deadly stillness" again rather than to salvation. Saturn and the tree merge (as in the epic simile depicting how Thea's words fail to awaken the branch-charmed forest) in their stillness: the tree's leaves are "hush'd" like Saturn, and the trees' "arms" describe a serpentine Saturn. In fact, his stoniness almost becomes at last an identifiable statue, the Laocoön. If his presence looks noble, his voice gives him away. Keats explains that only one aspect of Saturn's countenance—his lips—tell the truth. Speech cannot deceive, however it tries: "only his lips . . . told the truth." When Saturn and Thea get up to leave, Thea "stretched her white arm through the hollow dark" (1.455), making it finally clear that Saturn's speech has not turned the dark void into the fruitful garden.

I have been suggesting that the alternative to Thea and Saturn's ineffectual language is the poet's. Keats effects, it seems to me, a more powerful and meaningful contrast between Saturn and the poet than was suggested by that between Saturn and Apollo in "Hyperion." It is apparent, I think, that Apollo's indolence—he calls himself "idle" (*PW*, 3.106)—represented a problematic relationship to the notions of rest and labor achieved in the first two books of "Hyperion." The rather sudden and too easy influx of power and knowledge into Apollo's brain failed to represent a completely successful alternative to the Titans. In "The Fall of Hyperion," however, Keats frames the central story of the empty luxury of the Titans with a story of hard labor. If, as I have been suggesting, the empty rhetoric of Saturn is implicitly compared to a different notion of the poet's language, one can grasp this only by understanding that the poet's language is the product of his labor.

Keats insistently makes clear that the dream process is no luxurious daydreaming, and he does this, strategically, before the poet's dialogue with Moneta on dreamers and poets. The poet-dreamer at first finds himself in a happy dream, indeed the very dream that we have identified as the most congenial to Keats. He finds himself in a garden of plenty, a world of well-ordered space that serves the functions of comfort and even protection, as well as being a bountiful feast. The "trees of every clime" make a protective "screen" around the poet, and within this as within a further enchanted circle he finds "an arbour" with "a feast of summer fruits" (*PW*, 1.19–29): "Still was more plenty than the fabled horn / Thrice emptied could pour forth, at banqueting / For Proserpine return'd to her own fields" (1.35–37). This is the kind of simile of exaggeration seen in the description of Saturn's primal scene, but turned around; if the words there attempted to describe a lifelessness beyond words, here they hope to capture through hyperbole an almost supernatural sense of plenty. It is a short-lived moment in the poem, and there are signs everywhere of its vulnerability. Certainly the images of Proserpine, and subsequently Eve, tell of paradise lost, and the fear of emptiness is betrayed in the compulsive nature of the images of plenty and in Keats's obvious attempts at the denial of emptiness: the fabled horn, if it pours forth three times and still more, each time is "emptied," and the "empty shells" (a curiously suggestive image if we recall Saturn's wish for the hollow shells to be strung for music) of the fruits tasted suggest that a limit can be reached even in this paradise. Soon the poet loses this garden in one of Keats's favorite tropes, the dream-within-the-dream, but the new dream (of the temple, and the story of Saturn) is in direct antithesis to the first, and is in fact nearer to nightmare. It enforces upon the poet a hard labor (as opposed to the happy discovery of the fruitful summer garden at hand), with a harvest of wisdom that is suffering.

In the approach to the altar in this new, stark landscape, Keats announces the theme of labor in all its richness: the altar is "To be approach'd on either side by steps, / And marble balustrade, and patient travail / To count with toil the innumerable degrees" (*PW*, 1.90–92). The toil of the climb holds out the promise of a further labor, with "travail" having both its meanings of general toil and the specific labor

of childbirth. The theme is insistent from here on: "the hard task proposed" (1.120) is the climbing of the steps, and "Prodigious seem'd the
toil" (1.121). In the midst of this labor is an imagery always glancing at,
and missing, Saturn's entrancement. After the drink in the garden, for
example, "down I sank, / Like a Silenus on an antique vase" (1.55-56),
and while apparently falling into a temporary stupor, the poet eventually
starts up as if with wings. A "numbness" plagues him and "Slow, heavy,
deadly was my pace" (1.129), but he is able to climb the stairs. "The
cold / Grew stifling, suffocating" (1.129-30), but he shrieks in defiance
of this silencing. There is, significantly, an agony of speech the poet
must undergo: there is a "cold grasp / Upon those streams that pulse
beside the throat" (1.124-25), and he wonders "What am I that another
death come not / To choke my utterance sacrilegious?" (1.139-40). In
short, the poet's labor fights at once the inertness and silence of Saturn.
The poet knows he has been "saved from death" (1.138), and this refers
back to the theme of salvation in the prologue: his ability to speak (at
first only "shriek," 1.126) and to attend to the speech of Moneta is his
only salvation.

Moneta's speech to the poet turns completely on the notion of labor.
She praises humanitarians in what really amounts to an inverted criticism
of those who "rest":

> "None can usurp this height," return'd that shade,
> "But those to whom the miseries of the world
> "Are misery, and will not let them rest.
> "All else who find a haven in the world
> "Where they may thoughtless sleep away their days,
> "If by a chance into this fane they come,
> "Rot on the pavement where thou rottedst half."
>
> (*PW*, 1.147-53)

It is of course an argument whose meaning travels in two directions: we
think of Saturn's deadly sleep, or Hyperion's haven, and of the numbing
sleep the poet has just escaped through toil. The poet, not connecting
his recent toil (which, I suppose, has seemed somewhat gratuitous, and
certainly not in the interest of humanity) with Moneta's speech, asks if
there are not many who "like slaves to poor humanity, / Labour for
mortal good" (1.158-59). His attempt at discriminations leads Moneta
to an interesting discrimination of her own on the kinds of labor:

> Thou art a dreaming thing,
> A fever of thyself—thing of the Earth;
> What bliss even in hope is there for thee?
> What haven? every creature hath its home;

> Every sole man hath days of joy and pain,
> Whether his labours be sublime or low—
> The pain alone; the joy alone; distinct:
> Only the dreamer venoms all his days,
> Bearing more woe than all his sins deserve.
>
> (1.168-76)

A shocking turn: the dreamer is not, after all, laborless, and is in fact par excellence a laborer. But he is one who bears woe, and seems like the fallen Titans lost in a world of continuous, but unproductive, bearing and labor. The narrator, once again pressing Moneta to a further discrimination, begins by declaring the usefulness of the poet—"sure not all / Those melodies sung into the World's ear / Are useless" (1.186-89)—and the passage ends with Moneta's famous distinction between dreamers and poets.

The basic idea of the Hyperion poems is a language of power. I should explain first that Keats in fact used such a phrase, and second that, like me, he borrowed it. Keats quotes and paraphrases at great length the part of Hazlitt's *Letter to Gibson* that defines the language of power: "The language of Poetry naturally falls in with the language of power. I affirm, Sir, that Poetry, that the imagination, generally speaking, delights in power, in strong excitement, as well as in truth, in good, in right, whereas pure reason and the moral sense approve only of the true and good" (*L*, 2, 74-75). While Keats seems in full agreement with Hazlitt here, the Hyperions refute, or at least revise, Hazlitt. The argument between philosophy and poetry that plays so important a part in Keats's poetics, with ever increasing importance after "Endymion" and as he approaches "The Fall," moves him at times to give up poetry precisely because of Hazlitt's meaning: the Muse seems promiscuously to give herself to the flashiest bidder, and finds (in the quoted words of Hazlitt) "in grandeur, in outward shew, in the accumulation of individual wealth and luxury" (2, 75) something irresistible. Poetry associates itself arbitrarily with good and evil, truth and illusion, and if a choice is necessary, it will sacrifice truth to a happy illusion. In the Hyperion poems Keats begins to define the language of power differently: it has left the fallen Titans precisely because they no longer represent the truth. But it must be granted that in its grossest form the idea does appear in "Hyperion" in a version close to Hazlitt's. In the Titans' debate the power of language is simply the ability to persuade, to steal center stage, to overpower another's words and the audience with rhetoric and even with loudness. Clymene, "wording timidly" (*PW*, 2.251), is the foil to Enceladus's powerful speech:

So far her voice flow'd on, like timorous brook
That, lingering along a pebbled coast,
Doth fear to meet the sea: but sea it met,
And shudder'd; for the overwhelming voice
Of huge Enceladus swallow'd it in wrath:
The ponderous syllables, like sullen waves
In the half-glutted hollows of reef-rocks,
Came booming thus.

(2.300–7)

Enceladus's attack on "baby-words" (2.314) and the passage's description of a linguistic power-play is half comic. Behind these apparent and
superficial differences in the powers of speech is a general and profound
loss of power that all the Titans share. Keats eventually pushes Hazlitt's
concept so far that he contradicts it—the failure of the Titans' speech,
its powerlessness, derives from a failure to represent the truth about the
universe.

The image of Saturn, with his words trying to fill the hollows of the
time-eaten oaks, is a crucial representation of Keats's ability to undermine the obsessive need out of which his earlier poetry grew. First, it is
an obvious enough reaction against Hazlitt's dictum. While the speech
shows poetry's "tendency to immediate excitement or theatrical effect,
no matter how produced" (L, 2, 75), we are clearly moved to object to
Saturn's speech on these grounds: it is empty excitement, theatricality
with no value and no truth. In fact, to turn the tables on Hazlitt, it
seems a perfect example of what Keats heard Hazlitt call "the devouring
egotism of the writer's own mind—to fill up the dreary void with the
Mood of their own Minds."[5] Hazlitt evidently took a dim (and restricted)
view of what is, for this tradition of writers, the central set of terms and
acts. Second, if the overbrimming ontological power in which a few
words ("Let there be . . .") create an entire world is so often the model
of the romantic poets, the Hyperions reveal that God himself is a lie, a
mock power: he is in fact the emptiness he pretends to fill. Milton's
God—"I am who fill / Infinitude"[6]—is a fiction as much as Saturn or any
other of man's gods: "For as one part of the human species must have
their carved Jupiter; so another part must have the palpable and named
Mediatior and saviour, their Christ, their Oromanes and their Vishnu"
(L, 2, 103).

The gods are an anthropomorphic projection of man: we define ourselves by their hypothetical powers and we define them by our most extreme desires. To picture their fall is to liberate ourselves finally, even if
it is into an empty world. None of this is to undermine the power of
language itself, but rather to suggest that the gods, like man, are

instruments through which the divine word works. This is a view un-shared by Wordsworth, whose God or at least some divine mind always provides the model for the divine language that the poet copies or reveals. It is close to Heidegger's portrait of the great German poet of the fallen gods, Hölderlin: "The power of the Father has departed from the gods, from man, and alone remains existent in the Word."[7] The gods, like men themselves, pass on, but the Word lives on eternally. What the Hyperions discover is that the gods are no longer connected to the divine word and its power. It is clear that the universe is worded, or at least requires the Word in some profound sense: we hear in "Hyperion" of "Nature's uni-versal scroll" (*PW*, 2.151), of the "Unwearied ear of the whole universe" (3.65), and of that guide to the universe, an "old spirit-leaved book" (2.133). Nature seems a written transcription of some divine power (Nature as God's Book), or a great ear awaiting the linguistic commands that direct it, or a world interpretable only by a mysterious language or book. The Titans' language, which at once directed and interpreted the universe, now is ineffectual. The gods seem like men, lost in a mysterious universe without the key to its interpretation: "No, no-where can un-riddle, though I search, / And pore on Nature's universal scroll / Even to swooning, why" (2.150-52).

The Hyperions are not simply concerned with the power of the word to create *ex nihilo* (Keats's early obsession), but with its interpretive power, its power to translate a mystery. When Keats devalues the various gods men have created in their own image—Christ, Jupiter, and Vishnu—he suggests that man's relation to the unknown divine power (the disem-bodied Word behind all these personified gods) is still a reading of a sacred text: "I will call the *world* a School instituted for the purpose of teaching little children to read—I will call the *human heart* the *horn Book* used in that School—and I will call the *Child able to read,* the *Soul* made from that *school* and *hornbook*" (*L,* 2, 102). Experience becomes the ability to read, and our connection with God is a full reading of his creation. In the Hype-rions, the Muse serves a similar purpose of instruction: hers is a divine nar-rative, and she translates its mysteries for the poet. Moneta seems an embodiment of language itself. But there is another central fact here, and this is that she is a foreign language, even a dead language—"the pale Omega of a withered race" (*PW,* 1.287). It is through her power to speak this language and to translate it, and through the poet's power to receive, understand, and transcribe it, that the divine narrative passes out of the sphere of the unknown to become history, accessible to all men. But we are on the brink of a serious danger here: language seems always on the verge of a final death, its meaning buried once and for all beyond under-standing.

That Moneta's language can be translated is encouraging, but that it needs translation at all sounds an ominous note about all language. The heavens and their movements in "Hyperion" are represented, for example, as a language that man can no longer read. They are

> hieroglyphics old
> Which sages and keen-eyed astrologers
> Then living on the earth, with labouring thought
> Won from the gaze of many centuries:
> Now lost, save what we find on remnants huge
> Of stone, or marble swart; their import gone,
> Their wisdom long since fled.
>
> *(PW,* 1.277–83)

The imagery of marble and stone, consistently a metaphor for the Titans, suggests that the fallen gods represent a story long lost. Like the Elgin marbles that so moved Keats's imagination, the gods represent the same lost culture, a remnant of a former wisdom. The consistent imagery of Egypt, Greece, and the Druids in fact is an emphatic reminder (as it is in *Women in Love*) of cultures that have died, reminding us, for example, of "When Sages look'd to Egypt for their lore" (1.33). Both the marbles and these stone-gods, if they speak to Keats, speak to him through the mists and fogs that dominate these poems and can tell only a fragment of their story. What comes down to us through the ages, then, are Keats's two fragmented epics and the syntactically fragmented vision that ends "On Seeing the Elgin Marbles": "a billowy main—/ A sun—a shadow of magnitude."

The Titans are part of Greek civilization, of Homer and Hesiod, and even in this remind us that languages die, that Keats could enter these realms of gold only through translation. If "persuaded of the power the knowledge of any language gives one" (he is trying to read Ariosto at the time, *L,* 2, 212), he rarely attains such power, and must postpone until the next world his dream of communication: "one of the grandeurs of immortality—there will be no space and consequently the only commerce between spirits will be by their intelligence of each other—when they will completely understand each other—while we in this world merely comp[re]hend each other in different degrees" (2, 5). Only then can there be a final escape from what he earlier called "the jabbering in the Tower of Babel" (1, 155). Keats's language, then, is the opposite of Wordsworth's universal music of humanity, understood by all men. Language in the Hyperions is seen inevitably as a foreign idiom, a fragmentary sentence from a dead language, if not an impossible hieroglyphic. Keats's hieroglyphics also stand in opposition to Wordsworth's geometric language: the first is a language of signs entirely lost, a wisdom now hidden from men, while the latter is a comprehensible system of signs and symbols that has lasted down to the present day. In fact, in Keats's poems there is a realization of what Wordsworth feared words might become, namely, hieroglyphics.

The extended time of history (so apparent in the Egyptian, Greek, and Druid imagery), which makes relics out of the Greek gods, is analogous to the momentary passage of time in the poet's life when the lived moment is frozen into art, divorced from life. It is like Thea's experience of time in "Hyperion," "O aching time! O moments big as years!" (*PW,* 1.64). Keats realizes at once that what he is presently penning may someday become a hieroglyphic itself and, what is more, that art, rather than the salvation of experience, may be its sepulcher. The Titans are consistently referred to as "images," and one of the major discoveries of the Hyperion poems is that the death of any poet's images (Homer's or Hesiod's) is the death of every poet's. Keats's sympathetic participation in the suffering and fall of the gods is appropriate because he is suffering the death of his own life, his own art. Every poet creates a mythology that is destined to become an unknown language, and at this point in his career it became untenable for Keats to create (like Blake, for example) a new one. Instead, his language is directed at reviving the fallen mythology of Greece only to watch its gods fall again, and seeing in it the superannuation of every poet's images. If the Titans are images, they are called in "Hyperion" "scarce images of life" (2.33).

In this way all labor, if it does not end in death, certainly involves it:

> As I had found
> A grain of gold upon a mountain side,
> And twing'd with avarice strain'd out my eyes
> To search its sullen entrails rich with ore,
> So at the view of sad Moneta's brow,
> I ach'd to see what things the hollow brain
> Behind enwombed.
>
> (*PW,* 1.271–77)

The poet's labors in "The Fall" are those of the prospector (recalling Keats's advice to Shelley about loading every rift of his subject with ore), but the anatomical imagery suggests the intimate connection between birth and death, those "creations and destroyings" (3.116) Apollo experiences. The harvest, what we purchase with our labor, is the gold of last things, and to be "pregnant with poetic lore" (*L,* 1, 106) is not an escape from the deathly void. All works of art are heir, like the marbles, to "the rude / Wasting of Old time," but more than historical time there are those moments big as years that make art an incomplete, even an incorrect, transcription of experience. Like the young poets Keats once talked of, if not dead before conceived, every work of art is dead after.

Keats's equivocations over the spoken versus the written word suggest this fleeting moment in which the poem dies. He desperately attempts to make the impossible happen, to have this voiced dialogue between Moneta and the narrator always have the power and spontaneity of speech, even when he knows that, like the ancients, he is a scribe of a soon-to-be-forgotten language. In the Hyperions Keats sought a voice that paradoxically could be momentary and eternal, of the present moment and for all time. There is a primitive, deeply personal association in Keats's mind between voice and power. His sensitivity to Tom's inability to speak—as in the descriptions of the Titans, a general feebleness is connected with a weak voice—looks like personal wisdom when Keats becomes fatally ill himself. Even when his writing is virtually at a standstill, he protests (ironically enough, in a letter) that he can still speak: "you must not mind about my speaking in a low tone for I am ordered to do so though I *can* speak out" (2, 250). It is in this sense that Keats asks Reynolds to separate the wheat from the chaff, "the true voice of feeling" from "the false beauty proceeding from art" (2, 167). The true voice of feeling is the original voice in which all art has its beginning, but with which it inevitably loses some connection. Like Shelley's fading coal, the original brightness of inspiration can never be recaptured.

These remarks on the Hyperions have led me to some apparent contradictions that are, I think, true to the nature of Keats's speculations, which he admitted could go from feathers to iron. In "The Fall of Hyperion," the gods' loss of power is framed by the poetic endeavor to spell dreams and to save imagination from dumb enchantment through words. Language becomes a means of salvation for the poet. At the same time a curious undercurrent of skepticism, almost as a corrective to what the poet sees as a growing self-complacence similar to the gods', runs through the poems. Even with Keats's bold new requirements for poetic vision fulfilled (that it be closer to nightmare than to the dream of wish fulfillment and that it involve the anguish of hard labor) still some teasing thought that art, no matter how one guards against it, may be no more than deceit, unsettles these poems. It is, of course, the kind of imagination that Keats, self-analytically, described often: its goal is "to make up one's mind about nothing—to let the mind be a thoroughfare for all thoughts" (L, 2, 213), and its practice is to mistrust all its own speculations. It thrives on a sublime tentativeness, and it is wedded to a historicism that is distinctly modern.

In his most optimistic mind Keats saw history as a benignant power that allows "a grand march of intellect" (L, 1, 282). Such a view of time is countered in the poems in any number of other views: in the picture of Moneta "deathwards progressing / To no death" (an indirect criticism

of the nineteenth-century view of progress, *PW*, 1.260–61), in the plot
structure that sees son warring against sire, or in the "sublime pathetic"
passages on the unhappy labor of the parent gods (in Oceanus and Tethys,
or in Tellus). But even the "grand march of intellect" is a severe limitation
on the individual. "A mighty providence subdues the mightiest Minds to
the service of the time being" (*L*, 1, 282), and necessarily makes of the
greatest works of art fragments, links in a chain of truth. The Hyperions
dramatize these attitudes toward history and art. Keats fears, for example,
that his language in them is artful, artificial, and his endeavors to move
as far away from Milton and toward the voice of feeling do not seem a
clear way out:

> I have given up Hyperion—there were too many Miltonic inversions
> in it—Miltonic verse cannot be written but in an artful or rather
> artist's humour. I wish to give myself up to other sensations. En-
> glish ought to be kept up. It may be interesting to you to pick out
> some lines from Hyperion, and put a mark X to the false beauty
> proceeding from art, one || to the true voice of feeling. Upon my
> soul 'twas Imagination I cannot make the distinction—Every now
> & then there is a Miltonic intonation—But I cannot make the divi-
> sion properly. (2, 167)

As soon as the words are written, the enchantment of art is already on
them and seems to alter them, to mask them before the author's very
eyes. All kinds of misgivings seem to crowd in on Keats at once, for
every language is destined to die (English is in need of being "kept up"),
and even at the present moment he is unable to divide the artful from
the authentic. While these misgivings certainly contributed to Keats's
inability to complete the poems, I wish to emphasize that they are part
of the texture and drama of the poems. It would be foolish to argue that
the poems were left unfinished intentionally, but there is something
movingly genuine about them as they stand. Contradicting that early
desire to cover the pages with 4,000 lines, Keats reaches the point where
he can say, "I have come to the resolution never to write for the sake of
writing, or making a poem, but from running over with any little knowledge and experience which many years of reflection may perhaps give
me—otherwise I will be dumb" (2, 43).

The skeptical underthought and the fragmentariness of the Hyperion
poems seem Keats's only defenses against the subterfuge of art. The
Hyperions become an early precursor of those deliberately "incomplete"
works that dominate the twentieth century, the open-ended novel and
poem and play. They anticipate Yeats's state of mind when he rhetorically asks, "Who does not distrust complete ideas"? (*A*, 480). If Wordsworth
is more closely connected to Keats in this matter than we first might

realize—after all, his finished poem is only a prelude to a longer work that never gets written, and this prelude itself tentatively searches for a right poetic idiom and theme—still Wordsworth finishes it, and is granted that godly view from atop a world when he looks down in book 14 and judges his creation good. Wordsworth's characteristic question to himself, "What need of many words?" (P, 1.105), is an apparently practical question answered indirectly with fourteen books of verse. It betrays a theoretical question about the long poem in romanticism in general, and most emphatically about Keats's fragmentary epics: if words are the herald of a new world, is there ever any end of creation, any seventh day of rest? Keats eventually realizes that it is impossible "to tear from the book of Life all blank Leaves" (L, 1, 140). The blank emptiness that interrupts the Hyperions' words is part of the space they fill, or rather, part of the space they fail to fill. The empty page creates a curious frame around them, and in its own way is an articulate reminder that the void is permanent, that words are its interruption and not vice versa.

4

KEATS

> *Dreaming is on the whole an example of regression to the dreamer's earliest condition, a revival of his childhood.*

> *But dreams give us more than such optative clauses. They show us the wish as already fulfilled; they represent its fulfillment as real and present. . . . A thought expressed in the optative has been replaced by a representation in the present tense.*
>
> Freud

If the Hyperion poems achieve at least part of their effect by being fragments, the meaning of "The Eve of St. Agnes" depends precisely on its ending. To understand this ending, however, we have to go back to the beginning, to the actual writing of the poem and the first critical response to it. Woodhouse's comments on "St. Agnes" explain Keats's intentions for the ending, and in so doing manage to suggest an explanation that elucidates in one stroke both the poem's complicated narrative structure (including its ending) and the contradictory interpretations that have become part of its controversial and voluminous critical history: "[Keats] has altered the last 3 lines to leave on the reader a sense of pettish disgust, by bringing Old Angela in (only) dead stiff & ugly.—He says he likes that the poem should leave off with this Change of Sentiment—it was what he aimed at, & was glad to find from my objections to it that he had succeeded.—I apprehend he had a fancy for trying his hand at an attempt to play with his reader, & fling him off at last." (*L*, 2, 162–63). Keats's revision of the last stanza actually amounted to no more than a rather grotesque description of the Beadsman's death; Angela is described essentially in the same way in both versions, that is, as "dead stiff & ugly."[1] This minor revision simply made obvious the effect that the last stanza had originally produced with more subtlety and art, and was wisely discarded. In Woodhouse's reaction there is something clearly like the response that Keats intended the published ending of the poem to have. Indeed, several modern critics have, like Woodhouse, been unsettled by the poem's dark conclusion, and some have even argued that the poem ends tragically.[2] It seems clear that even without the revision, "St. Agnes" ends with a significant shift in tone, and that Keats's decision to end his poem with a "Change of Sentiment" was part of an original and abiding intention. After all, the subject matter of the last stanza has always remained the same—the lovers' entrance into the winter storm, the nightmare-ridden revellers, the imagery of demon and coffin-worm, and the deaths of Angela and the Beadsman—and is indeed dark for a happy romance. What is crucial here is that Keats was satisfied that the poem divided Woodhouse, that it caught him between a final sense of darkness and an otherwise pre-dominant sense of warmth and gaiety (what Woodhouse calls a "mingling of sentiment and sneering").

Unfortunately, modern criticism has obscured this dual response by offering one side or the other. The popular view sees the poem as a triumphant hymn to young love, and, if more profound than "Endymion," still in the basic mode of that happy romance.[3] The other side of the argument is represented by Jack Stillinger's well-known essay, which criticizes Madeline's dreaming and mocks Porphyro's sincerity.[4] Stillinger admits that, in his desire to uncover the poem's darkness, he exaggerates his case by undermining the lovers with a series of comparisons to famous literary characters and types outside the poem. Perhaps because these comparisons too often take him beyond the poem he is led to doubt that any unity or consistency exists in "The Eve of St. Agnes." In any case, both modern positions are exclusive: the general effect of the poem is one of happy romance and there are clearly intended notes of dismay at crucial points in the poem. We cannot ignore the richness and warmth of the lovers' passion; neither can we ignore the winter cold at the beginning and end, the deaths in the last stanza, and Madeline's deception and dis-appointment. We would do well to return to Woodhouse's explanation that Keats intended to end his poem with a change of sentiment, and see what value such a reading has.

It seems clear today that both the effect and meaning of "The Eve of St. Agnes" lie somewhere between the two positions modern criticism has taken. Stuart Sperry, Jr., one of the most recent critics of the poem, has sought out just such a middle ground. He argues that certain psycho-logical tensions within and between the characters are the key to the poem's complicated tone. For Sperry the poem is above all dramatic (he points to Keats's deep interest in the drama), and it is these complex dramatic tensions, he maintains, that deepen the romance.[5] Keats's interest in the drama notwithstanding, the characters of the poem do not seem, in my opinion, able to bear complex psychological interpretation. Furthermore, Sperry neglects what is for me the central problem of the poem—the turn in sentiment at the end. I think that if we emphasize the narrative side of the poem, rather than its dramatic aspects, we will be able to approach this problem satisfactorily. After all, the problem is essentially one of narrative structure: why does the teller of the tale suddenly change the tone of the poem, and what effect does this have on his audience? I am suggesting that critics have largely overlooked, first, that we are guided through this tale by a distinct narrator and that the poem's apparent contradictions in tone and theme are the result of this narrator's changing perspective on his story; and second, that these shifts in tone may be a conscious and clever manipulation of the reader's emotions.

My first point is that we continually neglect to distinguish Keats's narrators from Keats himself and from each other, even though it is clear, for example, that Keats's reworking of the Hyperion poems hinges on this crucial problem or that the narrator of "Endymion," with his intrusions into the poem, becomes a figure for the romancer and thereby significantly deepens and complicates the poem's central action.[6] The second point is one that Woodhouse suggests: he suspects that Keats "had a fancy for trying his hand at an attempt to play with his reader, & fling him off at last." The unsettling effect of the conclusion begins to look like an integral part of the poem when we realize that it parallels the central action. By this I mean that the reader's surprised awakening in the last stanza from a simple romance of happy love (that is all the poem has pretended to be) resembles Madeline's own awakening to a cold winter storm and the prospect that she has been deceived. In short, what I am suggesting here is that Madeline's dream is not the only one that is interrupted in the poem's concluding stanzas: the poem is a dream of happy love for the narrator-romancer, and one for which the reader willingly suspends his disbelief. Critical attention in the past has been focused almost solely on the lovers' quest; more important is the way in which Keats has made his narrator and his reader share in the experience of the lovers.

Freud astutely recognized in fictions and romance this same triple structure: he speaks of the invulnerable hero, whom he labels His Majesty the Ego, and explains how the successes of such a figure are the reassuring enactment of both the artist's and the audience's wish fulfillments. Freud in fact attributes much of the pleasure of art to the writer's positioning us where we can enjoy, without the anxiety of reproach, our own daydreams.[7] Keats's poem turns out to be an ironic anticipation of Freud's formulation. Here, as in the Hyperions, is Keats's new poetic formula, the dream become nightmare. Moreover, the turning point of Keats's poem, its dramatic center, is not the ever-increasing power of the dream, or the dream come true, but the disillusioned awakening of Madeline, the narrator, and the reader. Finally, and perhaps most importantly, Keats provides anything but a simple and secure environment in which the reader can daydream without reproach. Keats's poem manages a revolutionary reaction to the subterfuge of art, an exploitation of the aspects of art's deceitfulness, but turned around on the reader. This is, then, a remarkable case of the tables turned: the reader becomes the dupe and the artist becomes the truth-teller. Art becomes its own cure and, rather than allowing the reader a comfortable hiding place, subtly moves him, as it does Madeline, into the difficult world of reality.

While too little critical attention has been paid to Keats's narrators, happily they call attention to themselves at crucial points in the poems. They address the reader directly and make requests of him; they offer philosophical advice on the action of the poem, and even maxims; they engage in wishes and they dream like the characters themselves. In short, the narrators are a significant part of the action of their poems, dramatis personae in their own right. The narrator of "St. Agnes" is no exception. He is engaged in a quest himself—the creation of a romance—and thereby describes, as it were, the poem's subplot. He is caught, like most storytellers, between the worlds of imagination and reality, and it is here that he is most like Madeline. Certainly Keats himself often enough draws the analogy between poetry and dreams to justify this comparison of the narrator and Madeline. If the crux of the poem is Madeline's dream and its relationship to reality, the narrator seems involved in the same experience: his romance is a poetic dream of long ago, of ancient chivalry and young love, and the poem asks in what sense this dream is true. His role in the poem is that of the romancer, and true to his type he catches our attention by happily revealing his creative powers: he works intently and successfully, it seems, to turn his story away from hardship and suffering and the cold of winter toward passion and delight. This narrator, while describing the cold winter night, the Beadsman, and the revellers, gladly turns to the center of his story, Madeline: his story is of love, not piety or revelry, and he can successfully "wish away" (PW, 41) what he wills. Some stanzas later, another request of the narrator's is answered when he implores his reader's silence, and the warrior-guests' blindness, so that Madeline's lover may have safe entrance into the castle: "He ventures in: let no buzz'd whisper tell: / All eyes be muffled, or a hundred swords / Will storm his heart" (82–84). The narrator's fate seems tied to the lovers': quite simply put, his romance depends on the success of Madeline and Porphyro's love. It may sound as if I have forgotten that the lovers are only characters in his tale, but actually it is the narrator who seems to have forgotten this. He exclaims with delight —"Ah, happy chance!" (91)—at Porphyro's lucky meeting with the good-intentioned Angela, and often seems to hang over Porphyro's shoulder, anticipating the lover's pleasure: "Now prepare, / Young Porphyro, for gazing on that bed; / She comes, she comes again, like ring-dove fray'd and fled" (196–98). His characters and their quest assume a life of their own as the narrator seems to believe, quite innocently, in the actuality of his own tale. He exclaims again with wonder and delight, sharing the lover's joy, as he describes Porphyro gazing on the sleeping maid: Porphyro "'tween the curtains peep'd, where, lo!—how fast she slept" (252). This narrator, then, enters the action of the poem in two important ways: first, through his requests and wishes, and second, through his excited and exclamatory involvement in the lovers' quest.

That the narrator's powers are couched in terms of wishes and requests suggests that they require some effort, that they are matched against some unstated reality that is always about to check them. And yet, in truth, we must admit that we always feel assured of his capabilities. So, while the narrator's wishes and requests all have about them a sense of effort, it is an easy effort: it seems clear that the victories of the imagination are easily won. The scene and entire focus of the poem do, in fact, turn to Madeline at his request, and obediently enough no sound is uttered, no threatening look is shot in Porphyro's direction as he enters the castle. The narrator seems proof of what the speaker of "Fancy" tells us, namely, that fancy is quick to bring, in spite of frost, all the delights of summer. Not only does the poem move, at his request, away from the cold of winter toward the warmth of young love (and the violets, roses, and exotic fruits and spices that describe that love), it also significantly turns away from recognizing time's natural passage. By this I mean that the narrator continually replaces, in the telling of his tale, the past tense with the present: it is what Freud calls in dreams the eventual change from the optative to the present tense. While the poem clearly begins in the dead of winter in the far distant past, much of it is told in the present tense, even with a sense of heated excitement. On the one hand, this suggests another victory of the romancer's: like all good storytellers he is able to make a tale of long ago seem a present reality. On the other hand, taken with his excited involvement in his tale and his own apparent belief in the reality and independence of his characters, this suggests that the narrator is becoming mesmerized by his own tale: he seems quite innocently to forget the distinction between fact and fiction. He simply slips into the present tense, because of his excitement, while telling a story of the past.

It is significant that the narrator's ability to "wish away" what he wills brings with it something like a narrowing of vision; he becomes "sole-thoughted" (*PW*, 42), almost obsessed by his own fiction. It is crucial to realize, then, that the narrator's own involvement in the events of his story is so strong that it is always questionable whether he is in control of his material, or vice versa. The poem's enigmatic reference to Merlin's doom, so long a puzzle to critics, may be a suggestion of the danger every magician-poet faces, namely, that of falling victim to his own spell. Madeline is placed in precisely the same situation. After all, she herself "the conjuror plays" (124), and the events of the poem, while clearly not tragic as in the case of Merlin, do show that her spell easily gets out of hand (the young girl receives from her magic significantly more than she bargains for). It has been pointed out, too, that her charmed sleep, when it is discovered to be "impossible to melt as iced stream" (283), becomes positively threatening.[8] In any case, the fluctuations between past tense and present tense throughout the poem are a key at least to the narrator's position: he is caught between recognizing the story as a fiction of long ago and suggesting (and half believing) that it is a present reality. In all these cases—in his wishes, his requests, his hovering between past and present—the narrator is poised between the two worlds of fact and fiction. His position, for the most part, seems secure: there is only the suggestion of a realm outside of the narrator's powers, and we learn of this world only by seeing him triumph over it (although some of his imaginative victories seem more like oversights).

It is in this light that I understand the poem's final stanza. By emphasizing the ineluctability of time, and by pointedly reversing his previous accomplishments, this stanza significantly limits the romancer's powers. The narrator seems, like the speaker of the "Ode to a Nightingale," to participate in a dream that abruptly dissolves in the end. The stanza begins by recording a final acknowledgment of objective time: though the penultimate stanza employs the present tense, this final stanza emphatically admits that "they are gone: aye, ages long ago / These lovers fled away into the storm" (*PW*, 370–71). This sudden and jarring distancing of the lovers accentuates the distinction between fact and fiction that the narrator has suppressed, and sometimes overlooked, all along. Moreover, the stanza is not simply set in the past, its subject is glaringly the passage of time: it reintroduces the cold of winter by describing the lovers' entrance into the storm; it describes Angela dead, "palsy-twitch'd, with meagre face deform," and the Beadsman likewise dead, among "his ashes cold" (376–78); and it reintroduces the "benightmared" (375) revellers whom, it now appears, the narrator can wish away only temporarily. Finally, the stanza's abruptness suggests the secret power of time: if the body of the poem has seemed a continual concession to romance and the narrator's fancy, this final stanza in one quick stroke disallows such concessions.

The narrator's experience is a microcosm of the central action of the poem. Particularly his "sole-thoughted" involvement in his dream of romance is elaborated upon in the story of Madeline and Porphyro. The narrator's ability to "wish away" the revellers, for example, is matched by Madeline's. She, like her creator, turns her back on these guests, and with "regardless eyes" (*PW*, 64) "heeded not at all" (59) the amorous cavaliers all about her. In short, "she saw not" (62). This emphasis on Madeline's narrowing vision (later in the poem she appears "Blinded" [240] by her dream-sleep, and Porphyro must work hard to "redeem / From such a stedfast spell his lady's eyes" [286-87]) suggests that her wishes and dreams obsess her. In fact, Madeline is so intent on her dream that she is startlingly described as dead to everything else: "all amort, / Save to St. Agnes and her lambs unshorn, / And all the bliss to be before tomorrow morn" (70-72). At first she seems willfully to blot out what she does not wish to see, but soon she seems (like the narrator) a victim of her own wish, "Hoodwink'd with fairy fancy" (70).

Porphyro is scolded by Angela for his reckless attitude in the castle of his greatest foe: like Madeline, then, Porphyro seems regardless of these warrior-guests, and of the dangers they hold for him. This intentness and eagerness account for the quick pace of the poem and the sense of haste throughout. If Madeline appears demure at the ball, her demureness is only a mask to hide her excited anticipation: "the hallow'd hour," though "near at hand" (*PW*, 66), has not yet arrived, and Madeline is "purposing each moment to retire" (73), but forcing herself to linger. If we look closely, we see the signs of this eagerness: the girl is clearly "Anxious," "her breathing quick and short" (65) as she impatiently awaits the magic hour. Porphyro is equally impatient: he experiences "tedious hours" (79) in expectation of gaining Madeline's chamber, and as he awaits the slow preparations of the aged Angela "the endless minutes slowly pass'd" (182). Finally, the lovers are not simply hasty out of mere impatience; they must hurry to win "all the bliss to be before tomorrow morn" (72)—Madeline to have her dream before St. Agnes's magic moon sets, and Porphyro to gain her chamber, and then escape before the dawn and the awakening of the warrior-guests.

This situation is reminiscent of Romeo and Juliet's race against time, and it seems clear that Keats did in fact have Shakespeare's play in mind. The lovers in both works are from feuding households, while the minor characters bear unmistakable resemblances to each other (the Beadsman and Friar Laurence, Angela and the nurse Angelica). There are more profound similarities that generally go unnoticed. Hunt's description of the contrary emotions out of which "St. Agnes" grew is perceptive in its own right, but also can help us see, indirectly, the poem's relationship to *Romeo and Juliet:* "He had, at the time of his writing this poem, the seeds of a mortal illness in him, and he, doubtless, wrote as he had felt, for he was also deeply in love; and extreme sensibility struggled in him with a great understanding."[9] This contrary knowledge—the death of his brother and his avowal of love to Fanny Brawne occurred only weeks before he began the poem—accounts, at least in part, for the poem's complicated tone and its theme of the necessary haste of young love. Moreover, Keats's obvious debt to *Romeo and Juliet* becomes more significant when we realize that he discovered in that play a mixed poetic mode that could marry sensibility and understanding. Keats saw in Shakespeare's play, and reproduced in his own poem, a mixed tone that begins with the props of romance—balls and feasts, love songs and exotic settings—only to deepen them with irony. It is no mere coincidence that Shakespeare's play has presented critics with the same problem we are facing in "St. Agnes:" both works seem headed for uncomplicated, happy conclusions, and each, to a different degree of course, disappoints our expectations. Shakespeare's play, as we well know, turns on certain memorable images and situations that reveal the lovers' desire to transcend time: Romeo's request in the balcony scene that Juliet, his sun, begin the day earlier; and Juliet's wish, later in the play, that the night come early and bring with it her Romeo. By establishing *Romeo and Juliet* as the model for Keats's poem, I wish to underscore not simply the mixed tone of "St. Agnes," but also its emphasis on this theme of time, for it does, like Shakespeare's play, deepen the romantic story of the mere impatience of young love into the story of man's struggle with time.

Madeline's charmed sleep, like Juliet's, is the most dramatic revelation of her secret desire to escape time. Madeline's bedchamber seems an innocent world of dreams that can protect her from the ceaseless forward movement of time. She is "regardless" (*PW*, 64) of the amorous cavaliers all about her and is anxious to retire because she seeks an ideal love in dreams. Madeline is impatient to enter a "poppied warmth of sleep" (237) that seems to defy time: she appears, in her dream-sleep, "blinded alike from sunshine and from rain, / As though a rose should shut, and be a bud again" (242-43). The syntax suggests what we already know: the full-blown rose is helpless to protect itself from the elements by becoming at will a bud again. Here the comparison between Madeline and the narrator becomes crucial: the dream that can transform the full-blown rose into a bud again is the precise temporal situation that the narrator seeks—to turn the clock back so that his Gothic tale of long ago, of a time of innocent love and chivalry, can replace a present reality.

Both Madeline's and the narrator's dreams, then, are attempted escapes into innocence. Juliet's sleep was a trick against time which unhappily delivered the lovers into time's hands. The results of Madeline's magic sleep, we learn at the poem's conclusion, are likewise at cross purposes with her desires. This sleep does not guard her entrance into an inviolable world of innocence; on the contrary, it delivers her into an adult world of responsibility, unprotected from cold winter storms. Indeed, the comparison of Madeline to the rose suggests what the poem ultimately establishes beyond a doubt, namely, Madeline's place in the world of natural process. Keats reveals the full implications of man's relationship to "the worldly elements" in a letter to the George Keatses. In imagery that reminds us of Madeline, he describes the vulnerability of the rose:

> Let the fish philosophise the ice away from the Rivers in winter time and they shall be at continual play in the tepid delight of summer. Look at the Poles and at the sands of Africa, Whirlpools and volcanoes—Let men exterminate them and I will say that they may arrive at earthly Happiness—The point at which Man may arrive is as far as the parallel state in inanimate nature and no further—*For instance suppose a rose to have sensation, it blooms on a beautiful morning it enjoys itself—but there comes a cold wind, a hot sun—it can not escape it,* it cannot destroy its annoyances—they are as native to the world as itself; no more can man be happy in spite, the world[l]y elements will prey upon his nature. (*L*, 2, 101, emphasis added)

The short life of a rose and the inefficacy of a fish's philosophizing are metaphors for man's limitations in a world that is universally prey to the fierceness of winter. "The Eve of St. Agnes" is organized around the basic analogy of this letter: all men, like the creatures of nature, are ultimately subject to time and the worldly elements.

We need not turn beyond the poem itself, however, for proof that Madeline's dream-escape into innocence is only an illusion, and that what the poem really dramatizes is her unexpected and hesitant entrance into experience. While Madeline's chamber seems a perfect protection against the winter that so often means death for Keats, it is pierced by a "wintry moon" (*PW*, 217) that reveals Madeline's vital kinship with the natural world, with everything beyond that chamber's walls. This "languid" (127) and "pallid" (200) moon, a veritable picture itself of time's progress, counts the minutes of objective time and, like the heavenly bodies in *Romeo and Juliet*, represents a universal scheme over which the lovers have no power. It is like the moon in "Hyperion," which, "with alteration slow," directs the "silver seasons four" (1.83–84), and even the fall of the gods.

This wintry moon penetrates the warmth of the chamber and makes it a
"chilly room" (275) and a "chilly nest" (235), and Madeline, through
this metaphor, a creature of nature. Indeed, throughout the poem Madeline is compared to the vulnerable creatures of nature: she is like a "ring-
dove fray'd and fled" (198), a "tongueless nightingale" (206), and a
"dove forlorn and lost with sick unpruned wing" (333). Shining through
a casement decorated with brightly colored fruits and flowers, the moon
casts "rose-bloom" (220) upon Madeline. This rose-bloom is a mark of
time: it is like "the stayne of Eve,"[10] and ironically contradicts Madeline's apparent budlike innocence by pointing to her imminent entrance
into experience. The casement is indeed "innumerable of stains" (212),
and her bed becomes the place in which her innocence is lost, not
guarded. The poem describes anagrammatically (through "stains" [212]
and "saints" [215]) and with rhyme (through "saint" [222] and "taint"
[225]) Madeline's change: it is a change, like the change in a single letter,
sometimes hard to detect, but of crucial importance.

While Madeline seeks, then, the dreams and protection afforded St.
Agnes's virgins and Blake's innocents, Keats ironically foreshadows her
loss of innocence. Finally, the red upon Madeline's breast is not only the
red of the natural world's full-blown rose, for in the midst of the decora-
tions on the casement "a shielded scutcheon blush'd with blood of
queens and kings" (PW, 216). The moon symbolically binds Madeline to
the blood of history and change and times past, to the mortality that
finds even great monarchs. I am suggesting, then, that the poem dramatizes its theme of time in two ways: first, by using the ideas of innocence and experience; and second, by defining experience as the world
of natural process.

These suggestions of Madeline's fall from innocence foreshadow the
climactic moments of the poem, Madeline's lovemaking with Porphyro
and her awakening. It is at this point that the poem becomes openly
ambivalent and seriously divides the reader. The most romantic moment
in the poem, when hero and heroine make love, leads immediately to
the most realistic moment: Madeline finds herself hastily awakened,
realizes that she has perhaps been deceived, and despite Porphyro's
assurances, leaves the castle "beset with fears" (PW, 352) to enter the winter storm. Madeline wakes immediately after her lovemaking with Porphyro because this love signals her entrance into a world beyond dreams.
This point in time is marked by the setting of St. Agnes's magic moon.
This setting moon declares the end of girlhood and dream-lovers for Madeline: St. Agnes's dreams are reserved for virgins only, and a new day, bleak
and stormy, awaits her. In her dream-sleep Madeline is "blissfully haven'd
both from joy and pain" (240); her lovemaking and subsequent awakening, however, introduce the young girl to the complicated world that

mixes joy with pain. While it is true that until this point Madeline's
dream is sovereign, and, as Sperry points out, reality (in the person of
Porphyro) must adjust to and become part of this dream, I wish to
emphasize that the action of these final stanzas significantly reverses
this movement by revealing the way in which the dream first is interrupted by, and then must accomodate itself to, reality. Porphyro's
insistence that Madeline awaken, the young girl's cries of dismay, the
lovers' haste, and their entrance into the winter storm all emphasize
the fact that this, alas, is no dream, to paraphrase Madeline's anxious
words. These events contribute to the darkening sense that culminates
in the last stanza with the narrator's own awakening.

The poem, then, does not describe simply the joy of a dream come
true; indeed, we neither see nor hear any joy expressed by Madeline
from the time she finally awakens. What the poem does describe, with
complicated ambivalence, are the consquences of real passion, and it
does so by emphasizing the distinction between such passion and mere
dreams: in short, a dream-lover would not necessitate Madeline's hurried and frightened entrance into the storm. This is what I meant earlier
when I said that Madeline receives from her dream-magic significantly
more than she bargains for. The world the poem describes, then, is one
in which dreams do come true; but it is precisely that transformation
of dreams into reality that brings with it the more difficult consequences
of the real world. Like Blake's Thel, Madeline originally shrinks from
accepting the love that involves her in mortality. She complains at the
sight of Porphyro all pallid and drear, and then, upon her final awakening, cries out in dismay when she realizes the consequences of her actions. Unlike Thel, however, she finally embraces this love, even though
she remains "beset with fears" (PW, 352). As in the poetry of Blake, innocence is nostalgically seen as a world of happy dreams, while our entrance
into experience presents us with realities that are at once less perfect and
more genuine. It is by passing beyond maidenhood and dreams, for example, that Madeline discovers the wonder of real love as well as the
responsibility and danger it involves.

The structure of "St. Agnes" cleverly involves the reader in its central
experience by catching him, as it does Madeline and the narrator, dreaming. At the beginning of the poem, the reader is soberly aware of the
powers of time. His first glimpse of the Beadsman, for example, abruptly
reveals that "already had his deathbell rung" (PW, 22). And with Angela he
meets "a poor, weak, palsy-stricken, churchyard thing, / Whose passing-
bell may ere the midnight toll" (155–56). Yet however clearly foreshadowed, the deaths of these characters in the last stanza disturb and
surprise the reader: we remember, for one, Woodhouse's complaints

about Angela all dead, stiff, and ugly. Because many of the events are told in the present tense, the reader himself eventually moves into the time of the fiction until he soon forgets the progress of objective time. This can be the only explanation behind the narrator's emphatic reminder in the last stanza that this has been a story of the distant past. In this light the deaths of the Beadsman and Angela are further reminders of the power of time.

It is also important to realize the power of the poem to make us forget what it originally predicted. The Beadsman and Angela, and their foreshadowed deaths, are forgotten in the colorful tale of love, and the reader becomes as sole-thoughted as the narrator, eager for the happy unravelling that is his due. The Gothic setting, the warm colors, the rich language, and the well-meaning spinner of the tale all entice the reader to suspend his gravest doubts—after all, he is in the world of the romantic fairy tale. Indeed, he is drawn into the tale by seeing the narrator's romantic requests easily answered. Not until the concluding stanzas do what have been subtle ironic suggestions become realized events, and then the reader himself is awakened from his dream.

I have already suggested how Madeline's lovemaking with Porphyro and her subsequent awakening are the most dramatic instances of the way the poem divides the reader, first offering him love's "solution sweet" (*PW*, 322) and then making him witness the girl's difficult awakening and entrance into the storm. And we have also seen how the poem's darkening tone culminates in the last stanza's emphasis on the ineluctability of time; Keats's revision of the last three lines was, evidently, to assure our final awakening. Woodhouse's divided response satisfied Keats, then, because it was, as Woodhouse tells us, what the poet intended. Modern criticism's division into two camps over the poem is simply an exaggeration of one response to the exclusion of the other. In a letter Keats wrote only several weeks after the poem there is a remarkable, though unintended, explanation of these surprises that the poem holds for heroine, narrator, and reader: "This is the world—thus we cannot expect to give way many hours to pleasure—Circumstances are like clouds continually gathering and bursting—While we are laughing the seed of some trouble is put into the wide arable land of events—while we are laughing it sprouts, is [i.e., it] grows and suddenly bears a poison fruit which we must pluck" (*L*, 2, 79). This passage explicitly describes what the poem enacts at several levels. The encounter with reality is seen essentially as an unexpected encounter with time, with natural process. The poison fruit that surprises us, and which we must pluck, is the fruit of experience. If this fruit presents us with the knowledge of our own mortality, it is also "soul-making" by discovering the knowledge of good and evil and of experience. Wisdom is foisted upon us, if you will, as it is upon Madeline and the narrator, or the way it is, to a greater degree, upon Apollo in "Hyperion."

What the poem ultimately does, it seems to me, is to record from different points of view the difficult adjustment between dream and reality. There is, for example, the serious danger that Porphyro may be completely absorbed into Madeline's dream: "Open thine eyes, for meek St. Agnes' sake, / Or I shall drowse beside thee, so my soul doth ache" (PW, 278–79). Indeed, we have already seen how Madeline herself is in danger of becoming completely mesmerized by her dream. On the other hand, some moments later, there is Porphyro's inability to blend successfully into Madeline's dream: he appears pallid and cold to the girl, and causes her to complain and almost fully awaken. A delicate balance is eventually achieved as Porphyro successfully enters, but does not completely succumb to, the dream. In the final stanzas we see another side of this problem of adjustment, namely, the surprises and shocks the imagination undergoes as it is made to embrace everything beyond itself. The burden is finally on the dreamer to awaken and enter the world: Porphyro cries to his "sweet dreamer" (334), "Arise—arise! the morning is at hand" (345), and again, "Awake! arise! my love, and fearless be" (350). In its involvement of the reader in this pattern of adjustment, first engaging his belief, then awakening him and revealing his credulity, the poem seems a precursor of the kind of narrative structure that dominates so many modern fictions: the reader participates in the limitations of the characters and narrator, and curiously learns only by sharing these limitations. The writer ironically involves the reader in a partial fiction to make him see, at the end, a truth.

The poem achieves this fuller sense of truth through subtle criticisms of a species of itself—the happy romance. Keats's use of the storm is a case in point. The reader must realize, because of the crucial significance of the storm at the end of the poem, that Porphyro encounters a storm long before the last stanza. The storm he encounters, however, seems introduced as a Gothic device and a colorful metaphor and, like the foreshadowed deaths of the Beadsman and Angela, it is easily forgotten by the reader: "All eyes be muffled, or a hundred swords / Will storm his heart, Love's fev'rous citadel" (PW, 83–84). It is clear that this storm is simply a metaphor and that Porphyro has nothing to fear from a storm that is essentially a literary device typical of romance. The narrator is sufficient protection against this metaphoric storm of swords, and seems to wish it away as he does the revellers. This storm, however, like the wished-away revellers and the forgotten Beadsman and Angela, reenters the poem, standing at its close once and for all. And it is here that the storm takes on a more serious character.

This final storm is, of course, the subject of unending critical debate. We know the extreme positions taken on it: some have argued that the lovers enter, through the storm, "some nebulous transcendence of their own," while others have argued that the storm is, quite simply, a tragic conclusion to the poem. Two critics have struck the right balance, it seems to me, by suggesting that the lovers finally enter a world of "difficulty, danger, and biting winds."[11] Given the poem's enactment of Madeline's loss of innocence, its discovery of her relationship to the world of natural process, and Keats's vision of "the worldly elements," the storm at the end is, in my opinion, the perfect objective correlative for Madeline's entrance into experience. The poem significantly moves from an elaborate Gothic metaphor (a storm of swords) to a realistic, dramatic event (a winter storm), and thereby underscores the distinction between fiction and reality. This rhetorical scaling down is equivalent to the syntactical distinctions between the hypothesis of fiction and the reality of experience. The poem ultimately replaces the conditional, optative, and imperative moods (whether the narrator's "These let us wish away," "let no buzz'd whisper tell," and "all eyes be muffled," or Madeline's implied wish, "as though a rose should shut") with the stark simplicity of the indicative, and similarly moves from the dreamy lapse into the present tense to the use of the past tense. Indeed, the poem presents a series of criticisms of itself, even of its own successes. It reverses the narrator's successful attempts at poetic dreaming and wishing, and also criticizes the reader's succumbing to its fictive powers. Finally, in its very rhetoric, the poem distinguishes between metaphor and realistic event. In "The Eve of St. Agnes," art is wary of art's own devices.

The key to Keats's major narrative poetry is a spirit of exacting truthfulness. Just such a spirit seems to check the narrator of "St. Agnes" by requiring of him a stark reintroduction of characters and themes he would gladly leave behind. A similar spirit urges the narrator of "Lamia" to truth: "And but the flitter-winged verse must tell, / For truth's sake, what woe afterwards befel, / 'Twould humour many a heart to leave them thus, / Shut from the busy world of more incredulous" (PW, 1.394-97). For Keats, verse begins to develop a high truthfulness that is beyond the reader's and even the storyteller's expectations. It does so in a curious way, by half granting their wishes. By this I mean that while all of Keats's narrative poems imaginatively reconstruct exotic settings and distant times, after "Endymion" they do so only to discover the failure of the nostalgic past. Art's high truthfulness, while it revives the past for us, reveals no Eden. "Lamia" and "Hyperion," the major narrative poems published with "St. Agnes" in the 1820 volume, work upon the reader in precisely this way. Both have characters and settings that, at first sight, suggest that they take place in happy lands where dreams come true. "Lamia" takes place, like all good fairy tales, "upon a time," before King Oberon "frighted away the Dryads and the Fauns" (1.1-5). "Hyperion" is set in "the infant world," inhabited by such grand figures as Thea, by whom "in stature the tall Amazon / Had stood a pigmy's height" (1.26-28). The events that occur in these settings, however, confirm that for Keats no time or place has been free from change and mortality: there is no Eden to recapture, nor even a stable heaven. Even "a primeval God" like Hyperion is helpless against time's natural processes: "Fain would he have commanded, fain took throne / And bid the day begin, if but for change. / He might not:—No, though a primeval God: / The sacred seasons might not be disturb'd" (1.290-93).

Keats sought accounts of an idyllic past in the popular histories of the time, but after reading Robertson's *History of America* and Voltaire's *Siècle de Louis XIV,* he had to confess that "even there they had mortal pains to bear as bad" (*L*, 2, 101). Keats's major narrative poems hinge, then, on this dramatic tension: while the poems explore the idea of an idyllic past, they finally are guided by a sense of uncompromising truthfulness. In this way Keats's poetry moved further and further away from becoming what he (at his most skeptical) feared poetry was, "a mere Jack a lantern to amuse whoever may chance to be struck with its brilliance" (1, 242). Though he feared that poetry was inferior to philosophy, he did not forsake it. Indeed, he developed a poetry that was philosophy's rival because it turned on the ultimate recognition of truth. And the place of "The Eve of St. Agnes" in this development is crucial. In it we experience one of Keats's finest ironies when we realize that, even as we temporarily enter the distant past that art revives, and even within the apparent framework of the regressive dream, we find to our surprise an enactment of the inevitable passage out of innocence.

5
W. B. YEATS

THE VISION OF EVIL AND POETIC OBJECTIVITY IN "NINETEEN HUNDRED AND NINETEEN"

> The only means of strengthening one's intellect is to make up one's
> mind about nothing—to let the mind be a thoroughfare for all thoughts.
>
> Keats

> All strange and terrible events are welcome,
> But comforts we despise.
>
> Shakespeare

> Building systems is childishness.
>
> Nietzsche

Yeats's early Shepherd poems are distinguished, critically, only by the consistent neglect they receive. "The Song of the Happy Shepherd" and "The Sad Shepherd" are passed over with hardly a glance or a word, notwithstanding Yeats's decision to place them strategically at the gates of his *Collected Poems,* mild shepherds of invitation rather than fiery archangels of protection. The Happy Shepherd's claim to hold the keys to a heavenly bliss has been neglected too long and, despite the fact that these poems bear, like so many of the undistinguished early lyrics, the unmistakable marks of a youthful poet echoing his masters—Blake and Shelley, as we might have guessed, and Wordsworth and Keats as well—still they are a particularly appropriate introduction to Yeats's work as a whole. What Yeats so often found true of the best of his early poems, namely, that they began to take on more and different meanings when set against his later work,[1] seems true here, and may even account for the decision behind their prominent position. In any case, I use the Shepherd poems as an introduction, both to certain esthetic problems in Yeats's poetry generally and more particularly to a poem that on the surface can hardly be said to share anything with these early lyrics. I will use these slight, apparently immature lyrics as background to one of

Yeats's most awesome and forbidding poems, "Nineteen Hundred and
Nineteen," a poem whose title signals a contemporaneity that immediately distances it from these early pastorals. But my purpose will become
clear. First, the Shepherd poems are an appropriate introduction to Yeats's
poetry because they suggest two alternate functions of poetry Yeats faced
early in his career, and through a fine irony contradict what he (at least
in his youth) may well have wished poetry to be—a simple escape from
the complexities and sorrows of life. Second, they can eventually lead us
to see in "Nineteen Hundred and Nineteen" the consequences of Yeats's
choice of one kind of poetry over another and how, despite a rather surprising consistency of image and idea between them and "Nineteen
Hundred and Nineteen," there appears in the later poem a new poetic
voice and tone, with a sure sense of poetic function.

     "The Song of the Happy Shepherd," on first reading and even on
closer inspection, is puzzling in its contradiction of what its title says it
is. It begins as a dirge, with the Happy Shepherd singing sadly of the
modern world and its lost innocence: "The woods of Arcady are dead, /
And over is their antique joy."[2] The poem's tone depends upon a central
tension: the shepherd is an exile, a pariah in a world of "Grey Truth,"
and his call to us, like the pastoralism in which it is couched, seems always strained, even somewhat strident. In fact, the irony of the poem
arises from Yeats's brilliant manipulation of the speaker's tone. While
the "antique joy" of the woods of Arcady is an image of lost innocence,
the present world is dominated by a curious, tainted innocence, making
"Grey Truth . . . her painted toy," and populated by "sick children,"
down to "the stammering schoolboy." The poem is complicated, then,
by a terminology that reflects back upon itself: the speaker dreams, it
would seem, of a genuine innocence, but the poem is often dominated
by a sick innocence, by a sense of puerility and mawkishness. The
speaker's place in this world is unclear because, while the title and pastoral framework suggest his genuine innocence, if we listen carefully to him
we discover something else. In his address to the sick children, for example, he includes himself (perhaps inadvertently) among their numbers:

> But O, sick children of the world,
> Of all the many changing things
> In dreary dancing past us whirled,
> To the cracked tune that Chronos sings,
> Words alone are certain good.

     When he speaks of the source of his solace—words—the happy shep-
herd betrays a sense of ambivalence, even bitterness, that is out of joint
with his apparent innocence. It is here more than anywhere else that he
seems to epitomize these "sick children": in his attempt to find his lost

health through a cure he does not fully believe in, he undermines the simplicity of his pastoral song with stridency and complaint. In fact, his logic contradicts itself. His argument attempts to prove that "Words alone are certain good," and is directed against "Word bemockers." He tries to show them how the illustrious deeds of yesterday have no permanent value, but he does so by making "words" a mere reduction of a former glory. The "entangled story" of "dusty deeds" is unable to capture the glory of the warring kings, and these ancient warriors are reduced to an "idle word" in the mouth of "the stammering schoolboy." The argument clearly undermines the efficacy of both words and deeds. Moreover, "the wandering earth herself may be / Only a sudden flaming word, / In clanging space a moment heard." This is the speech of a worldly cynic, not a happy shepherd. He either neglects or mocks, for example, the traditional view of nature as God's Word (is God's "Let there be light" a flaming word?) that informs Wordsworth's vision of nature: the earth may be "only" a flaming word lost in the universe's "endless reverie." There is no sacramental vision of nature here, neither is there a Blakean call to resurrection ("O Earth, O Earth, return! / Arise from out the dewy grass").[3] The speaker bewails the passing of a fiction; the woods of Arcady can never return because they have been ruined by "Grey Truth," or, as Shelley puts it, because "killing Truth had glared on them."[4] The veil of illusion is stripped from the golden age, and what is revealed is a thoroughly modern (not pastoral) universe, the heavens replaced by "clanging space," the music of the spheres by "endless reverie," and the *primum mobile* by "the cracked tune that Chronos sings." In this picture Chronos rules no golden age; he is simply the god of Time who hurries the world in a dizzying pace while the speaker seeks inviolability—innocence and youth. The poem thrives on this disequilibrium between its pastoral framework and a tone that is at once childish and urbane, an effect modelled on the rich and ironic interplay achieved by Blake in *Songs of Innocence and Experience.* The search for inviolability in a world ruled by time is also reminiscent of Keats's Madeline and her narrator, and of another genre—in the case of Keats, the romance—pushed to its limits so that it finally criticizes itself through a series of deliberate complications and ironies.

The shepherd's announcement that the woods of Arcady are dead, once we realize the argument of the poem, is not the mournful statement of the pastoralist, but a worldly warning. In fact, the happy shepherd seems filled with presentiments and warnings, his innocence always counterbalanced and interrupted by his suspicions. We are warned neither to "worship dusty deeds" nor to "hunger fiercely after truth" (innocent enough occupations, it would seem) for fear that such "toiling only breeds / New dreams, new dreams." The speaker announces that the

woods of Arcady are dead, it now seems, to force some kind of realization upon us. We are being told that the present world is incapable of
supporting our dreams, and that we must turn inward. The speaker is a
pastoralist who distrusts nature, and has faith only in himself. If one
can see how, in a fallen world, one must be warned against easy belief,
still the advice that "there is no truth / Save in thine own heart" seems
less than satisfactory, particularly when it becomes defined as a form of
mere escapism:

> Go gather by the humming sea
> Some twisted, echo-harbouring shell,
> And to its lips thy story tell,
> And they thy comforters will be,
> Rewording in melodious guile
> Thy fretful words a little while,
> Till they shall singing fade in ruth,
> And die a pearly brotherhood;
> For words alone are certain good:
> Sing then for this is also sooth.

The truth of the heart, says the simple shepherd, depends on guile. We are
bid to find the Wordsworthian shell of poetic inspiration. It is, however,
something less than Wordsworth's shell, which, while soothing the heart
of humankind, foretells its doom. Wordsworth's poetic inspiration, like
the high truthfulness of Keats's poetry, is beyond the manipulation of
man. If it is a solace, it is not an easy tool, and it recognizes (unlike the
shepherd) that nothing can bring back the hour of splendor in the grass.
The shepherd's shell, on the other hand, servilely meets the psychological
needs of the shepherd, even to the point of distorting the truth. In fact,
its very purpose is to reword "in melodious guile" the speaker's words.
The shepherd has no imaginative vision that cuts to the quick of the surrounding world and reveals a hidden paradise: he sings a poetry of escape
in which he seeks simply to forget the present. The final section of the
poem—the only one dominated by a pastoral vision—is undermined by
what has gone before. The shepherd admits that the "hapless faun" is
buried in a grave, but persists in the illusion that "he treads the lawn,"
or at least, he tells us, so "still I dream." The "twisted" and "echo-
harbouring" shell, like the drugged escape that "the poppies on the brow"
evoke, is a device of subterfuge, the twisted shell and his twisted words
of advice echoing the "entangled story" he warns against. If Keats chooses
to awaken Madeline from her poppied sleep, and to dramatize the difference between dream and reality in that way, Yeats suffers the shepherd's false rhetoric and contradictions, transferring his full awakening to
his companion in the poem that follows.

The Sad Shepherd in the companion poem is truly sad rather than falsely happy. Like Thel, he travels on a pilgrimage seeking something between solace and wisdom. This poem, however, turns *The Book of Thel* upside down in its description of a world of complete self-absorption. The irony is masterful, with the consequences of the Happy Shepherd's solipsism visited upon the Sad Shepherd. Not only do the lily, the cloud, and the clod of clay answer Thel, but they counsel her on the dangers of self-absorption. Here the Sad Shepherd calls to the stars to comfort him, "but they / Among themselves laugh on and sing alway." The sea likewise ignores him, and "swept on and cried her old cry still; / Rolling along in dreams from hill to hill." Next he cries his story to the dewdrops, "But naught they heard for they are always listening, / The dewdrops, for the sound of their own dropping." If it is the opposite of *Thel,* it is exactly the world of Shelley's *Alastor,* where "yellow flowers / For ever gaze on their own drooping eyes, / Reflected in the crystal calm"[5] of a stream: the poet in *Alastor,* like the shepherd here, finds himself in a world that mirrors in every direction his own solipsism. Finally, acting in our stead, the shepherd follows the advice that was given to the reader by the Happy Shepherd. We see enacted, then, not only the consequences of a world ruled by the solipsism of the Happy Shepherd, but also the direct results of his advice. The Sad Shepherd

> found a shell,
> And thought, *I will my heavy story tell*
> *Till my own words, re-echoing, shall send*
> *Their sadness through a hollow, pearly heart;*
> *And my own tale again for me shall sing,*
> *And my own whispering words be comforting,*
> *And lo! my ancient burden may depart.*

The "melodious guile" and comfort that the Happy Shepherd promised, however, prove a double fraud; the guileful escape actually fails to work. The shell "Changed all he sang to inarticulate moan / Among her wildering whirls, forgetting him." These "wildering whirls" remind us of what the Happy Shepherd seeks to forget, namely, that we and all things are "whirled, / To the cracked tune that Chronos sings." Finally, the world seems lost in "the endless reverie" (here self-reverie) that the skeptical Happy Shepherd fears is the truth about the universe.

The Sad Shepherd's poetic shell, then, is not a source of solace; instead, it produces an echo of his own true feelings that, in that final inarticulate moan, becomes a universal cry of loneliness and sorrow. In fact, the solace that is promised by the refrainlike "Words alone are certain good" disappears before the awful formless "inarticulate moan" that cries down at once man's attempts at language, order, and art. The false pastoralism of the poems is linguistically represented throughout in obtrusive and ineffectual archaisms—in pronouns like "ye," "thine," and "thy;" in words like "sooth" and "ruth;" in exclamations like "By the Rood;" and in the distinctly poetic "alway." This is anything but Wordsworth's timeless universal language; these archaisms appear like a foreign idiom in the poem, signalling the way it is divided against itself. Likewise, the words of the poem seem anything but the language Words- worth imagines, able to stave off the gathering waters about to drown the world. The shepherd's shell is not a prophetic voice out of the deep, a protection against the deluge, but a mere skeleton of life that conjures in its own architecture the terrifying nature of the sea, the whirling move- ment that knows no order. Earth is only a word, the poems are only words, and what power they have stems not from any magical musical- ity but from their dramatization of what stands beyond them—inarticu- late formlessness.

Both Shepherd poems hinge on the crucial image of the Words- worthian shell of poetry and on a definition of the function of poetry. Poetry is alternately defined (and the terms are very nearly Keats's) as a drugged state of dream escape or a surprising encounter with the un- deniable reality of one's own, and the world's, sorrow. One could argue that Yeats's poetic career was, like Keats's, a deliberate movement away from this first definition toward the second. "False beauty," a reaction to Keats's famous formulation about beauty and truth, becomes a signif- icant phrase that Yeats uses to remind himself of the dangers of the Happy Shepherd's advice. Appropriately, Yeats offers Keats's "Endym- ion" and its naïve pastoralism as an example of a poem that reveals the consequences of such beauty: "these images grow in beauty as they grow in sterility" (A, 313). "Endymion" is a youthful poem, then, that both Keats and Yeats use as a measuring rod throughout their poetic careers. Yeats's criticism of Keats is, of course, a thinly veiled criticism of the same urge he discovers in himself. The elegiac note sounded by "The Song of the Happy Shepherd" expresses Yeats's genuine desire for a world of innocent beauty, even while the poem undercuts the inno- cence that the shepherd recommends. "The woods of Arcady are dead" is, undeniably, a truth that stands behind the Collected Poems. What Yeats disputed in these early poems from the beginning, but more and more in the course of his career, was the inadequate response of his speakers to this truth: "it is almost all a flight into faeryland from the real world, and a summons to that flight. The chorus to the 'Stolen Child' sums it up—that it is not the poetry of insight and knowledge, but of longing and complaint—the cry of the heart against necessity" (LY, 63). The Shepherd poems contain only a limited insight: if they undermine the childish longing for a faeryland, they are unable to provide us with a more mature response to loss and suffering. Their value is negative rather than positive; it rests upon a special kind of irony, not vision. Keats's terminology becomes for Yeats (as it does for the whole tradition) the center of a problematic search for an authentic poetic form and content that will not sacrifice truth for beauty. In this search Yeats reinstigates, with his own examples, the battle of the ancients versus the moderns. He consistently praises Dante (and sometimes Villon or Shakespeare) in a criticism of the "false beauty" of his romantic fore-bears, and connects this false beauty with romanticism's lack of the Vision of Evil: "Had not Dante and Villon understood that their fate wrecked what life could not rebuild, had they lacked their Vision of Evil, had they cherished any species of optimism, they could but have found a false beauty" (*A*, 27). "False beauty" and the Vision of Evil are crucial ideas that Yeats uses to steer his poetic career away from "the cry of the heart against necessity" and the forced optimism of the Happy Shep-herd, toward the poetry of insight and knowledge; moreover, they form the basis of Yeats's discovery of an authentic poetic idiom in "Nineteen Hundred and Nineteen."

"Nineteen Hundred and Nineteen" begins with Yeats's recognition that he, his readers, society in general—the universal "we" of the open-ing stanzas—have accepted and even participated in the building of a cul-ture based on what he terms elsewhere "false beauty" and "false faith": "I know we make a false beauty by a denial of ugliness and that if we deny the causes of doubt we make a false faith, and that we must excite the whole being into activity if we would offer to God what is, it may be, the one thing germane to the matter, a consenting of all our facul-ties" (*E*, 31). False beauty and false faith, even more to the point, ex-plain the analogy between art and politics in the poem's first two stanzas:

> Many ingenious lovely things are gone
> That seemed sheer miracle to the multitude,
> Protected from the circle of the moon
> That pitches common things about. There stood
> Amid the ornamental bronzes and stone
> An ancient image made of olive wood—
> And gone are Phidias' famous ivories
> And all the golden grasshoppers and bees.
>
> We too had many pretty toys when young;
> A law indifferent to blame or praise,
> To bribe or threat; habits that made old wrong
> Melt down, as it were wax in the sun's rays;
> Public opinion ripening for so long

We thought it would outlive all future days.
O what fine thought we had because we thought
That the worst rogues and rascals died out.

As in "The Song of the Happy Shepherd," the first line appears elegiac.
Reading further, however, we realize that the tone of these opening
stanzas is emphatically bitter and ironic. While the Happy Shepherd's
bitterness arose from the loss of an innocence that the poem revealed
to be inauthentic, it is a measure of the speaker's wisdom here that he
is bitter at his implication in such a world. The golden grasshoppers and
bees, the famous ivories were, like our laws, "pretty toys" with which
we thought to amuse and protect ourselves. Our art, like our politics,
was essentially "ornamental," and "ingenious" where it might have been
wise.

The world Yeats describes, then, was one of "toys" and "tricks"
devised by an ingenious child. There is not, as there might be in Shelley,
for example, the elegiac passing of a golden age. The innocence is continually seen as childish, not childlike; it is regressive the way the Happy
Shepherd's was, and more importantly, dangerous. Every action betrayed
the same naïvete: "We pieced our thoughts into philosophy" the way a
child pieces together a puzzle; and the "great army" of trumpeters and
prancing chargers seems peopled with a child's toy soldiers, for it is "a
showy thing" like the ornamental bronzes. Our culture chose to react to
the forces of destruction and evil by childishly ignoring them or, more
precisely, by transforming them into playthings and toys. The child's
strategy is to fantasize, to daydream, and so to escape, and this is what
Freud says the poet shares with the child. In fact, the basis of Freud's
influential essay, "Creative Writers and Day-Dreaming," is just such a
comparison between the play of children and of poets. Yeats's poem is
of course no such daydream, but the criticism of it. Yeats makes the
result of this dream nightmare, and as with Keats a new esthetics is defined that owes more to the nightmare than to the dream. "Now days
are dragon-ridden, the nightmare / Rides upon sleep: a drunken soldiery
/ Can leave the mother, murdered at her door, / To crawl in her own
blood, and go scot-free." The apparently innocent irresponsibility of
childish daydreams erupts with a vengeance into a murderous irresponsibility (the soldier who murders the mother goes scot-free) and the nightmare becomes a horrible exaggeration of the dream. Its result is the
motherless child, the orphan suddenly thrust into a world of nightmare
without protection. This is a grotesque version of the fall from innocence that all men must undergo who live a false dream. The stanza ends
with a brilliant expression of the reality we are forced to face. The golden
grasshoppers and bees, the guardsmen's prancing chargers—the playthings

of the child's dream world—are suddenly transformed into the nightmarish dragon, but also, even more chillingly, into the all too realistic and petty weasel: we are "but weasels fighting in a hole." Yeats moves the reader from dream to nightmare, and finally to the unexaggerated and unromantic reality of everyday life.

The passage from innocence to experience is, of course, one view of the subject of the poem. The speaker is almost hyperaware of the world of change, with so grim a view of time that modern Ireland is no longer present, but past. The dialectic between past and present in this poem therefore takes an odd form. The apparently distant worlds of ancient Greece and modern Ireland are joined as a single past, the past of illusion, as opposed to the empty present where the poet stands. Yeats describes how a major part of our dream world consisted precisely in a pretty fiction about time. We were foolish enough to hold two contradictory views of time: we thought that while time stood still for us and we were protected from the circle of the moon by an inviolable innocence, the world at large moved forward toward the best of all possible worlds. We were, in other words, not simple Madelines naïvely seeking a lost innocence but more like the Happy Shepherd, who cynically predicts the world's corruption everywhere around himself yet attempts to secure himself in an island of illusion and dream.

This double view of time becomes one of Yeats's most bitter criticisms of the idea of progress, of the grand march of human history. Among the "toys" are

> habits that made old wrong
> Melt down, as it were wax in the sun's rays;
> Public opinion ripening for so long
> We thought it would outlive all future days.
> O what fine thought we had because we thought
> That the worst rogues and rascals had died out.

Time is seen at once as a punishment for the bad and a vehicle for the rewarding of the good: death was to single out "rogues" and "rascals" (even our language was tuned with pretty euphemisms, masking evil under the guise of a terminology meant for naughty children, like the word "mischief" in part 3), while public opinion was to ripen, to outstrip time itself, and to bear the fruits of law and order. It is the kind of conspiring autumn that makes Keats's bees think warm days will never cease, even though if autumn is here winter can not be far behind—a perfect climate for the ornamental bees and grasshoppers of Yeats's poem, imaginary creatures thriving in an imaginary and prolonged warmth. But the speaker knows "the winds of winter" and "how seasons run." Our innocent view of time is dramatically countered in stanza five with the speaker's wisdom: the nightmare makes us realize that "no work can stand, / Whether health, wealth or peace of mind were spent / On masterwork of intellect or hand." Still Yeats knows there are few "who can read the signs nor sink unmanned / Into the half-deceit of some intoxicant / From shallow wits." The intoxicant makes a connection between the weak and "the drunken soldiery," a drug that evidently turns us either to murder or to a deathlike somnolence, a kind of suicide. Moreover, our refusal to face this adult vision of time makes us "unmanned," and the innocence we have sought becomes what it must inevitably be in an adult world—impotence. This recalls Yeats's remark about "Endymion;" for him a beauty divorced from reality produces sterility, and innocence becomes sickness, as in the "sick children" of the Shepherd poems. Our "shallow wits" complete the picture, adding mental disorder to physical. The image of the child in this poem represents a regression in intelligence and sexuality.

These opening stanzas are dominated by Yeats's bitter tone, and by an absence of genuine elegy. After all, what has been lost is seen as false. As this first section closes, however, this bitterness does begin to modulate into the more universal mourning for the loss of all things that man creates. The poem becomes dirgelike as it asks, "Man is in love and loves what vanishes, / What more is there to say?" But Yeats seems to allow himself only a momentary expression of sorrow. The poem immediately turns bitter again: to combat the years of false faith, Yeats forces upon himself the bitter knowledge that comes of utter cynicism. He refuses the solace of sorrow, and acknowledges that it is not simply "the circle of the moon," some abstract notion of time, that undoes every masterwork, but we ourselves:

> That country round
> None dared admit, if such a thought were his,
> Incendiary or bigot could be found
> To burn that stump on the Acropolis,
> Or break in bits the famous ivories
> Or traffic in the grasshoppers or bees.

Yeats then forces himself to admit a truth that we have refused for too many years to recognize, and his question, "is there any comfort to be found?," becomes irrelevant as the poem directs itself, and its new poetics generally, beyond comfort. The first part of the poem reaches a standstill at this bitter admission.

The "traffic" of the last line of part 1—a violent action of the vulgar mob, "the multitude"—contrasts dramatically with the graceful dance that opens part 2. And yet the irony of this second section is that this graceful dance, which seems so different from the "burn[ing]" and "break[ing]" that end part 1, becomes similarly violent. The drowsy chargers and the trumpeters of part 1 erupt into the murderous soldiery. Loie Fuller's Chinese dancers, symbol of all that is fine and fanciful (with shining web, and floating ribbon of cloth) suddenly become, like the days of part 1, "dragon-ridden": "it seemed that a dragon of air / Had fallen among dancers, had whirled them round / Or hurried them off on its own furious path." This metamorphosis of an apparently naïve and harmless action into a furious one is the dominant image of the poem at this point. Art seems an attempt to order the destructive forces of evil, to transform them into the beauty of dance: the dancers transform the whirling that is time's destructive movement into the choreography of the dance. Yet art in this way embodies these destructive forces until they become its undoing. The dance is, after all, an orderly expression of the gyre; it is the artist's way of making comprehensible and beautiful the bitter reality that is life: "Life is . . . no orderly descent from level to level, no waterfall but a whirlpool, a gyre" (V, 40); "it is life itself which turns, now here, now there, a whirling and a bitterness" (52). As in "The Sad Shepherd," a chaotic whirling movement shocks and awakens the dreamer; it is a movement that has none of the dance's delicate precision or order, it is a furious movement that resists the order the artist attempts to impose upon it. Just as the shell has a will of its own, expressed in its "wildering whirls," and refuses to serve the shepherd's purpose, so this dragon power "hurried them [the dancers] off on its own furious path." All time, the second stanza of part 2 explains, is such a movement:

> So the Platonic Year
> Whirls out new right and wrong,
> Whirls in the old instead;
> All men are dancers and their tread
> Goes to the barbarous clangour of a gong.

The third section of the poem proceeds with the knowledge of parts 1 and 2. It returns to the themes of art and politics (part 1) with the certain knowledge that all people of every era are dancers in a terrible dance of change and destruction (part 2). Like so much of the poem, it attempts to describe and evaluate the possible responses to this knowledge. It does so through three stanzas that are carefully constructed upon a logic that at first may seem obscure. Stanza one presents the image of the swan as "the solitary soul," and in an elaboration of that image subtly suggests to the reader the two alternate responses to the knowledge of evil: "The wings half spread for flight, / The breast thrust out in pride / Whether to play, or to ride / Those winds that clamour of approaching night." The swan is delicately poised between two actions: to play, and to ride the winds of night. Like part 2, where the image of Loie Fuller's dancers immediately receives a kind of discursive elaboration, stanzas two and three of this section interpret, with supreme indirection, this image. The first alternative of the swan—to play—is the subject of stanza two, and becomes the poem's most explicit criticism of the artist and the politician: "A man in his own secret meditation / Is lost amid the labyrinth that he has made / In art or politics." This image of the labyrinth, particularly when connected with the artist's endeavor, reminds us of Daedalus, mythology's most famous artificer. The myth is for Yeats an emblem of the danger the artist is heir to. Even in the poem's first section Yeats suggests the myth obliquely: among the toys were "habits that made old wrong / Melt down, as it were wax in the sun's rays," an echo of the story of Icarus, and the consequences of the artist's trade used recklessly and childishly. The story of Daedalus's building the Cretan labyrinth certainly bears on the third section of the poem. Daedalus constructed the Cretan labyrinth, at King Minos's bidding, to hide the monstrous Minotaur from the sight of the populace. The Minotaur is the offspring of his wife and a bull, and is a disgrace to the king's family; in fact, it is like the dragon of part 1 of the poem, a mythical embodiment of evil. Lawgiver (Minos) and artist (Daedalus), then, conspire to hide the products of evil. It is an irony at once playful and deadly serious that this stanza, while reverently invoking Plato, should suggest the lawmaker and the poet as co-conspirators. This clearly returns to part 1's description of the artist's function as the artificer, the creator of guile, and it explains why the soul's first alternative in the face of evil is "to play:" it is the artist's choice to hide himself in his own secret meditation, his own system, his ingenious "toys" and "tricks." It is work as play, a mere game for self-amusement, an analogy Loerke will draw in *Women in Love*. The artist, Yeats reveals, is always in danger of finding himself "lost amid the labyrinth he has made," an ironic suggestion that such an artist becomes the embodiment of that evil he is trying to hide, the beast lost in the labyrinth. His ingenuity is a trap that he himself may fall into. The stanza finally explains that the labyrinth of work is no real solitude:

> Some Platonist affirms that in the station
> Where we should cast off body and trade
> The ancient habit sticks
> And that if our works could
> But vanish with our breath
> That were a lucky death,
> For triumph can but mar our solitude.

The labyrinth of work is the false alternative of the solitary soul: it actually prevents the soul from achieving solitude.

The third and final stanza of this section returns to the second alter-native of the soul. The introductory image of the swan's potential action —to play or to ride the winds—becomes transformed into the swan's choice of action: "The swan has leaped into the desolate heaven." The swan's potential action modulates into a past action—what the swan, if it is to embody the solitary soul's activity, has always chosen. This leap is the active acceptance of the destructive winds, and the solitude that necessarily follows upon that acceptance. There is about this leap a simple directness that is the opposite of the circuitous path of the dancers or of the artist's ingenious labyrinth, forms designed to avoid and obscure the forces of evil. The dance, with its whirling movements, is certainly an image of the labyrinth; it is a "web" in which the dancers unwittingly become "enwound," like the artist lost amid the labyrinth he has made. The leap of the swan is a flight above the labyrinth, like Daedalus's final leap into the sky. It is clearly not, however, an escape from evil. It represents simply the acceptance of evil, and the discovery of evil at its source. This leap represents the man who, instead of trying to escape evil only to find himself suddenly its victim (parts 1 and 2), *chooses* to ride the winds of night. It becomes the single action the soul can take to reach "the desolate heaven." This image of the swan's leap, while it presents Yeats with the first positive alternative of the poem, arouses in him its own kind of violence:

That image can bring wildness, bring a rage
To end all things, to end
What my laborious life imagined, even
The half-imagined, the half-written page;
O but we dreamed to mend
Whatever mischief seemed
To afflict mankind, but now
That winds of winter blow
Learn that we were crack-pated when we dreamed.

This wildness and rage, however, subside into bitterness again. The half-written page is not torn up, but leads into parts 4 and 5. The knowledge of the swan's leap is not acted upon; indeed, the poem significantly regresses. Part 4 is a brief return to the image that sums up Yeats's bitter-ness: "the weasel's twist, the weasel's tooth." And part 5 is the clearest example of the kind of testing of response that I suggest is the poem's central technique. The speaker, in his bitterness, turns to mockery; he mocks the great, the wise, and the good, but finally, and most impor-tantly, he mocks mockers as he exhausts this kind of response.

It is best, at first, to understand part 6 as a reworking of the earlier sections of the poem. The trumpeters, the drowsy chargers, and Loie Fuller's graceful dancers return, but they are so transformed that we

may not recognize them. They are no longer images of a dream fulfillment, but rather of a shocking nightmare. They are the "signs" Yeats
speaks of earlier; they hide and mask nothing, they openly announce
evil:

> Violence upon the roads; violence of horses;
> Some few have handsome riders, are garlanded
> On delicate sensitive ear or tossing mane,
> But wearied running round and round in their courses
> All break and vanish and evil gathers head.

The drowsy chargers of part 1 erupt into violent action, and make way
for this section's first embodiment of evil:

> Herodias' daughters have returned again,
> A sudden blast of dusty wind and after
> Thunder of feet, tumult of images,
> Their purpose in the labyrinth of the wind.
> And should some crazy hand dare touch a daughter
> All turn with amorous cries, or angry cries,
> According to the wind, for all are blind.

Loie Fuller's dancers are replaced by Herodias's daughters; the dance of
floating ribbon becomes a dance of passion that fulfills the anticipatory
violence of the horses that precedes it. This is the dance of Salome,
motivated equally by passion and destruction: every touch inspires the
daughters to turn, in the violent dance that sounds like a "thunder of
feet," "with amorous cries, or angry cries." The poem's final image
makes clear that even amorousness here becomes fierce anger, destruction, and evil:

> There lurches past, his great eyes without thought
> Under the shadows of stupid straw-pale locks,
> That insolent fiend Robert Artisson
> To whom the love-lorn lady Kyteler brought
> Bronzed peacock feathers, red combs of her cocks.

Part 6, then, is orchestrated into three movements: with the "running
round and round" of the horses, the "thunder of feet" of the dancers,
and the final "lurch" of Robert Artisson, it becomes a violent, and even
grotesque, version of the earlier dance. It builds into an ever increasing
emphasis on the sensual: there are the details in the description of the
riders (they are "handsome," their horses have "delicate sensitive ear or
tossing mane"); there are the "amorous cries" of the daughters; and
finally there is the fiend and his sexual victim, the lovelorn Lady Kyteler.
This emphasis on sexuality is the natural climax to the poem. It, like the

nightmare vision of which it is so large a part, is the only antidote to the dreamlike regressiveness that has been described earlier. Keats's and Yeats's dreamers share this: sexuality is the awakening, the entrance into adulthood. The real alternatives this poem presents, then, are "to sink unmanned / Into the half-deceit of some intoxicant" (to find, in dream, an easy impotence) or to surrender to a nightmare of violent sexuality— to the daughters of Herodias, to the fiend Robert Artisson. Nightmare becomes defined as the rape of innocence, and the image of Robert Artisson expresses this fully: he is a nightmare, an incubus.

If part 6 is the kind of reworking I have described, it is also startlingly different from all the other sections. Part 6 is absolutely impersonal. Through its other sections the poem is colored, even dominated, by the speaker's thought, his emotion, and his varying reactions to the problem of evil. We have seen him bitter at his own personal failure and at society's; we have seen him grow elegiac and grandiloquent on the question of loss; we have seen him take the stance of mockery, and then turn around and mock mockers; and we have seen him madden in rage and wildness. Part 6 significantly contains no such personal emotion. In fact, the poem's process is an exhaustion of personal emotion. The most significant technical device of "Nineteen Hundred and Nineteen" is a testing of the different responses to the problem of evil until all of these responses are exhausted. Only this exhaustion of all that is personal can lead Yeats to the Vision of Evil that is the poem's crowning achievement: "Does not art come when a nature, that never ceases to judge itself, exhausts personal emotion in action or desire so completely that something impersonal, something that has nothing to do with action or desire, suddenly starts into its place, something which is as unforeseen, as completely organized, even as unique, as the images that pass before the mind between sleeping and waking?" (A, 332). There is no better description of the process of "Nineteen Hundred and Nineteen" and its concluding section. The argument of the poem is no argument at all, and its form emerges precisely from what has seemed to be its somewhat arbitrary and formless arrangement of parts. The poem's progress is slow, often wandering, and perhaps even digressive. Yet if we understand that it is precisely through an allowance of emotion that emotion is exhausted, we will see the coherence. "Nineteen Hundred and Nineteen" is a poem that is about, among other things, the discovery of proper poetic form, and it becomes, finally, an illustration of that form. When we ask why Yeats, after understanding the meaning of the swan's leap, does not act upon it immediately, why he does not then have the Vision of Evil, we fail to understand this form. There is certainly an avoidance of the final vision, a preference to lapse into the bitterness of part 4, or even the mockery of part 5, each of which is an easier response than the surrender to the Vision of Evil. Yeats knows that belief in evil must always be unwilling, and yet without it the greatest poetry is not possible: "Is it that these men, who believe what they wish, can never be quite sincere and so live in a world of half-belief? But no man believes willingly in evil or in suffering. How much of the strength and weight of Dante and of Balzac comes from unwilling belief, from the lack of it how much of the rhetoric and vagueness of all Shelley" (*E*, 277)?

Yeats's many alternatives in "Nineteen Hundred and Nineteen"—the continued intoxication of the dream, bitterness, mockery, tearing up the half-written page in wildness—are all rejected only after they are tried, and tried again sometimes, until he discovers through this lengthy process the Vision of Evil. Yeats called each of the six sections "poems" (*CPY*, 455), and each is, in a way, another beginning in the search for an adequate response. Yeats's sense that each of these sections exists as a separate entity, as a poem, is part of this process of exhaustion: "every moment, in feeling or in thought, prepares in the dark by its own increasing clarity and confidence for its own executioner" (*M*, 340). Each section, then, is an orchestrated movement that prepares the way for what, paradoxically, cannot be foreseen and yet is inevitable: in this sense something "suddenly starts into its place, something which is as unforeseen, as completely organized, even as unique, as the images that pass before the mind between sleeping and waking."

This exhaustion of desire becomes for Yeats, to return to the problem that began my discussion of "Nineteen Hundred and Nineteen," a crucial moment in his discrimination between classical and romantic writers. The argument settles finally into criticism of Shelley and praise of Dante: "Shelley was not a mystic, his system of thought was constructed by his logical faculty to satisfy desire, not a symbolical revelation received after the suppression of all desire. He could not say with Dante, 'His will is our peace,' nor with Finn in the Irish story, 'The best music is what happens'" (*EI*, 421–22). The system of thought that Shelley constructs is the private labyrinth of the artist: it prevents revelation and supplies what Yeats elsewhere calls "fantastic, constructed images" (*V*, 144). For this reason, Shelley lacks the Vision of Evil. This sense of the labyrinthine construction of the artifact is opposed in Yeats's mind to "revelation," that state in which the poet sees the unavoidable truth. Yeats trades, at the end of "Nineteen Hundred and Nineteen," the labyrinth of secret meditation for the "labyrinth of the wind." This image of the wind, like the "thunder of feet" that accompanies it, removes all sense of artifice and makes clear that the forces of evil are like a force of nature itself: this is indeed "the winding movement of Nature" (*M*, 340), the whirling gyre.

Both Keats and Yeats, then, find their antidotes to childish illusion not only in sexuality, but in a natural world so violent that it exorcises

art: the cold winter storm in "The Eve of St. Agnes" is matched by
Yeats's knowledge that we can not "bar that foul storm out," or that
"levelling wind." Moreover, the "labyrinth of the wind" is not a "private"
structure to solace and protect an individual, but rather a force that effects all people, and that the solitary recognizes and accepts. Indeed it
is precisely because of this recognition and acceptance that one is solitary. Civilization, as "Meru" tells us, is built upon illusion: the solitary,
like the hermit atop Mt. Meru, potentially undermines civilization because of this knowledge. And this is the best explanation of that analogy
between politics and art that underlies so much of "Nineteen Hundred
and Nineteen": "A civilisation is a struggle to keep self-control. . . . The
loss of control over thought comes towards the end; first a sinking in
upon the moral being, then the last surrender, the irrational cry, revelation—the scream of Juno's peacocks" (V, 268). Politics, and art as we
often understand it (and as Yeats criticizes it in this poem), are predicated upon the kind of order that stems from control over thought.
Yeats uses the imminent downfall of a political order, really of a civilization, in the year 1919, to symbolize a radical poetics that he finds
absent in romanticism—a poetics that is based upon and succeeds only
through the loss of control over thought.

The poem ends in an atmosphere of surrender: Herodias's daughters
are the tools of the wind, the lovelorn Lady Kyteler clearly has sur-
rendered to her passion, and the peacock feathers and combs are the
most obvious manifestations of sacrifice. Passion becomes the best example of the loss of control over thought, and is a sign of what Yeats
calls "the last surrender." In this light the phrase "evil gathers head,"
preceding the entrance of Herodias's daughters, has a grotesquely literal
meaning: the vision of evil necessitates a surrender of mind that becomes,
in the most literal sense, a beheading. Finally, these surrenders to passion
are of course like the poet's own surrender of control. In a poem that
has been so dominated by personal emotion and reaction, it is not difficult to see how part 6 becomes this surrender for the poet. Even the
poem's relapses and digressions can be explained more fully by understanding this final goal of the poet. These relapses are part of that relaxation of will that Yeats is after: rather than directing the poem to some
predetermined conclusion, the poet seeks a kind of purposelessness that
ends in part 6. If the beginning sections follow the argument the poet is
making, through the ultimate relaxation of will the poet writes a poem
whose final form is externally imposed, not by his own poetic purpose,
but by a force beyond him, a vision that he awaits in all humility: "I
think that we who are poets and artists . . . must go from desire to weariness and so to desire again, and live but for the moment when vision
comes to our weariness like terrible lightning, in the humility of the

brutes" (*M,* 340). It is incorrect, then, it seems to me, to read the ending of the poem as apocalyptic. It is, if anything, the exact opposite; it is an apotheosis of time, of change, of a destruction that does not issue in a new heaven and earth, but rather "Whirls out new right and wrong, / Whirls in the old instead." The poet is not exalted through vision. He escapes nothing except falsehood; he surrenders everything to the powers, and process, of time.

It should be clear by now that I am on the verge of seeing as the model for Yeats's poetic activity in this poem a kind of "objectivity" that critics think Yeats largely dismissed as incompatible with poetry. The well-known distinction in *A Vision* between objectivity and subjectivity, be-tween primary and antithetical phases, would seem to deny, at least at first, that such objectivity could give one of Yeats's poems its charac-teristic form. Subjectivity (or the antithetical phases) represents "our in-ner world of desire and imagination," while objectivity (or the primary phases) "exhibit[s] the actual facts, not coloured by the opinions or feelings" (*V,* 73). It is clear even from these simple definitions that, while the antithetical phases, because of their association with imagina-tion, are most clearly the poet's, the avoidance of desire and the attempt to reach beyond personal opinion and feeling are at once the characteris-tics of "Nineteen Hundred and Nineteen" and of objectivity. In fact, looking more closely at the criticism of Shelley that bears so directly on this poem, we begin to see that Yeats's fear that art can take the form of subterfuge makes him equivocate somewhat more than critics have guessed in his praise of subjectivity, and rejection of objectivity, as the basis of his own poetry.

    While critics have emphasized Yeats's understanding of the poet as maker and transformer, they have largely neglected his interest in pas-sive mediumship. It is true that Yeats's earliest thought is influenced by the Blavatsky Lodge and the Golden Dawn, both of which emphasize control of the will. From 1911 through the writing of "Nineteen Hun-dred and Nineteen," however, Yeats's thought is sparked and nurtured by spiritualism. This new interest is reflected in his major prose works of the time (it plays an extraordinarily large role in *Per Amica Silentia Lunae* and is an essential part of the system in *A Vision,* not to mention its connection to Mrs. Yeats's automatic writing) and it clearly serves as the central intellectual background to the poetic form of "Nineteen Hundred and Nineteen." The consequences of this interest, for example, lie at the heart of Yeats's criticism that Shelley was not a mystic and that his system of thought was constructed by his logical faculty to satis-fy desire. In fact, Yeats consistently connects authentic image making with a discipline that purges the initiate of desire. He goes on, immediately after his criticism of Shelley, to explain the authentic mode of revelation:

> If the experimentalist had an impassioned purpose, a propaganda, let us say, and no critical sense, he might become obsessed by images, voices, that had, it seemed, for their sole object to guard his purpose or to express its contrary and threaten it. The mystic, on the other hand, is in no such danger; he so lives whether in East or West, whether he be Ramakrishna or Boehme, as to dedicate his initiatory image, and its generated images, not to his own but to the Divine Purpose, and after certain years attains to the saint's miraculous life. (*EI*, 422)

Shelley is criticized, then, for not having enough of the mystic's, or saint's, objectivity. Shelley's personal purpose shapes the image according to his will, and this is the labyrinth of secret meditation that Yeats fears.

By the time we reach *A Vision*, the saint seems to possess none of the qualities of the poet, but here and throughout *Per Amica* he has a quality required of the poet. *Per Amica* in fact offers example after example in the elaboration of this idea that the poet has much to learn from the saint.

> If you suspend this critical faculty, I have discovered, either as the result of training, or, if you have the gift, by passing into a slight trance, images pass rapidly before you. If you can suspend also desire, and let them form at their own will, your absorption becomes more complete and they are more clear in color, more precise in articulation, and you and they begin to move in the midst of what seems a powerful light. (*M*, 344)

This suspension of the critical faculty and all willed mental activity is a version of Keats's negative capability. In *Per Amica*, where the passivity of the mind is most strongly counselled, it is often couched in the parlance of the seance room. The vision of the artist, or the life of the spirits, becomes defrauded without passivity: the spirits become "subject to a kind of drunkeness and are stupefied, old writers said, as if with honey, and readily mistake our memory for their own, and believe themselves whom and what we please. We bewilder and overmaster them" (*M*, 363). Instead, to be connected to Anima Mundi, to the Great Memory, "we become mediumistic" (362).

The kind of passivity that is the saint's in *Per Amica* becomes the hallmark of objectivity, or the primary phases, in *A Vision*. The central difference is that its most brilliant descriptions are no longer of the saint (who becomes a rather flat archetype of moral obedience), but of the

fool. If one correctly understands what is for Yeats the profound relationship between objectivity and subjectivity, it becomes clear that he
means the poet to assume at least some of the characteristics of the
primary personality. The antithetical poet, it will be remembered, finds
his mask in everything that is opposite to him, and in the late plays we
see more clearly and boldly than anywhere else how the fool becomes,
for this reason, a figure for the poet. Yeats's characterization of the fool
describes a particular mode of poetic activity, and one strikingly relevant
to "Nineteen Hundred and Nineteen":

> He is but a straw blown by the wind, with no mind but the wind
> and no act but a nameless drifting and turning, and is sometimes
> called "The Child of God." At his worst his hands and feet and
> eyes, his will and feelings, obey obscure subconscious fantasies,
> while at his best he could know all wisdom if he could know any-
> thing. The physical world suggests to his mind pictures and events
> that have no relation to his needs or even to his desires. (V, 182)

This is, of course, a version of that passivity characteristic of mystic and
saint. The fool here becomes a medium for the wind's message, just as
the poet in "Nineteen Hundred and Nineteen" finds himself, like
Herodias's daughters, an instrument of the wind—"Their purpose in the
labyrinth of the wind." The fool is the medium for revelation precisely
because he is without need, without desire. Indeed, he is the nearest incarnation to that "complete passivity, complete plasticity" (183) that
characterizes Phase 1. In Phase 1 "mind and body take whatever shape,
accept whatever image is imprinted upon them, transact whatever purpose is imposed upon them, are indeed the instruments of supernatural
manifestation, the final link between the living and more powerful beings" (183). Yeats uses similar terms to describe both the mental activity of the mystic that allows the reception of images and this phase of
complete plasticity: those who properly suspend desire "seek to become,
as it were, polished mirrors" (M, 344), and in the objective phases man has
"the steellike plasticity of water where the last ripple has been smoothed
away" (V, 82).

　　If we can get beyond Yeats's esoteric terminology, we will see that
such definitions do not describe an unusual mode of poetic activity. In
fact, unlike the language of the seance room, spirits, and mediumship,
the terms "objectivity" and "subjectivity" do bear a relationship to (and
may even be meant to direct us to) the English epistemological tradition
and to the argument in Romanticism that sees the poet alternately as
passive and active. There is, for example, Keats's advice that "we should
rather be the flower than the Bee": "let us open our leaves like a flower
and be passive and receptive" (L, 1, 232). The Aeolian lyre is the symbol

around which the tradition's arguments often center: the instrument
was particularly attractive to these poets because its music could literally be attributed to nature rather than to art.[6] Coleridge describes the
experience in a well-known poem named after the instrument:

> Full many a thought uncall'd and undetain'd,
> And many idle flitting phantasies,
> Traverse my indolent and passive brain,
> As wild and various as the random gales
> That swell and flutter on this subject Lute![7]

If the romantic poets and Yeats become, like the Aeolian lyre, passive
to the influences of nature, Yeats is not inspired by the "gentle breeze"
that greets Wordsworth in the opening line of *The Prelude*. Instead, he
experiences in "Nineteen Hundred and Nineteen" the "dusty wind,"
the "levelling wind," the "winds of winter," "Those winds that clamour
of approaching night." In any case, Phase 1 seems at least a partial description of Yeats's state of mind at the end of "Nineteen Hundred and
Nineteen": "a tumult of images" is impressed upon his mind because he
has reached a state beyond desire, and he thereby becomes an "instrument of supernatural manifestation." The poet becomes the tool that is
at the same time the musical instrument. The poet who is all desire becomes the desireless fool: this is, according to the great plan, the way in
which the poet discovers everything opposite to himself. The objective
phases, by definition, are selfless, while the antithetical phases attempt,
paradoxically, to achieve self-expression through self-sacrifice, quite
often in fact through the mask of saint or fool.

Robert Artisson is the poem's clearest figure for such a poetic
medium. He reminds one particularly of the mindless fool who is but a
straw blown by the wind, "his great eyes without thought / Under the
shadow of stupid straw-pale locks." A civilization reared on the foundation of thought—"O what fine thought we had because we thought /
That the worst rogues and rascals had died out;" "we pieced our thoughts
into philosophy;" "Parliament and King / Thought . . ."—collapses in
the face of the stupid fiend. While Artisson is an embodiment of evil, his
thoughtlessness becomes for Yeats a refreshing escape from a maze of
complicated and contrived thoughts. The vacuity sensed in Artisson—
even his name's curious suggestion of the artist—makes him a representation of a unique and grotesque poetic medium. (He was also known to
Yeats as the Son of Art,[8] a new Icarus, reckless as ever, but all too effective in evil designs.) But then Yeats realized that the artist, and a culture
in general, if sick of desire, can begin "to long for the arbitrary and accidental, for the grotesque, the repulsive and the terrible, that it may be
cured of desire" (*V*, 295). This is the kind of objectivity tried by Yeats

in order to cure art of its subterfuge and the poet of his desire. It is, to paraphrase Keats, the kind of poetic activity that can create, with equal delight, an Imogen or an Iago. It is Yeats become the chameleon poet. Artisson represents everything the poet has not been, and even something that he is, in part, in the process of becoming. "Nineteen Hundred and Nineteen" is a work of art that directs itself toward everything beyond and outside itself: in this way it escapes from the narrow and enclosed labyrinth of private meditation.

Objectivity, in this view, is seen as a careful check on the subjectivity of the poet; it is, as we have seen, a description of image reception that allows a kind of truth sometimes impossible for the poet of desire. What it lacks, of course, is the poet's understanding and means of expression: the fool, who at best knows all wisdom, is without the poet's gift of articulation. He reminds one of Keats's savages, who have dreams as beautiful as the poet's, but "bare of laurel they live, dream, and die; / For Poesy alone can tell her dreams" (*PW*, 403). Actually, Phases 1 and 15 are criticisms of each other. While Phase 15 is clearly a model for the artistic process, it nevertheless becomes almost too artificial in its other-worldliness and its insistence on the fulfillment of desire: "Because the 15th Phase can never find direct human expression, being a supernatural incarnation, it impressed upon work and thought an element of strain and artifice, a desire to combine elements which may be incompatible, or which suggest by their combination something supernatural" (*V*, 292). The antithetical phases are criticized under the term "automa-tonism," and Shelley once again is the central example: "*Antithetical men* (Phase 15 once passed) use this *automatonism* to evade hatred, or rather to hide it from their own eyes; perhaps all at some time or other, in moments of fatigue, give themselves up to fantastic, constructed images, or to an almost mechanical laughter" (144). Automatonism, which the poet sometimes mistakes for poetic invention, is clearly distinguished from it, and is seen as the subjective man's escape from fact.

Moreover, Yeats has shaped his system so that Phase 15 (almost as a guarded afterthought) includes the Vision of Evil.[9] In a description of a phase that is so given over to fulfillment of desire, it is odd, to say the least, to find this sentence tucked away toward the end, with the Vision of Evil broken up as a phrase and without its capital letters: "Even for the most perfect, there is a time of pain, a passage through a vision, where evil reveals itself in its final meaning" (*V*, 136). The sentence seems gratuitous and out of place, and I believe introduced here as a safeguard: it is the insistence on Yeats's part that every poet, though devoted to the fulfillment of his desire in images of the entirely beautiful, pass through such a vision. It is a more comprehensible view, I think, to understand that Yeats saw in subjectivity the danger of the "sterile beauty" of "Endymion," and that objectivity was its best antidote. The example of Nietzsche is helpful. Yeats explains that the writers of the phases surrounding 15 are lost in their antithetical dream: Blake, Coventry Patmore, and Nietzsche, for example, "were begotten in the Sistine Chapel, and still dream that all can be transformed if they be but emphatic; yet Nietzsche, when the doctrine of the Eternal Recurrence drifts before his eyes, knows for an instant that nothing can be so transformed and is almost of the next gyre" (299). The Eternal Recurrence is like the Platonic Year of "Nineteen Hundred and Nineteen," and the recognition that the world is untransformable, of course, is an objective check on the self-absorbing dream of the antithetical poet. The poet seems destined to alternate, tragically, between the subjective dream (of the Happy Shepherd) and the objective awakening (of the Sad Shepherd). But wisdom has come with this knowledge, and a poetic idiom able to support it.

Even with the restricted view of Yeats's career I have confined myself to in this chapter, we can see how he has transformed the rather fey dreaming of the shepherd, and the pastoral equipment of the early Shepherd poems, into a vision of the present civilization's imminent downfall, with artist, politician, and citizen alike seeking comfort in dreams and subterfuge. The "dreary dancing" to Chronos's cracked tune that the Happy Shepherd thinks he can hold back from becomes a universal dance of destruction that no one can avoid: "All men are dancers and their tread / Goes to the barbarous clangour of a gong." Finally, the melancholic and vague sense of loss and suffering in the Shepherd poems has matured into the awful Vision of Evil, and the shepherds' childish complaints have been replaced by the more complicated "unwilling belief" in evil. A Vision describes the tragic tension between desire and necessity: "Life is an endeavor, made vain by the four sails of its mill, to come to a double contemplation, that of the chosen Image, that of the fated Image" (V, 94). In "Nineteen Hundred and Nineteen" Yeats forsakes the chosen Image for a terrifying look at the fated Image; like Dante, he is able to redefine desire, "to desire whatever happens" (A, 273). As an example of the loss of control over thought, the poem is a surrender to something like Nietzsche's Eternal Recurrence. It is the subjective thinker's acknowledgment, perhaps only for an instant, that the world cannot be transformed according to his will and that he must submit himself to the power beyond him that "Whirls out new right and wrong, / Whirls in the old instead."

Yeats reaches the same point Keats does—the half-written page—but completes it. For Yeats the half-written page is a sign of trepidation, a shrinking back from the Vision of Evil, while completed it is a testament of one's acceptance, like Dante's "His will be done" or like Nietzsche's reaffirmation of the classical "amor fati": "My formula for greatness in man is *amor fati*: the fact that a man wishes nothing to be different, either in front of him or behind him, or for all eternity. Not only must the necessary be borne, and on no account concealed,—all idealism is falsehood in the face of necessity,—but it must also be *loved*."[10] It is the courageous step beyond personal comfort, the declaration that the artist may stand in the world beyond daydreams and not "sink unmanned / Into the half-deceit of some intoxicant." But clearly the words do not fill the page to hide its blankness; they are, in fact, like Keats's words, a revelation of the void. Yeats, in a characteristic gesture of sexual submission (a literal following of Nietzsche's advice to love necessity), admits "The last kiss is given to the void." Keats and Yeats dramatically alter the points of the poetic compass they inherit from Milton and Wordsworth. Milton's heaven is a divine effluence that transforms the void into paradise, and Wordsworth's romantic reading of this text changes it only somewhat: a divine mind and its divine words (God and the Word, the poet and his words) are able to survive the desert void and the approaching deluge, indeed they are able to recreate the ordered universe after any cataclysm. But Keats and Yeats picture heaven differently. In Keats it has become Wordsworth's desert, "Deserted, void," and the Muse is no longer imagination's rich daughter singing of an endless plenitude, but instead Moneta, "Priestess of this desolation" (*PW*, 227, 408). Similarly, a "desolate heaven" is the place of Yeats's song, where the levelling winds make the poet an instrument of the Vision of Evil. Finally, unlike Wordsworth, neither Keats nor Yeats rises in a divine gesture to admire his work. In fact, the only certain knowledge that underlies the work of both is precisely that work's vulnerability. Wordsworth still has hope "Of building up a Work that shall endure" (*P*, 14.311). Keats's poems acknowledge the superannuation of every poet's images, the hieroglyphics every language becomes, and Yeats admits that "no work can stand, / Whether health, wealth or peace of mind were spent / On master-work of intellect or hand." If Keats and Yeats are accorded divine vision, they become gods with a fatal flaw, brooding over the destruction of their own creations.

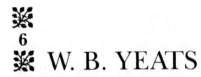

6
W. B. YEATS

"HER VISION IN THE WOOD" AS TRAGIC ART:
A "HOLLOW IMAGE OF FULFILLED DESIRE"

I must say to the Muses what the maid says to the Man—"take me while the fit is on me"—Would you like a true Story? "There was a Man and his Wife who being to go a long journey on foot, in the course of their travels came to a River which rolled knee deep over the pebbles—In these cases the Man generally pulls off his shoes and stockings and carries the woman on his Back. This Man did so; and his Wife being pregnant and troubled, as in such cases is very common, with strange longings, took the strangest that ever was heard of—Seeing her Husband's foot, a handsome one enough, look very clean and tempting in the clear water, on their arrival at the other bank she earnestly demanded a bit of it; he being an affectionate fellow and fearing for the comeliness of his child gave her a bit which he cut off with his Clasp knife—Not satisfied she asked another morsel—supposing there might be twins he gave her a slice more. Not yet contented she craved another Piece. 'You wretch cries the Man, would you wish me to kill myself? take that!' Upon which he stabb'd her with the knife, cut her open and found there three Children in her Belly."

Keats

He has just done a drawing of me which is very charming, but by an un-lucky accident most damnably like Keats.

Yeats

I have shown how "Nineteen Hundred and Nineteen" turns on the distinction between a dream in the past—"we were crack-pated when we dreamed"—and a present nightmare—"Now . . . the nightmare / Rides upon sleep" (*CPY*, 205–6). In *Per Amica Silentia Lunae*, following in the footsteps of Freud (and perhaps outstripping them, at least in his understanding of art), Yeats explores the relationship between dream and art, and develops what is for me among his most significant definitions of art. *Per Amica*, which Yeats called "a kind of prose backing to my poetry" (*LY*, 625), begins by demonstrating the function of wish fulfillment in

109

both life and art. He tells the following anecdote: "I have sometimes told one close friend that her only fault is a habit of harsh judgment with those who have not her sympathy, and she has written comedies where the wickedest people seem but bold children. She does not know why she has created that world where no one is ever judged, a high celebration of indulgence, but to me it seems that her ideal of beauty is the compensating dream of a nature wearied out by over-much judgment" (*M*, 326). Beauty here is given a Freudian definition through two significant concepts that dominate *Per Amica;* it is a dream, and as such it compensates for what the woman lacks in life. It is only one step further for Yeats to see a similar process at work in the serious artist: "There are indeed certain men whose art is less an opposing virtue than a compensation for some accident of health or circumstance" (327). Synge, of course, becomes the prime example here: "Condemned to the life of a monk by bad health," he delighted "in fine physical life;" "gentle and silent," he created "voluble daredevils who 'go romancing through a romping lifetime'" (327).

The problem that immediately presents itself, following my reading of "Nineteen Hundred and Nineteen," is that in *Per Amica* Yeats explains what he took great pains to deny in that poem, namely, Freud's view that art is, like dreams, a form of wish fulfillment. Yeats goes on in *Per Amica,* however, to make an important discrimination. He gives two definitions of art as wish fulfillment and then elaborates upon them, once again distinguishing between Dante and an English Romantic poet:

> Some thirty years ago I read a prose allegory by Simeon Solomon, long out of print and unprocurable, and remember or seem to remember a sentence, "a hollow image of fulfilled desire." All happy art seems to me that hollow image, but when its lineaments express also the poverty or the exasperation that set its maker to the work, we call it tragic art. Keats but gave us his dream of luxury; but while reading Dante we never long escape the conflict. (*M*, 329)

These definitions, which have been given little attention by critics and have even been misunderstood by them,[1] will be the guiding terms for the rest of my discussion of Yeats's poetry: happy art is simply a dream, a wish fulfillment; tragic art, while still "a hollow image of fulfilled desire," reveals the tragic circumstances at its source. It is clear that Yeats has misrepresented Keats, who is of course the master of the kind of ironic relationship between dream and art that Yeats calls "tragic art." In Keats, after "Endymion" (for "Endymion" is often the poem Yeats chooses in his criticism of Keats), the luxurious dream is always significantly qualified: it turns into nightmare in "La Belle Dame sans Merci;" it is openly criticized and becomes a version of a nightmare of suffering (as it does in "Nineteen Hundred and Nineteen") in "The Fall of Hyperion;" it is interrupted and forced to embrace everything beyond itself in "St. Agnes;" and it vanishes, only after revealing the despair out of which it grew, in "Ode to a Nightingale." In fact, I know of no better model for Yeats's "tragic art" than the Nightingale Ode. I have quoted these passages from *Per Amica* because, like the nightmare Vision of Evil, the acknowledgment of art as a kind of dreamy wish fulfillment and the deliberate criticism of this view become the basis for another of Yeats's strategies against the subterfuge of art.

"Her Vision in the Wood" is one of the finest examples of the complicated way Yeats develops the basic analogy, and the ironic discrepancy, between art and the simple wish fulfillment of dreams. It is a poem that, while extravagant praise has been given it, has received to date no complete reading, and really little more than scattered notes. Critics have called it "the most neglected of all Yeats's masterpieces," "one of his best poems," and finally what I take to be damning praise (because it increases the sense of confusion and neglect that has surrounded the poem by mistaking its position in the *Collected Poems*), "one of the few considerable poems in *Words for Music Perhaps*."[2] A complete reading of the poem must take into account one further passage from *Per Amica*, which directly comments on the subject of the poem given in the title, and that is the dream-vision:

> The doctors of medicine have discovered that certain dreams of the night, for I do not grant them all, are the day's unfulfilled desire, and that our terror of desires condemned by the conscience has distorted and disturbed our dreams. They have only studied the breaking into dream of elements that have remained unsatisfied without purifying discouragement. We can satisfy in life a few of our passions and each passion but a little, and our characters indeed but differ because no two men bargain alike. The bargain, the compromise, is always threatened, and when it is broken we become mad or hysterical or are in some way deluded; and so when a starved or banished passion shows in a dream we, before awaking, break the logic that had given it the capacity of action and throw it into chaos again. But the passions, when we know that they cannot find fulfillment, become vision; and a vision, whether we wake or sleep, prolongs its power by rhythm and pattern, the wheel where the world is butterfly. (*M*, 341)

Yeats's starting point here is clearly something like the Freudian interpretation of dreams, which he largely accepts. Dream and vision are subtly distinguished in the passage. The dream, because its recipient has not forgone the passion it represents, is distorted. The vision, which comes to the personality that recognizes fulfillment is impossible, is un-distorted, and even has the order of a work of art: it has "rhythm and pattern" (terms that Forster was to make famous in his discussion of the novel). Whether dream or vision, however, it represents desire fulfilled. What is crucial for the reading of "Her Vision in the Wood" and Yeats's poetry in general is that Yeats uses the same language in *Per Amica* to describe both art and dream-vision: both are fulfilled desires. Yeats is simultaneously developing a theory of art and a psychology, and we must keep this in mind when we read the poem.

In "Her Vision in the Wood," the central irony—and it is an extraor-dinary one, given this background—is that the speaker has a dream-vision that is clearly not fulfilling:

Dry timber under that rich foliage,
At wine-dark midnight in the sacred wood,
Too old for a man's love I stood in rage
Imagining men. Imagining that I could
A greater with a lesser pang assuage
Or but to find if withered vein ran blood,
I tore my body that its wine might cover
Whatever could recall the lip of lover.

And after that I held my fingers up,
Stared at the wine-dark nail, or dark that ran
Down every withered finger from the top;
But the dark changed to red, and torches shone,
And deafening music shook the leaves; a troop
Shouldered a litter with a wounded man,
Or smote upon the string and to the sound
Sang of the beast that gave the fatal wound.

All stately women moving to a song
With loosened hair or foreheads grief-distraught,
It seemed a Quattrocento painter's throng,
A thoughtless image of Mantegna's thought—
Why should they think that are for ever young?
Till suddenly in grief's contagion caught,
I stared upon his blood-bedabbled breast
And sang my malediction with the rest.

That thing all blood and mire, that beast-torn wreck,
Half turned and fixed a glazing eye on mine,
And, though love's bitter-sweet had all come back,
Those bodies from a picture or a coin
Nor saw my body fall nor heard it shriek,

Nor knew, drunken with singing as with wine,
That they had brought no fabulous symbol there
But my heart's victim and its torturer.

(*CPY*, 269-70)

The speaker's experience has some of the qualities of both dream and
vision. The speaker herself seems nearly mad or hysterical (a sign, according to Yeats, of the dream), but the image she sees before her has the
beauty and order of vision, especially of artistic vision. The poem is certainly predicated upon Yeats's Freudian observation that "the passions,
when we know that they cannot find fulfillment, become vision."

Stanza one establishes quite simply that the speaker is seeking the
kind of compensatory dream-vision that I have described. The stanza is
composed of two rather elaborate sentences, both of which reveal, in
different ways, her desire. The word "Imagining" is used twice in a single
line, both times at crucial positions—at the beginning of a line and at the
beginning of a sentence, and therefore capitalized both times. It emphasizes the source of compensation the speaker seeks: imagination is to
suppress the painful reality of her old age. The mention of wine in this
context reminds us of a similar double escape, through Bacchus and the
wings of Poesy, that Keats seeks in his visionary escape from the weariness, the fever, and the fret. The first sentence openly describes this
imaginative leap: the woman imagines what she most lacks—men. The
second sentence describes an act of violence, the tearing of her body,
which does not represent her acceptance of her lot of suffering and the
pain of old age. Quite the contrary, it is used as an intoxicant to allow
her to forget her circumstances: "I tore my body that its wine might
cover / Whatever could recall the lip of lover." It is also a violent inflic-
tion to make her body produce the blood that is the sign of fertility in
woman.

The most complicated fact about the poem is that the woman both
finds and does not find what she seeks. Stanzas two and three do in fact
present the speaker with a vision in the wood: it is, on the face of it, a
dream of wish fulfillment. She sees an image of the wounded Adonis,
who traditionally holds out the promise to man and nature alike of
rejuvenation and fruition. Yeats could even have seen the myth in Keats's
"Endymion," where Adonis spends the winter dreaming of his Venus,
only to awaken in the spring to the splendid truth of his dreams. "Her
Vision," however, ends with the failure of this vision. The climax is
anticlimactic, robbing the speaker of the just rewards of vision, namely,
a happy wish fulfillment. In fact, the poem ends more like a nightmare,
with the speaker's shriek and her physical collapse, from which she does
not awaken. The poem does not reach out toward some future of bliss,

the way Keats's "Endymion" and Yeats's own "Sailing to Byzantium" do; it is abruptly concluded, with no sense of future whatsoever.

I should now turn to the sources of this irony, that is, precisely why the vision is unfulfilling, beyond the surmise (given my reading of "Nineteen Hundred and Nineteen") that Yeats is deliberately avoiding a form of art that is based on a pattern of wish fulfillment. It is certainly true that the two poems share an ironic response to the Freudian association of art with dream fulfillment. The brief outline I have just given of the poem's process, while it is oversimple in most respects, has one saving grace—its literalness. Critics have made certain assumptions about the poem's dramatic situation that are patently incorrect and that obscure the source of its irony: "It is a very peculiar Venus, in her old age and knowledgeable in the painting of the Quattrocento."[3] Two clues have led to such a reading: "The beast that gave the fatal wound" is generally and correctly identified as the boar that killed Adonis, and the ceremony enacted in the poem is seen as modelled after the Adonis festival of the ancient world. These two observations, correct as they are, have unfortunately led some readers to assume that the poem is a direct rendering of the Venus-Adonis myth. I have quoted the above interpretation because it directs us, precisely through its false assumptions, to the heart of the poem's irony: the poem's complex irony arises in the disparity between the Venus-Adonis myth as we know it and as it traditionally functions, and the dramatic situation Yeats has put before us. My simple outline of the poem hesitantly identified its characters, cautious not to equate them with Venus and Adonis. The man carried in on the litter is just that, "a wounded man" who reminds us of Adonis (I called him an "image of Adonis"). The speaker is a woman—that woman of "A Woman Young and Old," now old—about whom we know little more.

Yeats was familiar enough with Frazer to know, for example, that at the Adonis festivals it was usually an image of the god that was mourned: "At the festivals of Adonis . . . the death of the god was annually mourned, with a bitter wailing, chiefly by women; images of him, dressed to resemble corpses, were carried out as to burial."[4] The concluding and shocking realization of the speaker, however, removes the man even further from Adonis; the man is neither Adonis nor even a "fabulous symbol" (a mere image of Adonis). He is, first and last, the speaker's lover, "my heart's victim and its torturer." In Frazer once again we find the explanation of these circumstances: "There is some reason to think that in early times Adonis was sometimes personated by a living man who died a violent death in the character of the god."[5] The woman, likewise, is "a very peculiar Venus" because she is no Venus at all; that is, she is understood precisely as she fails, dry timber that she is, to be the ever young and beautiful goddess of love. There is in "Her Vision," then,

an extraordinary look at the Venus-Adonis myth and at myth in general;
myth is viewed from without rather than from within. We do not understand it in the traditional way, through the eyes of the mythic figures.
Rather, it is seen, painfully, through mortal eyes. Its efficacy and meaning all but disappear at the poem's conclusion in the face of private
experience. The existence of the myth at all in the reader's mind makes
the speaker more pitiful in the final distance that stands between her and
the mythic archetypes.

Yeats dramatizes here a painful and tragic division in everyone. "A
Woman Young and Old," the group of poems with which "Her Vision in
the Wood" is meant to be read, plays magnificent variations on this
theme. The brilliance and life of the series, I believe, arise from its
avoidance of the systematic archetypes of *A Vision*. The series dramatizes
the woman at once as the particular girl who declares that the source of
her love is "That his hair is beautiful, / Cold as the March wind his eyes"
(*CPY*, 266) in the opening lyric, "Father and Child," and as the woman
of "Chosen" who describes how she found that momentary "stillness"
in "the whirling Zodiac" when, "Struggling for an image," she was both
herself and "the maternal midnight," and her lover's heart "my heart did
seem" (268). In "Chosen" this reconciliation becomes a moment of the
past recollected (or imagined), and the reconciliation between image and
person, between archetype and individual, is made somewhat suspect by
that word "seem." "Her Vision" undercuts the remembered moment of
"Chosen" by showing the speaker's lover sacrificed into archetype,
removed ultimately beyond her sphere. He is on the verge of moving
into a further life that denies the joy and pain (the "bitter-sweet")—
Yeats uses Keats's favorite formulation—of experience. For Yeats this
double suggestion of the particular individual and the mythic archetype
is part of a paradox about the human condition that he tirelessly restates:
"I am always, in all I do, driven to a moment which is the realisation of
myself as unique and free, or to a moment which is the surrender to God
of all that I am" (*E*, 305). It is stated less personally, for all people, in *A
Vision:* "Every action of man declares the soul's ultimate, particular
freedom, and the soul's disappearance in God; declares that reality is a
congeries of beings and a single being; nor is this antinomy an appearance imposed upon us by the form of thought but life itself which turns
now here, now there, a whirling and a bitterness" (*V*, 52). "Her Vision"
pictures these turns, now here, now there, in the double nature of its
characters. The wounded man, for example, literally "half-turns" to the
woman in revelation of his division. Part of him remembers, and reminds
her of, "love's bitter-sweet." The other part of him is already distant
from that love. His "glazing eye" describes that process, enacted before
us, of the man's receding into the myth, becoming like "Those bodies

from a picture or a coin" and unlike the speaker. The bittersweet of love calls him back momentarily to the taste of life, to the particular events of life and to the woman who was his lover. But already fast upon him is the intoxicating ceremony that makes him over into Adonis and calls him to his own individual death and rebirth as the mythic archetype. The poem describes, from the point of view of the speaker, the same process, but in reverse. She is momentarily caught up in the ceremony: "Till suddenly in grief's contagion caught, / I stared upon his blood-bedabbled breast / And sang my malediction with the rest." This "stare" is like her lover's "glazing eye" (such eyes are always the sign for Yeats of a visionary otherworldliness). The last stanza of the poem, however, dramatically reverses this process as the woman becomes dissociated from the "stately women" of the ceremony, the communal dance and song ending, at least for her. It is her recognition of her lover that precipitates her fall back into individuality, into suffering and grief.

Even if I were to give the poem a reading that revealed the speaker as a traditional figure from the myth, the poem would still dramatize this distinction between the soul's disappearance in God and its radical particularity. The poem opens with an ambiguity, brilliantly rich and suggestive, that helps identify the speaker from another angle: "Dry timber under that rich foliage, / At wine-dark midnight in the sacred wood, / Too old for a man's love I stood in rage / Imagining men." The subject of this rather elaborate sentence, "I," is postponed until the latter half of the third line. "Dry timber," then, does not become identified as a metaphor for a human subject until that point, and is taken simply as that—dry timber. The speaker is curiously like and unlike the natural world: she is dry timber whereas the wood has rich foliage, but that she is a kind of timber at all, and is mistakenly taken as nothing but timber until the end of line 3, suggests a confusion between the world of nature and humanity. The Venus-Adonis myth contains such a confusion, one in fact that Yeats was often drawn to. His poetry and prose alike delight in accounts of tree-spirits, and of men and women transformed into trees. If the speaker of "Her Vision" is identified in this way she becomes Myrrha (from myrrh tree), Adonis's mortal mother. Yeats quotes Spenser, "the mirrhe sweete bleeding in the bitter wound" (*EI*, 377), reminiscent of the bittersweet wound of love in the poem. Frazer explains the story of Adonis's birth in this way: "A faint rationalistic colour was given to the legend by saying that his mother was a woman named Myrrh, who had been turned into a myrrh-tree soon after she had conceived the child."[6] We have here, then, the grieving, aging mother weeping over the death of her son. Such a reading, while it makes the speaker a figure of the traditional myth, is still an unconventional view of the myth; it has indeed the status of a countermyth because it provokingly misses the point. We still see the myth through a mortal's eyes.

Moreover, just as the mortal woman-lover inevitably reminds us of Venus, this mortal mother reminds us of the Mother Goddess who, whether we look to Frazer or to the Neo-Platonic readings of the myth, is a more significant figure in the myth than Venus herself. The Mother Goddess is a figure that Yeats often refers to. She appears as "the Great Mother" in "Colonus' Praise," a poem wholly evocative of "Her Vision," where "Immortal ladies tread the ground / Dizzy with harmonious sound" in "The wine-dark of the wood's intricacies" (*CPY*, 215). She appears once again as "the Great Mother" in "Parnell's Funeral," another poem that evokes ancient ceremony and sacrifice (though Dionysius instead of Adonis is the presiding god) with a similar imagery (like the "Stamped boy and tree upon Sicilian coin," 275). And she appears memorably in Yeats's notes to his *Autobiographies,* where he retells the myth he uses in "Parnell's Funeral": "the Myth of the Child Slain and Reborn," that is, "the tree as Mother, killing the Tree as Son" (the man in the poem is her heart's victim). The Tree as Mother becomes, in these notes, associated with "the Mother-Goddess": "She is pictured upon certain Cretan coins of the fifth century B.C. as a slightly draped, beautiful woman, sitting in the heart of a branching tree" (*A,* 578).

The introduction of this idea of the Mother Goddess explains one aspect of the poem, that is, how the speaker can be viewed as both the man's lover and his mother: the Mother Goddess is at once mistress and mother. But the implications are deeper. In "Her Vision in the Wood" there is the tantalizing association of the Mother Goddess, who slays Adonis and then works his resurrection. What we do not have—and this is the significant point—is the all-powerful and immortal goddess herself; she exists only as an ironic figure in the background, casting a deadly shadow across the substantial figure of the woman, telling us (and almost reminding her) of what she is not. The woman may seek to forget, though there are everywhere the ghostly reminders of her limitations, of her mortality. The Mother Goddess is the symbol of the rich foliage, of a transcendent summer that knows no end. That we see the speaker both as Myrrha and as the Mother Goddess has the same effect as seeing her as mortal lover and Venus. The mythic archetypes become the ironic underthought of the poem. Yeats has drawn his view of the myth from a peculiar perspective, one that even goes counter to the practice he admires in Shakespeare: "The heroes of Shakespeare convey to us through their looks, or through the metaphorical patterns of their speech, the sudden enlargement of their vision, their ecstasy at the approach of death. . . . They have become God or Mother Goddess, the pelican, 'My baby at my breast,' but all must be cold. . . . The maid of honour whose tragedy they sing must be lifted out of history" (*EI*, 522–23). Quite the contrary, the speaker of this poem is planted firmly in history: it is precisely that she is in history, and not in the eternal present of myth, that is the most significant fact about her. She is dry timber, and seems not to participate even in nature's renewal, not to mention an eternally fruitful present. She cries out, not coldly, but *hysterica passio*—like Lear before tragic ecstasy descends upon him—precisely because she does not become the Mother Goddess. While she is the mother who has borne the son, her anguish is sounded loud and clear, and her son, who once fed upon her blood (and she on his), now seems hardly to recognize her. He passes ultimately beyond her, soon to be no longer even of the realm of flesh and blood, just as she is no longer the fertile and nourishing mother but the old woman with no other brood to bear and feed. The speaker of "Her Vision" does not become her fate, as is the case with Shakespeare's heroes, but is painfully divided from it.

The traditional interpretations of the Venus-Adonis myth that Yeats knew are clearly criticized in this poem. For Frazer the myth is an attempt on the part of a culture to comprehend, even to participate in the control of, the cycles of nature: the myth's meaning centers on the continual rejuvenation of nature and man. The Neo-Platonic interpretation of the myth, which Yeats encountered in Julian, centers precisely on the problem of multiplicity and unity I have raised. The wounding of Adonis is the Mother Goddess's check on his fall into multiplicity, into generation. His resurrection is his assumption back into the primal unity from which he fell. It is through vision, in this Neo-Platonic version, that one is led back to the principles from which one has fallen: vision is the best method by which to escape from the confines of the body. It is an interpretation, as we might expect, that declares the ultimate unity of the soul, its happy and final disappearance in God. For this reason the myth appears as a significant motif in, or more typically, provides the guiding framework for, a whole elegiac tradition that includes Bion, Moschus, and not least of all, Shelley: it is the symbol of grief turned to joy and celebration. Yeats's poem echoes Shelley's "Adonais": the woman tears her body so that "I could / A greater with a lesser pang assuage," just as in "Adonais" a mourning spirit attempts "to stem / A greater loss with one which was more weak."[7] Here the similarity ends, and Yeats's poem avoids the consolations of elegy, knowing too well the folly of being comforted. Shelley's poem has the mighty Mother mourn the death of her son, who turns out to transcend even her powers. If she is chained to Time (inferior to Adonais, still she is, unlike our speaker, the perfect fertility goddess, at one with the cycles of nature and reborn every spring), the soul of Adonais beacons from where the Eternal are. Yeats makes the mother of his poem more tragic (no mighty Mother is she), and even the transcendence of the Adonis figure, because of the poem's point of view, turns out to be tragic.

Yeats has refashioned the myth (and thereby avoided the elegy) to question its meaning: the focus of the poem falls not on the ultimate resurrection of Adonis, but on the woman's painful awareness of her own particularity, solitariness, and mortality; not on nature's rejuvenation, but on her decrepitude. It is, like some of Yeats's best poems, a poem of old age instead of a celebration of eternal spring. The woman is "dry timber" among "rich foliage," and while all of nature participates in the exultant renewal of Adonis, the woman is painfully excluded: the stately women neither hear her shriek nor see her fall. Like most myths, this one provides the group with a collective meaning, a sense of continuity: it integrates time (by connecting past and future, winter and summer, death and life) as well as integrating the community itself. At the same time, however, it makes the individual sharply aware of his predicament apart from the group. Indeed, in "Her Vision," the speaker is ultimately isolated from the group and the efficacy of the myth by the tragic revelation that the myth is insufficient for her. For Yeats, the meaning of this myth, and of any myth for that matter, stays vital only if it undergoes this kind of deconstruction, a kind of ritual sacrifice of itself. Its inadequacies, whatever they may be, must be revealed, for the sake of the myth itself: "Sexual desire dies because every touch consumes the Myth, and yet a myth that cannot be so consumed becomes a Spectre" (*YM*, 154).

I have examined the poem from two different but clearly analogous perspectives. One could even say that myth, as it is used by Yeats in this poem, is a mode of dream-vision. It is a classically accepted solution to the problems of discontinuity and death and is, finally, a public version of the more private and personal Freudian dream. However, each of these modes of compensation fails to function successfully for the speaker and is criticized by the poem. Now both dream-vision and myth have been used, particularly in modern literary criticism, as models for the work of art, either as its inspiration or its shaping form. It is not a difficult step to take, then, to see the poem as a reflection upon itself, upon its own process and function as art. Yeats makes us consider dream-vision and art as analogous functions in *Per Amica*, and in stanza one of "Her Vision" emphasis on "Imagining" as the central activity of the speaker reminds us of the artist's own experience. If the ceremonial figures in "Her Vision" represent a dream-vision or myth, they certainly are also meant to represent the product of the artist's imagination: they are "bodies from a picture or a coin;" they are like "A thoughtless image of Mantegna's thought." "Thought" and "image" are the particular terms Yeats employs to describe the artist's predicament. The artistic process, as shown in several passages in Yeats's prose and poetry, is the transformation of "thought"—the laborious processes that develop out of the particular experience, desire, joy, and pain of the artist—into "image."

This transformation is, for example, the key to Phase 15 of *A Vision:* "As all effort has ceased, all thought has become image" (*V,* 136). All effort ceases because all desire becomes fulfilled here. It is an artistic solution on a par with the compensations of dream and myth. But Yeats has presented, in "Her Vision," something beyond this systematic explanation: he has revealed to us, like few poets, the moment after the artist receives the vision that turns all "thought" into "image," and it is a tragic moment.

That the transformation of thought into image is described by Phase 15 tellingly pinpoints the artist's problem. Phase 15, Yeats insists, is a phase beyond man: "Phase 1 and Phase 15 are not human incarnations because human life is impossible without strife between the *tinctures"* (*V,* 79). The artist discovers himself tragically divided: he is of life, and his creation is beyond it. The artist, then, is the divided being *par excellence:* he is caught between the particularity of selfhood and the disappearance in God, the multiplicity of experience and the unity of art. He is, as Yeats describes, "more type than man, more passion than type" (*EI,* 509). Moreover, the image's apparent virtue—that it is self-delighting and self-sustaining—is seen in "Her Vision in the Wood" as only a further tragic circumstance of the artistic process. The image seems finally independent of its creator. This is the most subtly ironic commentary on the artist found in Yeats. The Shepherd poems directed the poet to a solipsistic intoxication and turned the tables on him by placing him in the midst of a natural world that was similarly unsympathetic and wholly self-involved. Here the artistic product has the same kind of self-absorption. One of the finest ironies of "Her Vision" is that while the speaker seeks intoxication through vision, she is torn by a clear-headed realization in the end, and it is the "stately women" who become "drunken with singing as with wine." The women are drunk with singing, with art: their grief is purely ceremonial, and the image they carry has become merely "a fabulous symbol" to them. Their singing is self-intoxicating the way Keats's art, according to Yeats, is: Keats "sang of a beauty so wholly preoccupied with itself that its contemplation is a kind of lingering trance" (*E,* 378). As part of the "image," these women are exempt from "thought": "Why should they think that are for ever young?" The women's trancelike intoxication prevents them from seeing the speaker fall or hearing her shriek. This shriek, heard against the women's singing, hysterical and jarring as it is, is the voice of wisdom; it embodies the final insight of the poem, namely, that raw experience is the source of all artistic creation. The poem, so preoccupied with forgetting, will not let us forget this. The Lethean intoxication of wine and song is contrasted with a new muse, a tragic Mnemosyne (not unlike Keats's), who makes the woman remember. This is no less than the classic anagnorisis, a sud-

den recognition that blazes through head and heart and produces the
characteristic peripeteia, a change in structure or movement that eschews
the ultimately triumphant rejoicing in eternal spring, the dreamy wish
fulfillment, the single self happily lost in the group's intoxication.

There is an alternative to this view of the self-absorbed and independent image, and that is the conception of "thought" and "image" as
contraries. I refer to the Blakean terminology that Yeats rehearsed so
often and reminded us he knew so well: "my mind had been full of Blake
from boyhood up and I saw the world as a conflict—Spectre and Emana-
tion—and could distinguish between a contrary and a negation. 'Contraries are positive,' wrote Blake, 'a negation is not a contrary'" (*V*, 72).
The image is usually seen, I think, as the solution to a problem, esthetic
or otherwise. It is the end point that is a successful conclusion to thought,
but, as solution, it is a negation of the problem. Critics have typically
seen the image as the poet's triumphant and apocalyptic escape from
time and the cares of labor, for example, in "Nineteen Hundred and
Nineteen" or "Among School Children" or "Sailing to Byzantium."
Yeats criticizes such a view in "Her Vision," most clearly by allowing us
to see that the image is no solution at all. Indeed, he reverses a typical
poetic technique by avoiding ending his poem with the image (as he does,
say, in "Among School Children"), and by showing the poet's state after
the birth of the image. The "wounded man," "that thing all blood and
mire," becomes to the stately women "a fabulous symbol." The image
is in danger, like the myth it depicts, of becoming a specter. The only
alternative it has is to remain in relationship, and that means conflict,
with its contrary: Phase 15 is not a human incarnation because "human
life is impossible without strife" (79), and Yeats, following Blake, reiterates "all things are from antithesis" (268), "All creation is from conflict" (*A*, 576). "Thought" and "image" are a rack upon which the artist
is both teased and tortured. He is pulled between their opposing forces,
as is all life:

> To such a pitch of folly I am brought,
> Being caught between the pull
> Of the dark moon and the full,
> The commonness of thought and images
> That have the frenzy of our western seas.
>
> (*CPY*, 169)

As painful as these contraries are to bear, they are at least fruitful.
They are clearly no escape from pain, however; to describe them in one
of Yeats's favorite formulations, they do not solve the antinomy, but are
its expression. And it is here that Yeats's happy artist, like Keats (to use
Yeats's example), gives us only his luxuriant dream. Morris is a genuinely

good example: "The dream world of Morris was as much the antithesis of daily life as with other men of genius, but he was never conscious of the antithesis and so he knew nothing of intellectual suffering" (*A*, 142). The tragic artist, unlike Morris, exposes the tragic source of his art. Even his most perfect, his happiest images, find and reveal their source in poverty, suffering, and pain. In this way the tragic artist prevents the image from escaping from life; the concluding lines of "Her Vision," and the poem's movement beyond the moment of the potentially compensating vision, accomplish this. Finally, Yeats makes a subtle discrimination between two kinds of artist, the one whose work is mere compensation and the one whose work is an opposing virtue: the image as solution is compensatory, the image as contrary is the opposing virtue the greatest artist seeks and bears.

The mythic subject of "Her Vision in the Wood" requires that we take up more fully the relationship between myth and art. To do so we must situate Yeats's demythologizing poem in its proper historical context, placing it after a crucial philosophical work on Greek drama, contemporary with anthropological investigations into Greek religion and drama, and before our own day's myth criticism. There is little doubt, in the first case, that Nietzsche's *Birth of Tragedy*, because of its special subject matter, stands behind Yeats's poem. But before I take up Nietzsche's work I wish to consider briefly first an English work inspired by it, Jane Harrison's account of Greek religion and drama, and second, the literary criticism of Northrop Frye.

Harrison, following Nietzsche, describes a dissociation of sensibility in the primitive rituals and drama of the Greeks. She characterizes it as a break between daimon and Olympian; it is a disease Greek religion dies of, and she calls it "Olympianism." While much of her work is more interested in Greek religion than Nietzsche's or Yeats's, still she puts the problem in esthetic terms that are directly relevant to my understanding of "Her Vision in the Wood": "The separation of god from worshipper, this segregation of the image that begot it, is manifestly a late and somewhat artificial stage, but in most religions it develops into a doctrine and even hardens into something of a dogma. Man utterly forgets that his gods are man-begotten and he stresses the gulf that separates him from his own image and presentation. . . . The Greeks being a people of high imaginative power are at the mercy of their own imaginations."[8] The separation between god and worshipper in the late stages of primitive ritual and religion is analogous to the separation, in art, between image and artist. This is in fact the precise analogy that lies behind Yeats's poem, with the same understanding of the deadly consequences of the act of separation. Harrison's emphasis on forgetting (she even explains that in such ceremonies the child forgets his mother) and on the human nature of the gods is also crucial. To use terms that would be perfectly congenial to her (particularly bearing in mind the chapter on the Aristotelian nature of primitive ritual that Gilbert Murray contributed to *Themis*), the anagnorisis of Yeats's poem is appropriately defined as the opposite of forgetting. It is based on the discovery of kinship, not unlike that in a Greek drama. There is the kinship between god and man (I have not forgotten that I distinguish between Adonis and the man, but if the ceremony is the Adonis rite then I am correct in seeing whatever god the rite celebrates as born from man), between lover and lover, between mother and son: the poem's emphasis on blood suggests this ever deepening kinship into blood relation. Harrison even puts the problem in terms Yeats would have been happy with because of their Blakean slant: "an Olympian is in fact in the main the negation of an Eniautos-daimon."[9] The strict immortality of the Olympians is what cuts them off from their creators (the Olympian in other words is defined as self-sustaining and self-begetting, beyond man and mortality), and rather than being construed as the contrary of the daimon, or even of man, "the Olympian who will not die to live renounces life, he desiccates and dies":[10] ironically, immortality itself turns out to be death, ultimate death.

Oddly enough, contemporary myth criticism, based so extensively on work like Harrison's and Murray's, is itself Olympian, committing the very error Harrison warns against—a further example, in the realm of literary criticism, of how myth becomes dogmatized. It is hard at first to understand how myth criticism develops into apocalyptic criticism, but Northrop Frye, an archetypal myth critic, gives a particularly relevant insight into this development in his discussion of Yeats's poetry. Frye's literary criticism, which strikes me as most successful when descriptive, turns evaluative, not only describing two different types of poetry—"cyclical" and "dialectical"—but choosing the latter as superior. The cyclical pattern seems more nearly related to ancient ritual and myth; it is "the assimilation of the death and rebirth of life in the human world to the natural cycles of sun, moon, water, and the seasons." The "dialectic," or as he later calls it, the "apocalyptic," enacts "a separation of happiness from misery, the hero from the villain, heaven from hell."[11] Frye is full of praise for those poems that "describe the direct passage across from ordinary life to archetype,"[12] and criticizes Yeats's prose on these grounds: "What we miss in *A Vision*, and in Yeats's speculative prose generally, is the kind of construct that would correspond to such a poem as 'Sailing to Byzantium.'... Such a poem is apocalyptic, a vision of plenitude which is still not bound to time."[13] While the example of "Sailing to Byzantium" does show the kind of poetry Frye admires, it is not very convincing. The poem ends with an apocalyptic wish, though the speaker can hardly be seen not bound to time. In fact, the poem dramatizes beautifully the idea of "tragic art" that I have been explaining, with the optative quality of the speaker's words devalued by his present condition. In any case, Frye praises those poems that end with an apocalyptic image, in other words the precise kind of poem that is being demythologized in "Her Vision in the Wood." The myth of the cycles, of winter and spring, death and rebirth, is crystallized by Frye into one single image that always ends with the resurrection and escape beyond mortality. The myth becomes idealized, and the discontinuity out of which it arises is masked and finally completely forgotten: "In this perspective the whole cycle of nature, of life and death and rebirth which man has dreamed, becomes a single gigantic image, and the process of redemption is to be finally understood as an identification with Man and in detachment from the cyclical image he has created."[14] It is a model based on something like Gilbert Murray's understanding of the Sacer Ludus, and of the entire tetralogy in Greek drama, that moved from the tragedies to a final, climactic satyr play.[15] But of course the dramas became individuated, and this break in form is a sign of the individual suffering in its tragic heroes. We certainly cannot claim these plays to be inferior to comedic satyr plays or see each individual literary work as incomplete or inferior unless related to a fuller apocalyptic pattern.

Moving backward in time we can see how indebted Harrison's and Frye's works are to Nietzsche's view of the double deity behind Greek drama—Dionysius and Apollo. Harrison's "Olympianism" is the complete triumph of the Apollonian, or what Nietzsche historically puts at the feet of Socrates, a triumph of a pure rationality that is deadly. Nietzsche describes myth's dangerous slant toward ideality this way: "But lest the Apollonian tendency freeze all form into Egyptian rigidity, and in attempting to prescribe its orbit to each particular wave inhibit the movement of the lake, the Dionysiac flood tide periodically destroys all the little circles in which the Apollonian will would confine Hellenism."[16] Nietzsche, who is truer to the term than Frye, sees a dialectic built into the very nature of myth that should assure it of its longevity, that should be its own solution. Yeats, on the other hand, sees in myth (and art) a natural proclivity toward ideality, abstraction, and doctrine. The myth, for Yeats, inevitably leads to the specter, and history seems to bear him out (even Nietzsche's example of Socrates supports Yeats's view, unless we make Socratic philosophy an unnatural deviation in a natural pattern).

Nietzsche and Yeats solve the problem of Olympianism, Socratic optimism and the fabulous symbol differently. Nietzsche mourns the death of myth, decries the mythless culture, and asks music (particularly

German music) to issue in the rebirth of myth. Yeats takes to heart more directly the meaning of the myth by turning the myth on itself and by using the myth's subject of sacrifice and victimage as the source of its own new form, its rebirth. The rebirth of myth then requires a sacrificial death, but one so large that only the entire myth will do. Myth and art are too easily compensations if not sacrificed. Nietzsche insists that the original form and function of the myth remain intact— "It then became the task of the dithyrambic chorus so to excite the mood of the listeners that when the tragic hero appeared they would behold not the awkwardly masked man but a figure born of their own rapt vision"[17]—while Yeats deliberately distorts such a convention in the myth. Yeats's speaker sees the man, not the god, and refuses all choric intoxication. In fact, by unmasking the god-man, she finally unmasks the myth itself. The continuity the myth enacts is broken by a discontinuity that, stated in its largest terms, is between the original myth and its retelling: if myth insures continuity, art in this case institutes a discontinuity between two versions of the myth. Yeats refuses the illusion that Nietzsche finally allows art, "a conception of art as the sanguine hope that the spell of individuation may yet be broken, as an augury of eventual reintegration."[18] It is as if Yeats has reconnected the myth to its true origin in sorrow, fear, and poverty: "The makers of religion have established their ceremonies, their form of art, upon fear of death, upon the hope of the father in his child, upon the love of man and woman" (EI, 203). Yeats's poem puts the fear of death back into the myth and shows a darker side to parental and erotic love in one integrated, complex action.

Finally, the direction of Yeats's poem seems inspired by one final reversal of Nietzsche's ideas. Yeats again agrees with a demythologizing element that Nietzsche criticizes. Nietzsche calls it "the incongruence between myth and word," and already one can guess how Yeats will make this incongruity the word's value, not its limitation. Nietzsche complains, "The myth, we might say, never finds an adequate objective correlative in the spoken word,"[19] and finds only in music such a correlative. This is why, in a previously quoted passage, he stresses the chorus's Lethean ability to make the individual forget his individuality and to see, dim-eyed, the god and not the man. Song and dance, in Yeats's poem, provide such a service, up to a point: they are communal activities that catch the speaker in their "contagion," but she eventually escapes this contagion for a more private suffering: the speaker falls (the opposite of the dance) and shrieks (the opposite of the song). Yeats puts Nietzsche's distinction between words and music this way: "Music is the most impersonal of things, and words the most personal, and that is why musicians do not like words" (EI, 268). When the women bring a "deafening music" into the wood, they temporarily deafen the speaker to her own words of suffering, the words she recites in stanza one. But her words, distinguished from their song, eventually enable her to draw herself out of the group. Rather than allowing the spell of music and dance to make her forget the awkwardly masked man and see a vision of the god (as Nietzsche suggests), the speaker's words name a horrifying human form—"That thing all blood and mire, that beast-torn wreck." The true beast in the story is eventually revealed not as the mythic boar (another deconstruction), but as the ravaging love between man and woman: the man's wounds, like the woman's, find their source in the torture and victimage that is love. The daimon may be fast becoming an Olympian, an *objet d'art,* but the speaker's words do their best to hurl down this god and break up this *objet d'art.* As if words were not enough, the speaker's shriek dramatizes a new depth (below the level of articulate words) to which the lyric poem allows itself to sink in order to stop mythologizing music. The speaker's shriek seems without consequence, apparently as fruitless as the woman herself; it neither captures the women's attention nor revives her lover. Still it is a declaration of passion that, for her and us, desecrates the ceremony, the music, even the desecrating word itself, and saves the myth even as it seems to destroy it.

Christianity provided Yeats with a vivid example of the fact that even desecration, when ritualized, becomes abstraction. Christ is one more fertility daimon, but by the pious frauds of religion he is crucified into mere dogma, standing for an ideality that is in its own way utterly Olympian. Like Keats, Yeats shows that the gods are man's own creation, dependent on him for their life and value; Christ, the man-god, is perhaps the best example. Both Keats and Yeats revive the dead gods, not by hiding this fact of their dependence, but by pressing it. The plan for "Hyperion" was to deify Apollo by submitting him to mortal suffering. The dying into life the god must undergo is of course Christlike. This Keatsian dying into life is the mythic subject of "Her Vision in the Wood" and is transcribed or formulated anew (in the sacrifice of the myth of sacrifice). Christ becomes for Yeats, too, the central symbol of the artistic process, but not until He is connected to primitive rituals of sacrifice. Yeats's claim that "the historical Christ [as opposed to the dogmatized God of modern religion] was indeed no more than the supreme symbol of the artistic imagination" (*EI,* 137) is convincing, to himself, only after he establishes the relationship between the Mass and pagan ritual: "A great work of art, the *Ode to a Nightingale* not less than the *Ode to Duty,* is as rooted in the early ages as the Mass which goes back to savage folklore" (*A,* 490). Yeats claims, "all our art has its image in the Mass that would lack authority were it not descended from savage ceremonies" (*EI,* 352). Yeats thinks back to the time when "the umbilical cord which united Christianity to the ancient world had not yet been cut, Christ was still the half-brother of Dionysius" (514).

The Mass is not just commemorative, as the stately women seem to take their ceremony: in fact its central focus, often lost in the forms of ceremony, directs us away from ceremony itself. I refer here to the idea of transubstantiation, the changing of the wine into blood, which is not the transformation of real event into symbol but just the opposite. Now we can begin to understand the imagery of blood and wine that is so insistent in "Her Vision." The images of tree (as myrrh-Myrrha and as cross) and blood (Adonis's blood is transformed into an anemone, Christ's into our life's blood), not to mention the central ideas of sacrifice and the compounding of man and god, allow Yeats to tell, once again, two stories at once. "Blood" and "wine" are in fact analogues for the more apparently esthetic categories of "thought" and "image" (the Mass is the symbol of the artistic process). Yeats, of course, knew the theological disagreement over transubstantiation: in fact the Protestant view, which held that the wine of communion was simply a symbol (even a "fabulous symbol") of the blood of Christ, may have led him to be "bored by an Irish Protestant point of view that suggested by its blank abstraction chloride of lime" (*EI*, 428)—a bitter alternative to the life-renewing Eucharist. The Mass becomes the symbol of the artistic process in a curious way, not by transforming real event into symbol, history into myth, but by reminding us of the blood in the image, of the historical in the midst of a timeless celebration. Both art and the Mass direct us from fabulous symbol back to life, from mere wine back to blood, from mere ceremony back to experience. The Mass, I must emphasize (as Yeats himself does), represents this only if correctly understood. Yeats, like the other writers in this tradition, was quick to criticize Christianity, and in fact dogmatized Christianity is just another example of the way the ritual of the daimon becomes abstract. Yeats adds a connection with Christianity to the historical perspective on the Socratic death of Greek culture given in *The Birth of Tragedy:* "Aristotle and Plato end creative system—to die into the truth is still to die—and formula begins. Yet even the truth into which Plato dies is a form of death, for when he separates the Eternal Ideas from Nature and shows them self-sustained he prepares the Christian desert and the Stoic suicide" (*V*, 271). Christ paradoxically can represent the death that is nonrenewing: "The tree has to die before it can be made into a cross" (*A*, 466). So Yeats must remind us of our true inheritance from Christ before the priests bowdlerized the testament: "It is still true that the Deity gives us, according to His Promise, not His thoughts or His convictions but His flesh and blood, and I believe that the elaborate technique of the arts, seeming to create out of itself a superhuman life, has taught more men to die than oratory or the Prayer Book. We only believe in those thoughts which have been conceived not in the brain but in the whole body" (*EI*, 235).

Abstraction is, finally, starvation. The Olympian refuses to be the daimon (or the fertility god) and the tribe dies, hungry and barren. The flesh and blood of Christ feeds his worshippers, but soon this is made out to be symbol only, and his worshippers go hungry or are fed a ration of chloride of lime. Christ is dogmatized into God (and we get no fertile land, but the "Christian desert"), Dionysius (or Adonis) into Olympian. But for Yeats all gods are revealed as shadows of a more original truth: "Whatever flames upon the night / Man's own resinous heart has fed" (*CPY*, 211). This heart feeds the resurrection in the Christian Mass because it is the source of the sacred blood and wine, and in the Dionysian ritual because it is torn out of the god to allow his rebirth. Yeats makes this heart the Eucharistic center of hunger and nourishment in everyone's resurrection: "for man and Daimon feed the hunger in one another's heart" (*M*, 335). As this idea is transformed, however, into its more particular form, the relationship between Muse and poet, it takes a tragic twist. The poet's heart, quite simply, feeds the Muse's. Yeats says that, when being directed by his instructors during the writing of *A Vision*, "if my mind returned too soon to their unmixed abstraction they would say, 'We are starved'" (*V*, 12). It is the poet who must "give concrete experience to their abstract thought" (12); it is the poet who must let the Muse feed upon him. We see the explanation of eternity in love with the productions of time, of Zeus's rape of Leda, given a Eucharistic turn.

But we must realize we have left behind one alternative for another, more tragic one (the basic form of "Her Vision" is a series of exclusive alternatives): in the Heraclitean formula that Yeats never tires of restating—"God and man die each other's life, live each other's death" (*CP*, 594)—god (or daimon) and man share an eternal dayspring. Each revives as the other weakens, and there seems no end to the alternating reciprocity; but this turns out to be a mythic version that, when translated into individual poet and muse, goes only in one direction, not in two. It becomes, suddenly for the poet, irreversible, and for this reason Yeats's description of himself is in terms remarkably close to the speaker's in "Her Vision" (right down to the image of a tree's "sap"): "The fascination of what's difficult / Has dried the sap out of my veins, and rent / Spontaneous joy and natural content / Out of my heart" (*CPY*, 91). The vampiric Muse (Nietzsche says, "One lives under the vampirism of one's talent"[20]), intoxicated on the wine-blood she drinks, like the stately women in "Her Vision," has no ear for tragic shrieks and no eye for mortal suffering. Yeats reflects on his Nobel prize medal: "It shows a young man listening to a Muse, who stands young and beautiful with a great lyre in her hand, and I think as I examine it, 'I was good-looking once like that young man, but my unpractised verse was full of infirmity, my Muse old as it were; and now I am old and rheumatic, and nothing to look at, but my Muse is young. I am even persuaded that she is like those Angels in Swedenborg's vision, and moves perpetually 'towards the day-spring of her youth'" (A, 541).

Moreover, there is no external Eucharist, no god beyond man (even the Muse now seems a fiction), that the poet in turn feeds off. This is the tragic discovery that the poet must feed off himself: "I am like the Tibetan monk who dreams at his initiation that he is eaten by a wild beast and learns on waking that he is eater and eaten" (EI, 519). This suggests the incestuous nature of the poet, symbolized in "Her Vision" in the doubling of mother and mistress. Yeats quite appropriately saw the poet, the bearer of poems, as a woman. He wrote to Ethel Mannin, "You are doubly a woman, first because of yourself, and secondly because of the muses, whereas I am but once a woman" (LY, 831). The poet begets upon himself the poem, feeds the child through his own lifeblood (poems become, in fact, a pelican's brood, but they exact the mother's death). Unlike the Great Mother, whose source of power and life is never ending, the poet is like the mother in "Her Vision." At first this relation of eater and eaten, like the reciprocal "victim" and "torturer" in the poem, seems to miss the sense of antithesis that Yeats insists is the source of creation, but Yeats imagines a crucial division within himself: "great poetry" is the result "of invisible warfare, the division of a mind within itself, a victory, the sacrifice of a man to himself" (EI, 321). And the sacrifice does not occur once only, but daily: "A writer must die every day he lives" (A, 457). In fact, Yeats warns against the single victory: "A poet, when he is grown old, will ask himself if he cannot keep his mask and his vision without new bitterness, even disappointment. . . . Then he will remember Wordsworth withering into eighty years, honoured and empty-witted, and climb to some waste room and find, forgotten there by youth, some bitter crust" (M, 342). Yeats demythologizes for himself, then, the poet's version of the mythic death and rebirth. The rich Eucharist becomes the single dry crust and the young poet becomes the old man (or woman) whose sap is dried out. And no matter how much of the blood is drunk or the flesh eaten, the poet's appetite remains unfulfilled. He sees the artistic imagination now not in any god, but in the tragic hero:

> Men did not mourn merely because their beloved was married to another, or because learning was bitter in the mouth, for such mourning believes that life might be happy were it different, and is therefore the less mourning, but because they had been born and

must die with their great thirst unslaked. And so it is that all the august sorrowful persons of literature, Cassandra and Helen and Deirdre, and Lear and Tristan, have come out of legends and are indeed but the images of the primitive imagination mirrored in the little looking-glass of the modern and classic imagination. (*EI,* 182)

The poem grows out of passion unfulfilled, or "a starved . . . passion" (*M,* 341).

Yeats claims that "when our whole being lives we create alike out of our love and hate" (*E,* 307). Beyond the well-known examples of this creative love-hate pictured in lover and lover, or in daimon and man, Yeats offers perhaps what is for him its most profound example—the poet's, at least the Irish poet's, relation to language: "Then I remind myself that though mine is the first English marriage I know of in the direct line, all my family names are English, and that I owe my soul to Shakespeare, to Spenser and to Blake, perhaps to William Morris, and to the English language in which I think, speak, and write, that everything I love has come to me through English; my hatred tortures me with love, my love with hate" (*EI,* 519). English is his language, and therefore is his parentage, whether he looks to his family name (father) or to the language he speaks ("his mother tongue," 520). The son is bound to this ancestry: "no man can think or write with music and vigour except in his mother tongue" (520). Yeats even presents the idea in an Oriental story (which anticipates Lacan's view, following Freud's Oedipal myth, of language as the father), once again ambiguously seeing language as a gift from the mother-father-lover: "My master lifted me up like the Divine Mother and hugged me to His breast and caressed me all over the body. Thereafter He gave me the Mantra (sacred words) and initiated me into the realisation of the Self" (479). Paradoxically, language is at once universal archetype and individual expression: the initiation into selfhood happens through words, and yet the words are a gift from the mother or father. The mother tongue is an almost divine ancestry, and often is cruel and harsh, making demands of conformity and tradition upon the child. Yet on the other hand, it is the only support the child has, the only source of nourishment and love. But by the same token the child has a gift for the parent—a new language, a language revived, regenerated through the generations it seems. Yeats's ideas about language and tradition make him think of "that supreme ceremony wherein the Mormon offers his wisdom to his ancestors" (*E,* 294). The family name can continue only through the new blood added to it.

Yeats directly grafts these synchronic and diachronic aspects of language onto the central myth of archetype and individual, of God and self: "Man incarnating, translating 'the divine ideas' into his language of the eye, to assert his own freedom, dying into the freedom of God and then coming to birth again" (*E,* 306). He compares this to "the assertions and surrender of sexual love" (306) and concludes with his statement about creation proceeding from love and hate. Here Yeats pictures man's translation of the Word into words as the source of both his individuality and his universality: the Word made Flesh is at once God become man and man become God. Language is surrender and self-assertion, victim and torturer. Like myth, it revives itself on this warfare. In fact, realizing that the dangers to language are always Olympian, Yeats rhetorically asks (actually it is, appropriately, the Heart that does the asking in an early version of the dialogue from "Vacillation"): "Can there be living speech in heaven's blue?" (*LY,* 790). The history of every nation's language, like the history of its religion or art, ends with death by abstraction, the death of living speech: "the death of language, the substitution of phrases as nearly impersonal as algebra for words and rhythms varying from man to man, is but part of the tyranny of impersonal things" (*EI,* 301); "every nation begins with poetry and ends with algebra" (*E,* 167). The poet can revive his language only through personal expression, which we have seen turn out to be, ironically enough, personal sacrifice: it is the sacrifice of the self for the mother (as the Muse feeds off the poet), for the mother tongue, for art, as well as the sacrifice of language itself, the Word made flesh, the Father giving up the Son. Yeats criticizes Wordsworth, whose universal language is a language of impersonality: "I discovered some twenty years ago that I must seek, not as Wordsworth thought, words in common use, but a powerful and passionate syntax" (*EI,* 522). Moreover, it is not simply a certain kind of syntax that Yeats seeks, but speech ("living speech") as opposed to writing: "I tried to make the language of poetry coincide with that of passionate, normal speech" (521); "I have spent my life in clearing out of poetry every phrase written for the eye, and bringing all back to syntax that is for ear alone" (529).

The fruitful contrariety (what Yeats calls creation out of love and hate) between *langue* and *parole,* between the written word handed down generation after generation like an inheritance, a literal testament, and the "living speech" or "living voice" (*E,* 202) (where, obversely, "the worth of his own mind becomes the inheritance of his people," 192) is always on the verge of breaking up, dissociating. In the famous passages on self and God from the prose works that I quoted earlier, there is a crucial distinction: in one Yeats says he is drawn to a moment that is the realization of himself as unique and free, *or* to a moment that is his surrender to God; in the other, less personal passage—he speaks of "one" instead of "I"—every action declares this freedom *and* this surrender to

God. It is the kind of ambiguity that continually deconstructs the myth of the poet: the Heraclitean myth translated into the myth of the poet becomes ironic, irreversible, signifying renewal for the Muse and exhaustion for the poet.

"Her Vision in the Wood" certainly shows an ironic side to Yeats's ideas about language. If poetry is to be a reconciliation between mother tongue and personal expression—Yeats's linguistic version of tradition and individual talent—in "Her Vision" he seems to dramatize the opposite, namely, music, language, and even inarticulate noise dissociated. The stately women sing an impersonal music, while the woman articulates an individual wisdom that finally becomes expressed in an inarticulate shriek. Shriek and music go in opposite directions, and break the poem apart. All art stops at the failure to reconcile personal and impersonal, individual and universal. The poem is abridged, sharply curtailed; it has no future, only a past (of love and fruition), and the end of the speaker's words is all too sudden and complete. Her shriek precipitates a sudden silence that signals the end of the poem, the end of all individual articulation, and the end of all imagining.

7

✻ E. M. FORSTER

THE VISION OF EVIL IN FICTION:
THE NARRATIVE STRUCTURE OF *A PASSAGE TO INDIA*

> *"Truth"*: this, according to my way of thinking, does not necessarily denote the antithesis of error, but in the most fundamental cases only the posture of various errors in relation to one another.
>
> No limit to the ways in which the world can be interpreted; every interpretation a symptom of growth or of decline.
> Inertia needs unity (monism); plurality of interpretations a sign of strength. Not to desire to deprive the world of its disturbing and enigmatic character.
>
> Nietzsche

Forster's point of departure in *A Passage to India* is remarkably close to Yeats's in "Nineteen Hundred and Nineteen": it is a correction of a tradition, and it rests upon a vision of evil. Forster charges that fiction traditionally has ignored, or at best has poorly handled, the idea of evil: "As a rule evil has been feebly envisaged in fiction, which seldom soars above misconduct or avoids the clouds of mysteriousness. Evil to most novelists is either sexual and social or is something very vague for which a special style with implications of poetry is thought suitable" (*AN,* 140). If Yeats chooses Dante as his model, Forster singles out Melville as the central exception to this traditional weakness: "It is to his conception of evil that Melville's work owes much of its strength" (140). Notwithstanding the similarities between Yeats and Forster on these points, the vision of evil provides Forster with a somewhat different set of problems to solve. The most elaborate description of these problems is, curiously enough, in Forster's preceding novel. Helen Schlegel's interpretation of the Fifth Symphony, justly one of the most celebrated passages in *Howards End* and indeed in all of Forster's fiction, may well betray what her sister argues is a naïve literalness: "She labels it with meanings from start to

133

finish; turns it into literature" (*HE*, 39). Still, it does explain a point of
view about all the arts that Forster himself shared. The goblins Helen
hears "merely observed in passing that there was no such thing as
splendour or heroism in the world," as they echo "Panic and emptiness!
Panic and emptiness!" Her "goblin walking quietly over the universe from
end to end" in fact seems a half-fanciful version of Forster's characterization of evil in Melville—Moby Dick's "slipping over the ocean and round
the world" (*AN*, 142). In any case, these goblins are not the whole of
this "wonderful movement" of the Fifth Symphony: "If things were
going too far, Beethoven took hold of the goblins and made them do
what he wanted." He does in fact make them all but disappear, it seems,
by so simple a technique as the change from minor to major key, and
"gusts of splendour" immediately replace them. The movement contains,
for Helen, two final alternations: the goblins return, but finally "Beethoven chose to make all right in the end" with more gusts of splendor.

As unsettling as the goblins are to Helen they are also the source of a
curious kind of solace: "He brought back the gusts of splendour, the
heroism, the youth, the magnificence of life and of death, and, amid vast
roarings of a superhuman joy, he led his Fifth Symphony to its conclusion. But the goblins were there. They could return. He had said so brave-
ly, and that is why one can trust Beethoven when he says other things"
(*HE*, 33–34). This final sentence, with Forster's characteristic irony, is
naïvely stated at the same time that it points to a profound concern of
Forster himself—namely, that the splendid beauty of an artist's work can
be believed only if that artist also openly admits to "Panic and emptiness!"
A vision of evil becomes a crucial clue to Forster's own trustworthiness as
a maker of fictions, a protection (as in Yeats) against the subterfuge of
art. The goblins who "merely observed in passing that there was no such
thing as splendour or heroism in the world" remind one of the echo in
A Passage to India; the echo murmurs, "Pathos, piety, courage—they exist,
but are identical, and so is filth. Everything exists, nothing has value"
(149). But lest we miss Forster's central concern, we must realize that
music, like lyric poetry or any other art, has its own special features and
techniques peculiar to it, like those "aspects of the novel" Forster took
care to outline and define.

Forster's major concern is the relationship between fiction and the
vision of evil. This is certainly the thrust of his complaint about the tradition of the novel, and it is the impetus behind *A Passage to India*. So, we
must translate the passage on Beethoven into universal categories applicable to all artists, and only then ask ourselves how these become relevant
to fiction: how does the artist protect himself against illusion? how does
he manipulate his audience to insure their belief? how does he manage to
shift his point of view and tone? Finally, and perhaps most importantly,

what is the relationship of evil, and nihilistic vision in general, to artistic expression, to beauty and form?

A Passage to India has inspired—perhaps instigated would be a better word—a relentless critical debate that cannot bring to a successful close even the most basic questions about the novel. The most typical form taken by the attempts to solve the novel's difficulties is for the critic to latch onto the particular aspect of the novel that seems most accessible, what Forster called its people, or characters. In their attempts to solve the novel's problems (or their own) critics have identified a single character, or set of characters, as their guide through the novel: Mrs. Moore, Godbole, Fielding, and others have been offered in essay after essay as models for our attention.[1] This seems, particularly as the list of characters grows, more symptom than solution. I use the term "guide" here deliberately to emphasize that crucial scenes in the novel do in fact center around this notion. Aziz's most embarrassing moments, for example, stem from his incompetence as a guide. Even after his ignorance about the caves becomes clear to his Western friends, he refuses to renege on his invitation to accompany them on a sightseeing expedition there, and the central events of the novel show Aziz sharing the responsibility of guiding with a local villager. The results of the guided tour are disastrous: both Aziz and the local guide lose Miss Quested. Both are unable, finally, to locate her in the maze of the caves, and the incident ends with a real act of violence (Aziz strikes the guide for a punishment) and an alleged one (Adela accuses Aziz of sexual assault), to say nothing of Mrs. Moore's frightening experience in the caves. In the last section of the novel Aziz finds himself once again offering his services as a guide (but with happier consequences) to Ralph Moore. He discovers, to his embarrassment, that "his companion was not so much a visitor as a guide" (*PI*, 313).

The novel subtly develops this notion of a guide in what becomes almost the novel's subplot, the adventure of the narrator (that aspect of the novel most neglected by critics). Helen Schlegel, rightly or wrongly, may hear Beethoven thinking in his music, but in fiction there is a more complicated situation still: the narrator, whom we do not simply equate with the author (Helen contends that Beethoven appears in person in his symphony to give the goblins a push), and his relationship to his characters, present a crucial problem in fiction that needs analysis. Forster sees the novel's special quality as its capacity to view the world doubly, through its narrator and its characters. Already with the opening chapter the parallel between the narrator and Aziz is clear. In fact, the opening chapters of both "Mosque" and "Caves" function as descriptions for the reader of aspects of this strange land. They are conceived as prologues, their tone is introductory, their matter is descriptive rather than dramatic.

The first is, quite simply, a brief tour of Chandrapore. The well-known opening chapter presents multiple views of the city, and seems almost to warn the visitor (or reader) that he has made an unfortunate choice in Chandrapore: "Except for the Marabar Caves—and they are twenty miles off—the city of Chandrapore presents nothing extraordinary" (*PI*, 7). The second section, "Caves," rounds out the opening description of Chandrapore by describing these extraordinary hills and the caves they contain. Both sections view the sites they describe with the visitor in mind: we hear in the case of Chandrapore what "new-comers" (8) are likely to experience, and in the case of the caves what occurs when "the visitor arrives for his five minutes" (125). The troubled and difficult passage to India, then, is at once the burden of Mrs. Moore and Adela, and of the reader. I emphasize the notion of guiding because it develops a suggestive significance in the novel. It reveals something about India, but even more about the novel itself, and it seems a fine description of the function of the narrator in his capacity to direct the interpretative act of reading. After all, the novel is a fictive world of astonishing complications, and shares with India its sudden changes in atmosphere and mood and its general capacity to elude interpretation. While critics of the novel have chosen one character after another to guide them through the world of the novel, it seems clear to me that Forster creates in *A Passage to India* a special relationship between narrator and reader. In fact, the narrator becomes a guide who attempts to accomplish for the reader what Aziz is unable to accomplish for his guests.

To understand the role of the narrator in the novel is to traverse the world of India with him (no easy task) and to see and hear its daily sights and sounds. It is a task far more encompassing than simply to understand (to return to the central strategy of the novel) his vision of evil. If both Yeats and Forster see civilization, and its culture of art and religion, as a mask for evil, a guileful act of self-subterfuge, still the picture of this world that a lyric poem and a novel give is, of course, extraordinarily different. The lyric poem, at least in Yeats's case, shrinks the inhabitants of this world into two types: the infantile dreamer (citizen, artist, and politician alike) who masks the evil, and the solitary poet courageous enough to accept the nightmare of time and of evil. But the numerous characters in *A Passage to India,* and its narrator, make special cases and various gradations. The testing of responses that is the heart of Yeats's poem is drawn out here, in Forster's novel, into as many responses as there are people, and more—the narrator alone is characterized by a widely varied series of viewpoints. Criticism's list of possible candidates for the author's viewpoint suggests the complexity of settling on a single model. If the varying responses are at least as complicated as in Yeats's poem, the object of evil is far more difficult to pin down in *A Passage to*

India. Yeats's use of a single symbolic personage, like Robert Artisson, to carry the weight of evil is something Forster knows cannot be done in the novel: he complains, for instance, that "a Lovelace or Uriah Heep . . . does more harm to the author than to the fellow characters" (*AN,* 141). Such factors make Yeats's Vision of Evil look theatrical, even artful (despite its function to demythologize) compared to Forster's (which is not allowed even the drama of capitalization). The most curious irony lies in the fact that fiction has so consistently failed to give a conception of evil: clearly it is the genre most capable of doing so, without mythologizing or romanticizing evil. Finally, *A Passage to India* quite naturally presents a larger picture of the world than a lyric poem does: the novel is a microcosm of everyday life. The vision of evil comes only after some hundred pages or so, and only after evil is seen to be delicately woven into the fabric of society. It may seem as if my discussion of the narrative structure of the novel, the largest part of this chapter, postpones for too long its core—the vision of evil and its relationship to art—but I must insist that the narrator's mode of perception, of everyday perception, his view of actions ridiculous and sublime, is the only prelude (if a long one) to the understanding of the novel's basic issues. In fact, even the most apparently irrelevant narrative act becomes subtly related to the vision of evil.

The narrator's function in the novel is defined most clearly at first as a kind of largeness of vision that offsets the smaller perspective of the individual characters. In a fairly typical passage we see that for Mrs. Moore and Adela, for example, a unity of experience that includes a single day's events is rare enough, while India is always defined as an entity beyond their ken: "Mrs. Moore continued to murmur 'Red knave on a black knave,' Miss Quested assisted her, and to intersperse among the intricacies of the play details about the hyena, the engagement, the Maharani of Mudkul, the Bhattacharyas, and the day generally, whose rough desiccated surface acquired as it receded a definite outline, as India itself might, could it be viewed from the moon." The narrator here suggests his own purpose in the novel. And as if that were not enough, he immediately displays the kind of distanced vision, or moon-vision, he recommends. The two women, tired after their long day in this inexplicable country, withdraw from it into the familiar world of Patience, a puzzling game whose rules they at least know, and in which they can relax with a sense of their own competence. As the day, now distanced from them, takes shape, the same process occurs, only on a far larger scale, in the novel's narrative voice: "Presently the players went to bed, but not before other people had woken up elsewhere, people whose emotions they could not share, and whose existence they ignored" (*PI,* 100).

This larger vision suggests India's "outline," if not its unity; or, let us say, it suggests a unity in disunity. Surpassing our expectations, it is an outline not merely of India, but of earth, and it reveals that the particular hopes and fears that these women feel are shared and unshared by people all over the globe. It is a vision of the unity of man's sense of his own self-importance, each person like every other because each thinks he is the center of the universe. This is a vision of earth from the moon—aloof, ironic toward man's self-importance, and yet sympathetic from a distance.

The narrator's voice, if I can generalize from this passage, is recognizable and even familiar. It is carefully modulated, reasoning, even wise—the kind of voice we associate with, say, George Eliot's novels. The narrator speaks with a breadth of understanding that suggests no limit to his vision. Much of his power in the novel stems from his ability to broaden the sphere of his central story, to include in it worlds of experience that his characters often miss. The characters, for example, are set against the backdrop of a teeming natural world: "It matters so little to the majority of living beings what the minority, that calls itself human, desires or decides. Most of the inhabitants of India do not mind how India is governed. Nor are the lower animals of England concerned about England, but in the tropics the indifference is more prominent, the inarticulate world is closer at hand and readier to resume control as soon as men are tired" (*PI*, 114). The effect here is the same as in the first passage. The narrator shifts the reader's attention away from Mrs. Moore and Adela, or in this case Aziz's friends, and focuses it on the world that surrounds them. Once again the narrator broadens the vista of his created world, and his voice carries with it the experience of different nations, even different natural creatures. It carries with it, as well, the implicit suggestion that the characters who are the central subject of the novel rarely have this further vision. In short, it provides the story with a significant context, and is a fairly typical form of irony in fiction. Aziz's friends talk politics, "while a squirrel hung head-downwards" (114) on a large unfinished house opposite Aziz's bungalow: it is, by itself, ample commentary on man's endeavors. There seems no limit to the narrator's vision. He extends his commentary to include even the sun: "Through excess of light, he failed to triumph, he also; in his yellowy-white overflow not only matter, but brightness itself lay drowned." The ultimate irony of the passage, then, is a curious kind of unity: "He was merely a creature, like the rest, and so debarred from glory" (115). It is a vision from the moon, if you will, in its cool objectivity and distance, and in its deliberate refusal to allow any romantic illusions about nature or the heavens to color it. Each thing is isolated in its own particular activity, each thing remains friendless: "He was not the unattainable friend, either of men or birds or other suns" (115). The scene, with squirrel and inglorious sun, becomes a significant commentary on man: Aziz's friends attempt "to recover their self-esteem and the qualities that distinguished them from each other" (114) when the narrator reveals, all too clearly, the quality they share even with an upside down squirrel and the inglorious sun.

Perhaps the two most celebrated passages in the novel—the great event itself, namely, Mrs. Moore's vision of evil in the caves, and her later view of Asirgarh—can be taken as typical examples of the narrative function in the novel. They need to be included here as stepping stones, for only in the light of the narrator's most typical function can we begin to see how other passages in the novel complicate this. At Mrs. Moore's entrance into the caves, the narrator presents some crucial information that the old lady lacks. Her singleness of vision, it is clear, is her limitation: she takes the caves for all, just as she previously took love and unity for all. The narrator, however, qualifies her experience in a central passage. The narrative begins in the past tense, supplying the reader with the details of plot: "She lost Aziz and Adela in the dark, didn't know who touched her. . . . There was also a terrifying echo" (*PI*, 147). A major shift in narrative voice occurs as the narrator distances himself from this time and place, and reveals the essential knowledge that Mrs. Moore lacks: "Professor Godbole had never mentioned an echo; it never impressed him, perhaps. There are some exquisite echoes in India; there is the whisper round the dome at Bijapur; there are the long, solid sentences that voyage through the air at Mandu, and return unbroken to their creator. The echo in a Marabar cave is not like these" (147). This is the kind of information that the party's official guide, Dr. Aziz, should be offering, but it is clear that what he neglects or is unable to tell the characters, the narrator tells the reader.

The narrator's universal present is an expression of the largeness of his vision, even of his ability to juxtapose one experience with another. It is essentially what happens to Mrs. Moore some hundred pages later. The narrator's catalogue of beautiful echoes is a version of Mrs. Moore's implicit realization that Asirgarh's beauty is as significant and real as the echo's emptiness: "There was, for instance, a place called Asirgarh which she passed at sunset and identified on a map—an enormous fortress among wooded hills. No one had even mentioned Asirgarh to her, but it had huge and noble bastions and to the right of them was a mosque. Ten minutes later, Asirgarh reappeared. The mosque was to the left of the bastions now. The train in its descent through the Vindyas had described a semi-circle round Asirgarh. What could she connect it with except its own name?" (*PI*, 209). She should connect it, of course, with the echo and the caves. Neither beauty nor ugliness, neither good nor evil is the single clue to the universe. If each momentarily excludes the other, that is more a sign of the limitation of the viewer than of the universe. It is because the perceiver sees singly that he is led, alternately, to believe simply in one or the other. Mrs. Moore's understanding is clearly threatened by her lack of information: "I have not seen the right places," she realizes as she thinks of all the places she would never visit, "neither Delhi nor Agra nor the Rajputana cities nor Kashmir, nor the obscurer marvels that had sometimes shone through men's speech: the bilingual rock of Girnar, the statue of Shri Belgola, the ruins of Mandu and Hampi, temples of Khajraha, gardens of Shalimar" (210-11). In this catalogue of places unvisited, Mandu is the most ironic because it is mentioned by the narrator in his description of echoes different from the Marabar echo. She realizes her tour of India has been incomplete, and Asirgarh taunts her: "'So you thought an echo was India; you took the Marabar caves as final?' they laughed. 'What have we in common with them, or they with Asirgarh? Good-bye!'" (210). It is a version of Godbole's explanation, many pages later, that the visitors of the Marabar failed to see the Tank of the Dagger, a work commemorating an act of sympathy and love, in close proximity to the caves. Asirgarh is a momentary illumination, almost too late, on the threshold of death; it explains the double view of life that Mrs. Moore might have had and shows her reaction to the caves as foolish, certainly exaggerated, in light of its narrowness.

The device of the train ride is one of the ways used in *A Passage to India* to insist on the necessity of multiple perspectives. It is used significantly at the approach to and departure from the caves, clearly connecting Mrs. Moore's experience at the Marabar with the later vision of Asirgarh. If Adela complains that the India she is seeing appears artificial and unreal, like the frozen pictures on an urn—"I'm tired of seeing picturesque figures pass before me as a frieze" (*PI*, 27); "She would see India always as a frieze" (47)—the train presents an image of a world in movement: "Astonishing even from the rise of the civil station, here the Marabar were gods to whom earth is a ghost. . . . The assemblage, ten in all, shifted a little as the train crept past them, as if observing its arrival" (137). It is at first no more than an optical illusion, but suggests, even if only through a trick of the eye, that India is alive—a view that turns out later, in "Caves," to be more true than we can guess at this point. The device of the train is even more important when the visitors leave the caves. With supreme irony we see the importance of perspective, and as we see it the characters are left fast asleep: "Mrs. Moore entered her carriage, the three men went to theirs, adjusted the shutters, turned on the electric fan and tried to get some sleep. In the twilight, all resembled corpses, and the train itself seemed dead though it moved—a coffin from the scientific north which troubled the scenery four times a day. As it left the Marabars, their nasty little cosmos disappeared, and gave place to the Marabars seen from a distance, finite and rather romantic" (161). Once again the reader is placed in a privileged position by sharing the narrator's double vision. Narrator and reader experience the terror of the caves with Mrs. Moore, but also, through the train ride, they see the caves recede into mere nastiness and then eventually disappear.

While this passage is a criticism of the limited view of the characters, it also criticizes what I have characterized as the narrator's power of vision: the distance that even the narrator seems to take pride in—the vision of earth from the moon—clearly has its liabilities. If one limited oneself to distanced vision, then all one would see of the Marabars is that they are "finite and rather romantic," as much a distortion as Mrs. Moore's vision of absolute evil in the caves. The point is made again and again in the novel, particularly with reference to the caves: "These hills look romantic in certain lights and at suitable distances" (*PI,* 126); "At this distance and hour they leapt into beauty" (190). We must then carefully redefine the narrator's function in the novel and the novel's description of complete vision; it is only insofar as largeness of vision can alternate between perspectives that it becomes a goal. If largeness of vision becomes defined, as it does in certain passages in the novel, merely as distanced vision, as moon-vision, then it is at best incomplete and often misleading. We learn, for example, that "Hinduism, so solid from a distance, is riven into sects and clans" (292). While the outline of India may be apparent from the moon, such a view may well be a falsification of what experience teaches. The Indians are tired of always being seen from that distanced English point of view:

> "Those high officials are different—they sympathize, the Viceroy sympathizes, they would have us treated properly. But they come too seldom and live too far away. Meanwhile—"
> "It is easy to sympathize at a distance," said an old gentleman with a beard. "I value more the kind word that is spoken close to my ear." (35)

Moreover, if the narrator's correctness of vision is playfully defined as a kind of vision from the moon, and distance becomes its prerequisite, he suggests an ideal vantage point that is located even beyond his own powers of imagination: "Beyond the sky must not there be something that overarches all the skies, more impartial even than they? Beyond which again . . ." (*PI,* 40). The sentence trails off as the ideal vantage point disappears beyond the limits of the known universe. Of course tradition has defined the ideal spectator of all earthly events as God, and it is a definition Mrs. Moore is ready with in the earlier sections of the novel: "God has put us on earth to love our neighbours and to show it, and He is omnipresent, even in India, to see how we are succeeding" (51). The novel at the same time, then, criticizes simple distanced vision and suggests a distanced vision that is superior to the narrator's. We must ask for further definitions and clarifications of this narrator's vision; we need to understand precisely the meaning of his largeness of vision, to distinguish it from God's, and to define its limitations clearly.

It is surprising, for example, that this narrator, who so self-confidently gives the catalogue of echoes in India, begins with what amounts to an admission of his limitations. If he can supply the reader with what Professor Godbole might have told Mrs. Moore, he seems unable to tell us—an unusual deficiency in an omniscient narrator—why Godbole fails to inform Mrs. Moore: "Professor Godbole had never mentioned an echo; it never impressed him, perhaps" (*PI,* 147). He is a narrator who goes dumb momentarily and whose vision, not about landmarks in India but about one of his own characters, proves curiously unreliable. His vision has certain inexplicable holes in it, and its strength turns out, on some occasions, to be weakness.

The opening paragraphs of the novel are an exploration of this idea of shifting perspectives. They stand at the head of the novel to remind the reader that the single point of view, even the distanced one, entraps him in a false vision of the world. These paragraphs announce a universe profoundly shaped by what is for Forster no less than a new philosophy that calls all into doubt. "The new economics," "the new psychology" (*T,* 284), the theory of evolution, and the theory of relativity all require what Forster calls the pessimism in modern literature. The modern writer, for example, "is in the grip of the modern idea of evolution, which teaches that all things alter" (*AE,* 144), the full consequences of which we will see in the opening of "Caves." "Psychology has split and shattered the idea of a 'Person,' and has shown that there is something incalculable in each of us, which may at any moment rise to the surface and destroy our normal behavior" (*T,* 68)—this new psychology may stand behind the narrator's reticence about certain of his characters. And "the idea of relativity, like the idea of the subconscious self, has got about and tinged their outlook" (276).

Einstein's theory did more than tinge Forster's outlook: it profoundly changed the universe he lived in by refuting absolute space, and thereby the absolute perspective of the Newtonian universe. The novel's opening paragraphs are a brief tour of Chandrapore, and the narrator is our surest guide, but the picture of the city is nonetheless unsettling. The description hangs on a dramatic difference of perspective: Chandrapore becomes two cities when seen from the streets of the city itself, then from "the high ground" of the civil station. In the first case the view is "abased," "monotonous": "Edged rather than washed by the river Ganges, it trails for a couple of miles along the bank, scarcely distinguishable from the rubbish it deposits so freely" (*PI,* 7). In the second case, the view alters drastically, even to the point of contradicting the first view: "On the second rise is laid out the little civil station, and viewed hence Chandrapore appears to be a totally different place. It is a city of gardens. It is no city, but a forest sparsely scattered with huts. It is a tropical pleasaunce washed by a noble river" (8). Taken together, these views of Chandrapore seem to invalidate each other, or at least to call into question the truth of each other. Moreover, Chandrapore becomes a labyrinth in which additional views reveal, not corroboration of the first view, but new information in the way of contradiction. The view from the civil station obscures aspects of the city, but even the city obscures aspects of its own nature: "bazaars shut out the wide and shifting panorama of the stream," and "though a few fine houses exist they are hidden away in gardens or down alleys whose filth deters all but the invited guest" (7). There is almost a perverse sense of obfuscation here. The victim of obscurity becomes, from another view, the offender, as we learn that "the toddy palms and neem trees and mangoes and pepul that were hidden behind the bazaars now become visible and in their turn hide the bazaars" (8). A car ride replaces the function of the train, and those who view the city from above "cannot believe it to be as meagre as it is described, and have to be driven down to acquire disillusionment" (8). The vision from the streets (the near vision) is misleading and the view from the civil station (the distanced vision) is also misleading.

I react to these views of Chandrapore ambivalently: if I take comfort in the narrator's ability to see both views, I wonder if his ability represents mine or something beyond me, just as God's is beyond his. The two views become a statement of the novel's theme of prejudice: the antagonism between the citizens of Chandrapore and the English at the civil station grows quite naturally out of the fact that each is limited to a particular, and necessarily false, point of view. We seem to totter on the brink of an impressionism, at this early point in the novel, that describes each individual (or, perhaps more insidiously, each race) imprisoned in a private world. Einstein's theory demonstrated to the world at the beginning of the twentieth century proof of the relativity of vision and seemed to confirm subjectivism in general, as well as the specific Kantian doctrine of the subjectivity of space and time. If we find disconcerting the fact that there are two views here that apparently invalidate each other, we begin to wonder how many other views, beyond those that are described, are possible. India becomes the symbol of a universe so large that Mrs. Moore wonders, "Let me think—we don't see the other side of the moon out here, no" (*PI,* 24). It is a world large enough to make one realize that vision is relative, but in which one must be content, finally, simply to see the "other side of the earth," "stick[ing] to the same old moon" (24).

Finally, a problem that looms large as the novel proceeds is hinted at in these opening paragraphs. We are on the verge of accepting the narrator's clear-sightedness as at least a partial solution to the novel's formulation of the problems of vision—we accept that a man must see the world from at least two points of view to see it at all—when we are made to acknowledge a reality that may remain finally unseen. We must distinguish then, not just between two different Chandrapores but between two different worlds: the seen and the unseen. The narrator I have been describing is a steady and patient observer, and not much more. In his own words, he has revealed in the opening paragraphs "everything that meets the eye" (PI, 7), but the novel, as it proceeds, suggests that this may not be sufficient. His view of the women retiring while people elsewhere are awakening or of what is "hidden" (7, 8) from one particular angle of vision in Chandrapore still emphasizes plain sight. In the first case he is calling upon what he has seen in the past, using his memory (Blake's criticism of memory appropriately suggests its limitation here for full vision). In the second, plain sight from a different position becomes the solution: the gardens that are hidden from the pedestrians, or the streets of Chandrapore that are hidden from the civil station by the trees, are hidden only because another object stands before them. Simple sight is an easy enough remedy, and it is what the narrator uses. While this theme of the hidden is announced in these opening paragraphs, it becomes dramatically transformed as the novel proceeds.

The novel investigates this idea of the hidden in a complicated comparison between two vastly different modes of perception. Like so much literature in this tradition, A Passage to India makes a subtle comparison between the values of science and religion, but often with unexpected results. The hills, and the caves they contain, seem inaccessible to all human value, and in mutual cooperation seem to resist the Hindu as the Hindu avoids them: "Hinduism has scratched and plastered a few rocks, but the shrines are unfrequented, as if pilgrims, who generally seek the extraordinary, had here found too much of it. Some saddhus did once settle in a cave, but they were smoked out, and even Buddha, who must have passed this way down to the Bo Tree of Gya, shunned a renunciation more complete than his own, and has left no legend of struggle or victory in the Marabar" (PI, 124). But curiously enough, where the Hindu mystic hesitates to tread, the geologist rushes in. Science, here the science of geology, is credited in this opening chapter of "Caves" with having certain powers of revelation that religion evidently lacks. In fact, it provides the narrator and the reader with a view of the caves—the most puzzling aspect of the novel—that religion, it seems, cannot: "The Ganges, though flowing from the foot of Vishnu and through Siva's hair, is not an ancient stream. Geology, looking further than religion, knows of a time when neither the river nor the Himalayas that nourished it existed, and an ocean flowed over the holy places of Hindustan. The mountains rose, their debris silted up the ocean, the gods took their seats on them and contrived the river, and the India we call immemorial came into being. But India is really far older" (123). Geology, then, presents a unique vision of the caves, and deepens our understanding of the requirements of vision. It directly parallels at the same time that it questions the narrator's double view of Chandrapore that opened part 1. Both chapters are introductory and descriptive; both hinge on the notion of perspective.

The opening chapter of "Mosque" is dramatically different, however, because of its insistence on "everything that meets the eye" (*PI,* 7). The opening chapter of "Caves" reveals what escapes simple sight. Here, if the observer will stand still, and if he is capable of doing so for "aeons" (123), a view of India is revealed to him that is hidden from most people. It is a vision that at once describes India changing imperceptibly (to our eyes) and changing on a grand scale (to the eyes of geology): "In the days of the prehistoric ocean the southern part of the peninsula already existed, and the high places of Dravidia have been land since land began, and have seen on the one side the sinking of a continent that joined them to Africa, and on the other the upheaval of the Himalayas from a sea. They are older than anything in the world" (123).

Furthermore, while the novel's first chapter emphasizes the notion of perspective, we have here an additional dimension of that notion—a view of the world in time. After all, chapter 1 describes essentially a static world; it is the observer who changes his position to see Chandrapore from the streets of the city or from above at the civil station. Even the devices of car and train are simple extensions of this idea of the observer's moving while the object remains stationary. The view of the caves from the train, where all ten caves seem to shift and move, is an optical illusion because the observer is doing the moving. Yet it does in fact suggest the scientific truth about them that we discover here: the caves and the hills are indeed moving. The vision of a world in flux dominates this chapter. Forster's irony, or science's, reveals, for example, that even these hills that are "older than anything in the world" must submit to a ceaseless and generally imperceptible change that leaves no thing or place the same: "Yet even they are altering. As Himalayan India arose, this India, the primal, has been depressed, and is slowly re-entering the curve of the earth. It may be that in aeons to come an ocean will flow here too, and cover the sun-born rocks with slime. Meanwhile the plain of the Ganges encroaches on them with something of the sea's action. They are sinking beneath the newer lands" (*PI,* 123). This is science's answer to Mrs. Moore; the caves and the hills are not absolute, their grandeur and mightiness will recede, and even they some day may be covered with slime. It is an ironic prediction of what Fielding, several chapters later, seems frivolously to hope: "I wish the Marabar Hills and all they contain were at the bottom of the sea" (167). The opening of part 1 complicated the sense of "the real India" (31) by provoking us to see that there were two Chandrapores (at least). But it, even as it strove toward completeness, was incomplete. It showed an essentially static world, and one that was visible to the untrained eye. Here "Himalayan India" and "India, the primal" vie for our attention, and the slow birth of another India is imminent. It is the final criticism of India as a "frieze," but it is also an India that is impossible for most people to realize.

If science reveals the hidden, its vision is essentially an amplification of simple sight, that is, the trained eye seeks the universe's secrets with microscope, telescope, and magnifying glass. What follows the opening chapter of "Caves"—namely, Mrs. Moore and Adela's tour through the Marabar region—begins to suggest that there is a world that may simply baffle the senses, trained or untrained, scientifically equipped or unequipped. Forster leads us to this world via a significant detour—a world of optical illusion. The Marabar hills are *par excellence* a world in which sense perception is hopelessly inadequate. Adela sees an object, for example, that may be a snake or may be the twisted stump of a tree. The party agrees it is a snake, "But when she looked through Ronny's field-glasses, she found it wasn't a snake, but the withered and twisted stump of a toddy-palm" (*PI,* 140-41). She is unable to convince anyone, and the episode remains unsettled: "there was a confusion about a snake which was never cleared up," "Nothing was explained" (140-41).

The entire landscape plays havoc with the senses: "Films of heat, radiated from the Kawa Dol precipices, increased the confusion. They came at irregular intervals and moved capriciously. A patch of field would jump up as if it was being fried, and then lie quiet. As they drew closer the radiation stopped" (*PI,* 141). Her closer vision, not vision from afar, is an aid. And yet later the exact opposite is true: as Aziz looks after an approaching car in search of Adela, he discovers to his surprise that "the car disappeared as it came nearer" (154). No rule of thumb will work in this land, and the guide is as hopelessly lost as the visitor. The landscape seems to deceive outright, or at least to confound all expectations: "The stones plunged straight into the earth, like cliffs into the sea, and while Miss Quested was remarking on this, and saying that it was striking, the plain quietly disappeared, peeled off, so to speak, and nothing was to be seen on either side but the granite, very dead and quiet" (141). It is a landscape of illusion, in which reality seems nonexistent, or suddenly to disappear, or to be hopelessly complicated and therefore completely elusive: "Everything seemed cut off at its root, and therefore infected with illusion" (140).

When we begin to compare the narrator's vision of the hills and caves with the characters' experience of them, the difference seems crucial, and not ironic in the way we have come to expect. We begin to realize that we cannot see the narrator's vision as simply superior. The narrator reports geology's discoveries in the opening chapter of "Caves" and proceeds to describe the caves in careful, even scientific, terms. The senses, for the narrator at least, seem an adequate guide: "The caves are readily described. A tunnel eight feet long, five feet high, three feet wide, leads to a circular chamber about twenty feet in diameter" (*PI*, 124). As the description continues, however, a note of mystification creeps in and unsettles the quiet and self-confident tone. If the hills confound the characters' senses, there is, on the part of the caves, an even more primitive frustration of man's desire for knowledge and understanding. It takes shape through a refusal to meet even the simplest requirements of the senses. At the hills one experiences "a spiritual silence which invaded more senses than the ear" (140), and in the caves the narrator begins to suggest that sight is helpless simply because there is nothing to see: "There is little to see, and no eye to see it" (124–25). In fact, his complete and scientific knowledge begins to disintegrate at a startling rate. Soon he tells us what "the visitor" sees when he "arrives for his five minutes, and strikes a match," then what "Local report declares," and finally, in the most flagrant disregard of scientific method, what is "rumoured" (125) about these caves.

The progress (or regression) of this opening chapter of "Caves" pinpoints a significant aspect of narration in the book in general. The narrator's movement from a kind of omniscience (his scientific vision) to a more limited view of the caves (his reliance on the visitor's view, and even rumor, as sources of information) is like those subtle modulations of narrative voice in which the experiences of the characters become, for a moment at least, the narrator's: "The bird in question dived into the dome of the tree. It was of no importance, yet they would have liked to identify it, it would somehow have solaced their hearts. But nothing in India is identifiable; the mere asking of a question causes it to disappear or to merge into something else" (*PI*, 85–86). What begins as a clear description of Adela and Ronny's viewpoint merges with what the narrator also seems to find true, and the large space that has continually separated them disappears. If the answers to such questions about the identity of the bird or the snake-tree remain clouded for the characters, they do so for the reader as well: no answer is forthcoming from the narrator (as with his curious lapse when describing Godbole with "perhaps"), and his vision, so helpful elsewhere, is simply withheld here, or is nonexistent, blinded and foiled like the characters' own.

A further example will show another side to this issue of the narrator as guide: "For instance, there were some mounds by the edge of the track, low, serrated, and touched with whitewash. What were these mounds—graves, breasts of the goddess Parvati? The villagers beneath gave both replies" (*PI*, 140). This is a version of the confusion over the snake-tree. But the double perspective, which has been the source of the narrator's powerful vision, becomes here simply obfuscation, doubt, and lack of understanding. These scenes in which we focus simply on the characters' limited vision, then, subtly refer back to principles that have been established through the narrator's vision. The limited view of the characters (their inability to identify the green bird, for example) modulates into what appears to be the narrator's agreement about India's elusiveness; their openness to the villagers' legends is like the narrator's own resorting to rumor and local report. The double perspective becomes ambiguous when it fails to provide, in certain experiences in India, the kind of information and wisdom that the narrator implicitly reveals it to possess. The clear-sightedness he implicitly recommends seems quite impossible to perform—textbook geology and tour manual directions are out of place here. Finally, the whole expedition to the caves becomes an ironic commentary on what the narrator provides as a model of vision in the chapter that opens "Caves." The particular examples I have looked at undercut most clearly what has been the visitor's best attempt at "sightseeing" (146): the guide, Dr. Aziz, is completely incompetent, and the landscape refuses to be seen in the normal sense of the term. But the failure of the characters in these episodes provides the narrator with the best evidence against evidence, with the best experience that "sightseeing," even with fieldglasses, may prove uninformative. We begin to realize—as the narrator himself does, through the experiences of the characters—that the world may not lay bare all its secrets to the steady and unswerving eye of science. Adela's fieldglasses, left behind in her escape from the caves and unable to help Aziz locate her, are the final symbol of the failure of this sightseeing party. The narrator's own distant perspective does not tell us as much as we learn by following the characters through the landscape. Finally, the viewpoints of the narrator and the characters are in a complicated relation to each other. His geological vision is a significant addition to our understanding of the caves, but so are the experiences of Aziz, Adela, and Mrs. Moore.

If chapter 1 seems like a foil, upset or at least seriously questioned and thereby deepened by the opening chapter of "Caves," this latter chapter now seems to serve a similar function. An experiment in vision, it moves us many paces ahead in its revelation of science's power; in retrospect, however, it seems less of a giant step than first appeared. The geologic vision, grand as it is, standing at the head of the novel's middle section, is undermined; it, like the Indian terrain, must submit to alteration. The novel's own movement in time again and again changes its method of vision and its focus of importance. The clarity of vision that is the narrator's seems most clearly associated here with the English point of view. And "Caves" makes us realize the limitation of the English perspective. Fielding, kind and reasonable to a fault, is limited by these very virtues: "clarity prevented him from experiencing something else" (*PI*, 118). What I have characterized as the narrator's vision—its clarity and reasonableness—may need even further definition. In the case of Aziz, for example, "the logic of evidence said 'Guilty'" (167). Evidence, in the legal and scientific senses, is scrutinized throughout "Caves," and is seen as an insufficient guide to a man's guilt, or the lack of order in the universe. The universe's direct frustration of our senses, in fact, may lead us to exercise other faculties. This is a point that Forster shares with the poets of vision, and particularly with Shelley's explanation that beauty "Exceeds our organs, which endure / No light, being themselves obscure":[2] "Perhaps the hundred Indias . . . are one, and the universe they mirror is one. They had not the apparatus for judging" (264).

At the novel's climax, in part 3, we begin to realize that religion offers a view of the universe that is, paradoxically, parallel and alternate to science's. On the one hand, "geology, looking further than religion," uncovers an important aspect of the caves. Religion, on the other hand, offers a glimpse of a hidden reality, but not through fieldglasses. Professor Godbole's vision of Mrs. Moore is the most dramatic example of this religious vision: "Chance brought her into his mind while it was in this heated state, he did not select her, she happened to occur among the throng of soliciting images, a tiny splinter, and he impelled her by his spiritual force to that place where completeness can be found. Completeness, not reconstruction. His senses grew thinner, he remembered a wasp seen he forgot where, perhaps on a stone. He loved the wasp equally, he impelled it likewise, he was imitating God" (*PI*, 286). Godbole sees the wasp because he has become, for the moment, Mrs. Moore. It is interesting that at his first meeting with the old woman Godbole performs the same spiritual act. "I placed myself in the position of a milkmaiden" (80), he tells Mrs. Moore, to perform his religious song. Once again the approach to God is made by placing oneself in another's position. The climax that the novel has been heading toward with great elaboration is here; the ability to see with another's eyes becomes the novel's definition of the approach to Godlike vision. In fact, any man who is able to see with more than his own eyes approximates God:

He had, with increasing vividness, again seen Mrs. Moore, and round her faintly clinging forms of trouble. He was a Brahman, she Christian, but it made no difference, it made no difference whether she was a trick of his memory or a telepathic appeal. It was his duty, as it was his desire, to place himself in the position of the God and to love her; and to place himself in her position and to say to the God, "Come, come, come, come." This was all he could do. How inadequate! But each according to his capacities, and he knew that his own were small. "One old English woman and one little, little wasp," he thought, as he stepped out of the temple into the grey pouring wet morning. "It does not seem much, still it is more than I am myself." (290–91)

It is at once the most metaphysical and the most practical answer to the problem of prejudice in the novel: a God is created who is neither Hindu nor Christian nor Moslem, or more precisely, who is at once Hindu and Christian and Moslem. To live the life of another is the novel's ultimate expression of love and sympathy: "to place himself in her position."

Godbole's imitation of God may help to redefine the precise relation in which the narrator stands to God. While Forster does employ romanticism's parallel between the artist and God, his skepticism is clear: "Were we equipped for hyperbole we might exclaim at this point: 'If God could tell the story of the Universe, the Universe would become fictitious'" (*AN,* 56). Forster's sense of hyperbole stems, at least in part, from his understanding of the distinction between the narrator's shifting, partially limited knowledge and the tradition's sense of God's absolute knowledge. Newton's name for absolute space is *sensorium Dei,* the visual organ of God; space quite simply the divine perspective itself. In the Einsteinian universe of relativity that the novel describes, however, the God of absolute vision no longer exists. The theory of relativity undermines vision *sub specie aeternitatis.* With the explosion of absolute space comes the death of God, the ideal spectator. Mrs. Moore's God of absolute knowledge—she reminds Ronny that "He is omnipresent, even in India, to see how we are succeeding" (*PI,* 51)—is, as even the old woman herself sadly realizes, unhappily out of place in India precisely because he is a God of a simpler time and place.

The godly perspective is comically and even bitterly undercut in the novel by its association with the British rulers: "At Chandrapore the Turtons were little gods" (*PI,* 28). Ronny's insistence on doing justice and keeping the peace causes Mrs. Moore to tell him, "Your sentiments are those of a god," and, "Englishmen like posing as Gods" (50). Also, "the Collector had watched the arrest from the interior of the waiting-room, and throwing open its perforated doors of zinc, he was now revealed like a god in a shrine" (162). In fact, the novel is replete with descriptions of a pantheon of gods able to match the Hindus'. These British

gods of complete partiality are matched by a god whose impartiality is
so great that it becomes indifference, almost unconsciousness. The
punkah wallah at Adela's trial is "a god" who "scarcely knew that he
existed and did not understand why the Court was fuller than usual;
indeed he did not know that it was fuller than usual, didn't even know
he worked a fan, though he thought he pulled a rope" (217–18). The
"beautiful naked god" (231), who represents "a male fate, a winnower
of souls" (217), is even unaware of the triumph of justice that takes
place in the court: "Unaware that anything unusual had occurred, he
continued to pull the cord of his punkah" (231). He stands "apart from
human destinies" (217), and "his aloofness" (218) and impartiality are
surely an ironic version of one side of the traditional God and the conventional narrator. He is counterbalanced by that god of complete
partiality who stands behind that minor pantheon of gods that Ronny
and the Turtons represent, namely, "the suburban Jehovah" (218)—
"God who saves the King will surely support the police" (211). Adela,
in fact, finds herself praying to this god: "Just as the Hindu clerks asked
Lakshmi for an increase in pay, so did she implore Jehovah for a favour-
able verdict" (211). While it is clear that these descriptions of God are
ironic, there is still some sense in which the narrator is related to God:
Forster makes a comparison between the two (even if he sees it as a
hyperbole), and gives the novel a growing sense of vision that ends in
Godbole's imitation of God.

The Hindu ceremony describes two alternate actions, Godbole's
imitation of God and God's imitation of man. The first is, among other
things, a description of the artistic process. Godbole's "senses grew
thinner" and his mind undergoes a "heated state" (*PI*, 286) similar to
that which Forster describes elsewhere, under the heading "Inspiration,"
in which the artist's "head grows hot" (*AE*, 119). In fact, when Forster
describes the creative process he compares it to the mystic's experience:
"There is something general about it. Although it is inside Samuel Taylor
Coleridge, it cannot be labelled with his name. It has something in common with all other deeper personalities, and the mystic will assert that
the common quality is God, and that here, in the obscure recesses of our
being, we near the Gates of the Divine" (*T*, 84). The artist experiences
the kind of annihilation of the self that Keats describes and the plasticity
Yeats describes, renamed by Forster "anonymity": "The poet wrote the
poem, no doubt, but he forgot himself while he wrote it" (84). This
is at once the core of the artistic process and the solution to the problems of ego and prejudice in the novel. The loss of self that allows the
narrator-author to share something with all men recreates him as God,
bringing him into existence as the Friend whom the Moslems await and
as the God whom the Hindus bid to "come, come, come, come."

But this leads to Forster's belief that deification occurs only as the exact opposite process takes place. The central action of the ceremony is God's incarnation: "Infinite Love took upon itself the form of SHRI KRISHNA, and saved the world" (*PI*, 287). God's incarnation becomes the novel's ultimate definition of love. If Godbole wants "to place himself in her [Mrs. Moore's] position" as all people should, God places himself in man's position as the ultimate act of sympathy. This is the farthest point perspectivism can go—God's relinquishment of the divine perspective for a human, limited point of view. It is used, once again comically, to suggest the failure of mercy and sympathy in the British, those gods who never relinquish their supreme position. Hamidullah knows that Aziz's fate at the hands of the English looks dismal, for "if God himself descended from heaven into their club and said you were innocent, they would disbelieve him" (269). Keats dramatizes this idea, in the Hyperion poems, for the whole tradition: the innocent and self-absorbed gods are toppled to make way for a god who understands suffering and mortality. Keats's growing awareness of this theme leads him to experiment with the role of the narrator in these poems. First he chooses an omniscient narrator, aloof and godly, and next he chooses a first-person narrator, mortal and suffering, and involved in the action of the poem rather than above it. Forster attempts to solve the problem with a narrator whose flexibility allows him to function in both roles. The godly perspective in both Keats and Forster becomes defined ultimately as the most universally human (and humane) position: it depends on the particulars of experience, it is knowledge enormous that never loses its connection with experience.

When Forster quotes with approval Shelley's belief that "imagination is as the immortal God which should assume flesh for the redemption of mortal passion" (*T*, 88) (clearly the statement behind his description of Shri Krishna's incarnation), he understands that God's incarnation is a sign of the imaginative act that all men may make and that the narrator in his novel does make *par excellence*. Forster's narrator is at once the God of the creation and the creation itself, the further vision and the nearer vision. The narrator exists as an independent figure as well as through the numerous incarnations of his characters (as Fielding, Aziz, Mrs. Moore, Ronny, and Adela). It is this double quality of the novel that Forster finds so appealing about the genre: "The speciality of the novel is that the writer can talk about his characters as well as through them" (*AN*, 84). The novel's narrative technique, then, if we are to be precise, rests upon (and grows through the tension between) two diverse activities. On the one hand, there are those isolable passages in which the narrator speaks singly, independently, and aloofly in an identifiable voice; on the other hand there is his perception of life through the medium of his characters. This is the best explanation of the diverse methods of narrative technique in the novel: it describes the distanced view, suggests at least one way in which the nearer view is achieved, and explains both those mergers of character and narrator and the slow elision in the narrator's vision in "Caves."

A Passage to India reflects on art in a complicated network of references —from Godbole's baffling song, which has only "the illusion of a Western melody" and soon becomes "a maze of noises, none harsh or unpleasant, none intelligible" (79), to the architecture of the Mediterranean, with its "beauty of form" and "harmony" (282), and to the trifling little *Cousin Kate,* the Club's rehearsal of its own small values and a retreat into a world of familiarity. Aziz's humble attempts at poetry constitute the most consistent pattern of references, however, and it is through a criticism of this poetry and the esthetic principles upon which it is based that the novel defines its own goals. Poetry becomes for Aziz and his friends, it would first appear, a perfect example of Forster's contention that art provides our sense of order. During a reading of Islamic poetry Aziz's friends experience a sense of unity: "India—a hundred Indias—whispered outside beneath the indifferent moon, but for the time India seemed one and their own" (15). Looking further, however, we realize that the poetry they recite and compose, while grander than *Cousin Kate,* is in its own way a retreat into a world of familiarity, simply an escape from the pressing problems of India. In this light it seems insular, proselytizing, and vapid. It gives them the "calm assurance . . . that India was one; Moslem; always had been; an assurance that lasted until they looked out of the door" (105). Such poetry "greeted ridiculous Chandrapore, where every street and house was divided against itself, and told her that she was a continent and a unity" (106).

This art flies in the face of reality. Its assurances, like those of Yeats's Happy Shepherd, contain no present vision, but only a futile lament for a simpler past; its truth is denied the moment one steps beyond its fragile doors. Aziz's friends are clear, but narrow, in their esthetic principles, and Forster is equally clear in his irony: "Pathos, they agreed, is the highest quality in art; a poem should touch the hearer with a sense of his own weakness, and should institute some comparison between mankind and flowers" (*PI,* 105). What is crucial here is that this is the kind of art that becomes the easy target of the echo, and Forster makes this doubly clear by repeating the Moslem's central esthetic requirement—pathos—as the first quality that the echo undermines: "'Pathos, piety, courage— they exist, but are identical, and so is filth. Everything exists, nothing has value.' If one had spoken vileness in that place, or quoted lofty poetry, the comment would have been the same—'ou-boum'" (149).

Lofty poetry, for all its comparisons between men and flowers, is easily assaulted by the echo. If all art is a target of the echo, that art based upon subterfuge opens itself to attack most easily. Forster's echo is an ironic inversion of the echo the Happy Shepherd hopefully predicts. The echo in Yeats is to reword a sad story by melodious guile, while the echo in Forster reduces all words and stories, lofty and common, to ou-boum. In fact, Forster's echo represents something that resists adornment altogether; it undermines lofty poetry, while it prevents man's attempts to mythologize and romanticize it. "Devils are of the North, and poems can be written about them, but no one could romanticize the Marabar" (150).

Western culture, in its religion and art, has been able to transform the darker side of life, but India rejects such transformations: "In Europe life retreats out of the cold, and exquisite fireside myths have resulted—Balder, Persephone—but here the retreat is from the source of life, the treacherous sun, and no poetry adorns it because disillusionment cannot be beautiful" (*PI*, 210-11). Poetry, a more sophisticated version of myth, seems equally impossible in India: "Men yearn for poetry though they may not confess it; they desire that joy shall be graceful and sorrow august and infinity have a form, and India fails to accomodate them" (211). The echo undermines the lofty poetry of Islam and the poetry of pathos, and even robs Mrs. Moore of a rich Western inheritance. The romantic setting of "Heaven, Hell, Annihilation," "that huge scenic background" that she imagines as the stage for all human endeavor, is emptied once and for all by the echo: "All heroic endeavor, and all that is known as art, assumes that there is such a background" (208), but the echo destroys that assumption. The novel presents, then, a vision of evil that refuses all attempts at subterfuge; it refuses to be represented as anything but itself, and undermines all religious and artistic attempts to mythologize, romanticize, and poetize it.

Language itself becomes the last, and perhaps finest, order that is undermined by the vision of evil. Forster subtly links the grandest and apparently most minute aspects of order—form itself, cosmically conceived, and the articulation of sounds into words: "There is something unspeakable in these outposts. They are like nothing else in the world, and a glimpse of them makes the breath catch. They rise abruptly, insanely, without the proportion that is kept by the wildest hills elsewhere, they bear no relation to anything dreamt or seen" (*PI*, 124). Clearly, the caves do not merely represent in some indirect way a vague assault on artistic value. More to the point, they represent everything that stands opposite to the main direction of the novel, all the way from its developing form down to the very sounds that order the novel's paragraphs, sentences, and words. The human alphabet is even unable surely to grasp or repeat the noise that is no language (a paradigm of art's attempt to describe what lies beyond art): "'Boum' is the sound as far as the human alphabet can express it, or 'bou-oum,' or 'ou-boum,'—utterly dull" (147). This dullness is, according to modern linguistic theory, the first barrier to language—language is built upon differentiation.[3] Forster insists on the caves' resistance to language: "Nothing, nothing attaches to them, and their reputation—for they have one—does not depend upon human speech" (124). The caves are the void, the barren wilderness that Wordsworth describes in the Arab dream, only they successfully resist the creative power of the Word. They seem, in fact, directly to combat it: Mrs. Moore discovers that Christianity's "divine words from 'Let there be Light' to 'It is finished' only amounted to 'boum'" (150). The Word that announces creation and order, then, is appropriately mocked in a barren land that somehow missed, because of its own inherent resistance to the Word, God's creative breath.

If the Word exists at all in this area, its might has been scaled down: "Truth is not truth in that exacting land unless there go with it kindness and more kindness and kindness again, unless the Word that was with God also is God" (*PI*, 245). This is said of Adela, whose words at the trial rest only upon cold justice and honesty. The Word's power in this novel is social, not cosmic, and it is one that seems to fail again and again. In fact, each social or religious group is marked by a speech pattern or language that separates it from the next; language in the novel is not even this kindly Word, but Babel. The British have the vapid language of the British empire, a string of clichés (masquerading as divine proverbs) repeated with a kind of echoing religious fervor: "My proverbs are: A penny saved is a penny earned; A stitch in time saves nine; Look before you leap; and the British empire rests upon them" (160). The Moslems' linguistic wisdom is mere precious subtlety and gamesmanship with words that does not possess the traditional power of the Word: "'There is no God but God' doesn't carry us far through the complexities of matter and spirit; it is only a game with words, really, a religious pun, not a religious truth" (276). Finally, the Hindu Sanskrit dramatically stands for no Wordsworthian universal language, but is the archetype of a language of exclusion: Godbole asks about one of Aziz's poems, "May I translate this particular one into Hindi? In fact, it might be rendered into Sanskrit almost, it is so enlightened" (294). This is poetry, not become the universal music of humanity, but become an esoteric language for the few. In any case, the lack of linguistic order that is represented by ou-boum comes to stand for a formlessness that knows no bounds. If the novel's form constitutes an ever widening series of relationships, at the center of the novel lies something that is by definition unrelated, proportionless, and formless. If the Word bestows order, on the universe and the world of the novel, here in these caves is the disorderly, what in fact lies beyond language itself. The narrator's goal of relatedness—of seeing everything in perspective and of articulating everything into relationship—meets its opposite in the hills and caves. The novel deliberately sets out to accomplish a paradox. The triumph of *A Passage to India*, it seems to me, depends on its form being made to contain the vision of formlessness without simply dissolving it.

One way of explaining the source of formlessness that is the chief feature of the caves is through the echo's reductionism, its singleness of voice and vision. Vision is, in the caves, self-absorbed. The typical Marabar "mirrors its own darkness in every direction infinitely" (*PI*, 125). As opposed to the vision that is an accumulation of an almost uncountable number of points of view, the echo is a voice that repeats over and over again a single sound, once again its own: "a Marabar cave can hear no sound but its own" (154), so ou-boum is its constant song. This is the echo encountered in Yeats's second Shepherd poem; it is a description of solipsism, the repetition ad infinitum of a single story of woe (although even that is to mythologize it and give it human content when it has none). It is the source of prejudice and egotism, a self-absorption that is mirrored, to different degrees, in all people. Indeed, the image of the caves is at least partially derived from Bacon's description of the Idols of the Cave: "For every one . . . has a cave or den of his own, which refracts and discolours the light of nature, owing either to his own proper and peculiar nature, or to his education and conversation with others, or to the reading of books, and the authority of those whom he esteems and admires, or to the differences of impressions, accordingly as they take place in a mind preoccupied and predisposed or in a mind indifferent and settled."[4] This is a classic description in British empiricist philosophy, as well as one of the major themes of this novel, and the great theme of the Victorian novel: an individual's particular experience limits him and becomes the source of a complicated labyrinth of prejudices that distort his vision. The novel states this almost as a truism in the example of "the shore-dweller who can only understand stability and supposes that every ship must be wrecked" (67). A man's own peculiar experience can become a prison-house, and this idea is used to characterize even how the English are divided from each other. In the case of Ronny and Adela, for example, "experiences, not character, divided them" (85). The novel, then, describes Bacon's belief that everyone has a cave or den of his own: Mrs. Moore declares, "I'll retire then into a cave of my own" (200), and the Marabars are certainly, on one level, the novel's embodiment of each individual's solitary prison-house, finally expressed in the arrangement of the caves—"isolated each from his neighbour by broad channels of the plain" (137).

The novel makes clear in several passages that the caves themselves are empty—in fact, "empty as an Easter egg" (*PI,* 125)—and that they contain neither good nor evil. Mrs. Moore recognizes after leaving them that "nothing evil had been in the cave, but she had not enjoyed herself" (148). The narrator explains about the deepest caves, "Nothing is inside them, they were sealed up before the creation of pestilence or treasure; if mankind grew curious and excavated, nothing, nothing would be added to the sum of good or evil" (125). The caves, then, are a vast receptacle for everyone's individual troubles, singleness of vision, and prejudice. It is these that echo. An echo is a repetition, and as such a mirror, a verbal mirror if you will, of the troubling voices that sound within each of us. An echo has no life of its own, but must be instigated by some external cause—in this case, the private troubles of the characters. Mrs. Moore's doubts about her God, for example, are not simply the result of the caves; these doubts are voiced well before she knows of the caves. The caves simply "echo" them. Adela is obviously troubled before she enters her cave: she carries with her the difficult burden of the double realization that she does not love the man she is to marry and that her Indian guide is strangely attractive to her. The trouble in the cave, for that reason, takes the oldest and most conventional form of prejudice—the white woman's accusation that she has been sexually assaulted by the black man. Godbole's explanation of the episode—that the action in the cave is performed by Aziz, by the guide, by Fielding, and by Godbole himself—is, if somewhat indirect, an explanation of the truth the entire novel is reaching toward, namely, that the cave's evil is neither inherent nor dependent on a single individual.

The incident at the cave expresses a severe limitation in each character, and shows an emptiness and darkness in each person's soul. It is a description, ultimately, of how people fall short of being God, the opposite of the vision of relatedness that makes a composite God of all men's wisdom and experience. The cave represents, to use Godbole's somewhat mythologized terms (Forster's notion of God is a philosophical construct, a hypothesis, unlike Godbole's Hindu doctrine), the absence of God, while the vision that the novel directs the reader toward, via the narrator, represents the presence of God. To see with a single pair of eyes, to reduce everything seen and heard to a monotony, and to take shadows and echoes for reality, expresses the most limited self, imprisoned in a cave. This is, of course, a version of Plato's allegory. Plato's cave has an echo that is the equivalent in sound of its shadows. The cave dweller, with legs and neck chained from childhood so that he can see only in one direction, takes these echoes and shadows as his only reality. This is the model for Forster's description of how the single viewpoint is necessarily distorted. It should be clear now that Bacon's description of the

Idols of the Cave is a translation into British empiricism of Plato's transcendent allegory. Bacon's light of nature is, in Plato, only one step in the ascent to the divine contemplation of the Idea of good. The complicated intertwining of scientific and religious values in *A Passage to India* flowers in this double historical association. Simple, empirical sight, and Platonic, heavenly vision are obfuscated in these caves, and the novel requires both for an escape from the prison-house of evil.

The novel comes closest to reconciling its different modes of vision at this point, with science and religion offering analogous viewpoints: to place oneself in another's position is like seeing from more perspectives than one. Still, to collapse these two views, to divest them of their standard equipment and diverse traditions, and to base Hinduism on the theory of relativity, or vice versa, is a step the novel shrinks from taking; Godbole and the geologist (or physicist, as the case may be) are not the same. It would, in fact, be counter to the spirit of relativity to collapse the variety of viewpoints into one. That there is any meeting ground at all between them stems from Forster's desire to see if the ideas of science are applicable to the world of human behavior.

Like Nietzsche, Forster sees science as the great demystifier of the modern world. His essays tirelessly report what is for him a new philosophy, with the physics of relativity its center. Science strips the universe of the meanings projected onto it, and at the same time strips the world of all human value. Man gives the dawn a symbolic meaning that is clearly illusory (if consoling), but one that India at least refuses to support: "It was as if virtue had failed in the celestial fount. . . . Why, when the chamber was prepared, did the bridegroom not enter with trumpets and shawms, as humanity expects? The sun rose without splendour" (*PI*, 137). The scientific explanation is forthcoming: it is "caused by dirt in the upper layers of the atmosphere that couldn't fall down during the night" (138). India's refusal to be romanticized makes it the perfect setting for Forster's novel. As in Yeats, the vision of evil involves a criticism of the romantic tradition, and in Forster at least this requires a setting beyond "dearest Grasmere. . . . Romantic yet manageable, it sprang from a kindlier planet" (138). Even Forster's reference to the scenic background of Heaven, Hell, and Annihilation is a criticism of English romanticism, namely, of the sublime backgrounds against which good and evil battle in Shelley's poetry.[5] India becomes the new world (despite its antiquity) where Einstein's discoveries are perceptible in everyday experiences.

While science empties the world of human value, Hinduism fills it: the first offers demystifying explanations, the second mystical interpretations. In the well-known essay on "Art for Art's Sake," Forster attempts to discover where order is found, and claims, "Not in the astronomical category, where it was for many years enthroned. The heavens and the earth have become terribly alike since Einstein. No longer can we find a reassuring contrast to chaos in the night sky and look up with George Meredith to the stars, the army of unalterable law, or listen for the music of the spheres. Order is not there" (*T*, 91). While the loss of astronomical order is clear, he explains that the mystic's sense of order is neither provable nor finally disputable. Art, in an argument reminiscent of Wordsworth's claim for poetry's inner order, becomes "the only material object in the universe which may possess internal harmony" (92). But *A Passage to India* is after something more complicated: it refuses to accept the beauty of artistic order without truth (once again we have the problem formulated in Keats's famous terms).[6] Art seems, at least in this novel, to be the arbiter between the two. It seeks not simply to impose order, but to arbitrate between the loss of order described by science and the mysterious order imagined by the mystic. This is no easy task. If science presents a dearth of meaning (that is, meaning applicable to the sphere of human desires and actions), then mystical interpretation, even interpretation of any kind, is a dangerous business. The reader finds sly warnings about the very interpretative act he is in the course of performing. Aziz's acts in particular are tenuous interpretations: he "decked it [the Mosque] with meanings the builder had never intended," "he tried to symbolize the whole into some truth of religion or love" (*PI*, 19); "In every remark he found a meaning, but not always the true meaning, and his life though vivid was largely a dream" (67). India becomes the land where the struggle between meaning and no meaning is most apparent. At his most skeptical Forster sees humanity destined to live in a world either with no meanings or false meanings, and the novel is an inquiry into the nature of meaning itself. The Hindu (or religious person in general) finds unacceptable the scientist's view of the gods as a contrivance, not to mention his sole reliance on materiality, while the scientist calls Godbole's vision mere hallucination. It reminds one of the tragic dissociation in "Lamia" between beauty and truth, between poetry and philosophy.

The view of meaning in *A Passage to India* is more complicated still, because it devalues even what can be seen as the strong points of both scientific and mystical vision. Even science has behind it some morality of its own, some interest, as Nietzsche showed. When Adela and Ronny try to interpret the tire tracks after the automobile accident, for example, their decision about the hairy animal is a comical example of the empiricist's refusal to acknowledge the mysterious, the unseen: all knowledge, and especially scientific knowledge, is a form of human control, and science is as tyrannous and illusory, in its dismissal of the realm of mystery, as is mysticism's reliance on a mysterious order. "I do so hate mysteries" (*PI,* 69) is science's slogan. The scientist collects data that proves him in control of the natural world. The English community, less sophisticated in the uses of science, still betrays, if outrageously, how prejudice comes to the aid of a race in the name of science: Mc Bryde contends "the darker races are physically attracted by the fairer, but not *vice versa*—not a matter for bitterness this, not a matter for abuse, but just a fact which any scientific observer will confirm" (218-19). Likewise, mysticism is not a successful alternative to science because it, when viewed carefully, does not offer models of human behavior or ways to act. Oddly enough, like science, it withdraws to a world beyond action. Both the scientist and the Hindu separate themselves from the realm of action. Forster distinguishes between the Protestant and the Hindu precisely on these grounds; whereas Protestantism is "an ethical code . . . applicable to daily life," "The Hindu is concerned not with conduct, but with vision." (*AE,* 220) Fielding and Godbole are of course the novel's representatives of these two types, sheer antipodes in modes of vision. We have already seen how Fielding's clarity of vision may stand in his way. Godbole's mysticism represents a negative tranquillity: "There seemed no reserve of tranquillity to draw upon in India. Either none, or else tranquillity swallowed up everything, as it appeared to do for Professor Godbole" (*PI,* 78). Through a deliberate act of apparent sympathy, he seems almost to lapse into the insentience of a stone (as, after Mrs. Moore and the wasp, Godbole's mind reaches toward a stone). From the point of view of human action, his seems a sympathy that is like indifference; he reminds one of the impartial punkah wallah at the trial. This is the traditional romantic formula of human life become so sympathetic to the objects of nature that it becomes them, like Lucy Gray, who neither hears nor sees because she has become a thing, as Wordsworth says, along with rocks and stones. This split in human personality and understanding is what the novel dramatizes—at least through its characters.

The narrator, I must quickly add, may be the solution here. After all, isn't he the reconciliation of both worlds, isn't he both Fielding and Godbole (literally, in that he plays both roles, and symbolically, in that he represents both kinds of vision)? Even my description of his powers of vision—some passages suggest a kind of omniscience, others a kind of myopia: the former seem to deify him, the latter to make him just another mortal—may suggest a kind of reconciliation, but I mean just the opposite. Too often readers iron out these differences, take their average, and locate the narrator vaguely between God and man. To do so is to lose the central quality of the text, to avoid its turns and twists; it is an interpretative act similar to reducing scientist and mystic to a "lowest-common-denominator" middle ground. While this may be an attractive solution, Forster resists it. He in fact praises narratives where the shift in the narrator's knowledge is felt dramatically, because they suggest the truth about human perception: "A novelist can shift his view-point if it comes off, and it comes off with Dickens and Tolstoy. Indeed this power to expand and contract perception (of which the shifting view-point is a symptom), this right to intermittent knowledge:—I find it one of the great advantages of the novel form, and it has a parallel in our perception of life. We are stupider at some times than others; we can enter into peoples' minds occasionally but not always, because our own minds get tired" (*AN*, 81). In the narrator, then, one should imagine not a simple reconciliation of the different modes of vision (whether practical or contemplative, mystical or scientific, mortal or godly), but a similar kind of shuttling between methods that is worked out on the level of character.

The lengthy series of narrative views I have described—(1)the distant moon-vision, (2) the nearer view, (3) the different static perspectives (that meet the eye), (4) the different perspectives in time, (5) the trained scientific vision, (6) the recourse to rumor and local report, and the failure of both the double perspective and the textbook geological view in certain lived situations, and (7) the view achieved by placing oneself in another's position—should not be taken as the solution to the problem of vision. There is here the kind of testing of response present in "Nineteen Hundred and Nineteen," except that in Yeats's poem the writer does reach the single right viewpoint. There is no such viewpoint in *A Passage to India*. The thrust of the novel's argument is to suggest several, really many, views that are irreconcilable, as well as to suggest that no single view is true. This fact depends on the nature of both the subject and the object; the subject's abilities change, from individual to individual, as well as from circumstance to circumstance, and the world is so complicated a place that it requires to be seen from many perspectives. The series of narrative views I have presented, then, is not to be taken as a solution to the problem of vision. If there is a solution, it is that there is no solution, because one view disputes another, and even these views are incomplete. This series of views suggests in fact countless views beyond our knowing—like the image of the arch beyond the next arch— and is the motive behind the narrator's question, directed less and less at his characters and more and more at himself, "How can the mind take hold of such a country?" (*PI*, 136). The reader learns something Adela never quite learns, namely, that "the real India" is, paradoxically, a fiction, as is the typical Indian: "There is no such person in existence as the general Indian" (266). And just as the typical or average Indian is a fiction, that narrator who becomes the average of his characters, or of his own distinct views, is a fiction. It is an abstraction, a philosophic position, an artistic stance that does not exist in life. The series of revisions that the novel imagines in its developing vision may take one closer to the truth, but it is a truth that is never quite entered into once and for all. This series of views functions, then, to raise the issue of vision to a higher plane. It is not so much an answer as a question given new status, contemplated in itself; the series of views is a contemplation of viewing. Here is a picture of the mind turned inward (even though it seems to view simply Chandrapore, or the caves), become its own object, and measuring its own resources. It is a mode of self-reflection that marks out the characteristic mental attitude of all the writers in this tradition.

Forster realizes that every strategy itself is always in danger of becoming sedimented, mythologized, or held up too easily as a solution to the problems the work has set out to contemplate. In *A Passage to India,* even as the vision of evil is demythologized, and the false art of pathos and solace is criticized, the narrator's eclectic point of view—what has seemed in its own way an antidote to mythology and to single vision— becomes more ambiguous than we at first realize. In this way the series of views is not a growing and harmonious solution to the problem of vision, but a structure that contains within itself its own contradictions and divisions, its own criticism of the last view. There is a tension in the narrative views that cannot be ironed out except in "a spurious unity" (*PI,* 88); scientist and mystic are antithetical, just as the individual narrative views are, and Forster may bring them tantalizingly close—as close as the two flames in the cave—but they cannot be one: "The two flames approach and strive to unite, but cannot" (125).

Forster's remarks in *Aspects of the Novel* may at first seem to deny this new ambiguity I am suggesting, particularly when they declare the difference between life and art, and suggest the novelist's superior vision: "In daily life we never understand each other, neither complete clairvoyance nor complete confessional exists. . . . But people in a novel can be understood completely by the reader" (*AN,* 47). Such a statement easily turns into Forster's warnings about confusing life and art: "When we try to translate the truth out of one sphere into another, whether from life into books or from books into lectures, something happens to truth, it goes wrong, not suddenly when it might be detected, but slowly" (106). Such remarks can even suggest a special kind of irony of their own: the gulf between life and art is so great that it is itself an irony, making the solutions art offers to daily life no solutions at all precisely because they are impracticable. In this view, the narrator represents a superior vision that is unattainable, and his relationship to his characters is like the relationship between Yeats's "hollow image of fulfilled desire" and the poverty out of which it grows. But the narrator himself suggests the impossibility of perfect sympathy: "How indeed is it possible for one human being to be sorry for all the sadness that meets him on the face of the earth, for the pain that is endured not only by men, but by animals and plants, and perhaps by the stones? The soul is tired in a moment" (*PI,* 247). No one real human being can, and the view of the narrator as simply superior to his characters, as a solution to vision (which I do not hold), is itself ironic. But if read correctly, even *Aspects of the Novel* suggests a different direction that Forster's fiction ultimately takes. *Aspects* is not a simple guidebook tour of aspects of the novel (the way *Passage* is not a simple tour of India). Read correctly, each aspect, from character to plot to structure, is not a simple surveying of a territory, not a laying claim to the strict boundaries of art, a demarcation of the line between art and life. The book is a plea for a special kind of gerrymandering, where territories are mixed and confused, not in the interest of one party, but of both.

In *Bleak House,* for example, Forster praises what turns out to be an attrition in the narrator's powers: "Chapter I of *Bleak House* is omniscient. . . . In Chapter II he is partially omniscient. . . . He can explain Sir Leicester Dedlock to us, part of Lady Dedlock but not all, and nothing of Mr Tulkinghorn. In Chapter III he is even more reprehensible: he goes straight across into the dramatic method and inhabits a young lady, Esther Summerson" (*AN,* 79). Dickens's novel of course provides Forster with a particularly good example of the series of roles Forster plays— omniscient narrator, limited narrator, and character. He calls this an "absence of view-point" (80), and praises similar absences in every aspect of the novel. The praise of Dickens leads him to praise Gide in the area of plot: "After all, why has a novel to be planned? Cannot it grow? Why need it close, as a play closes? Cannot it open out? Instead of standing above his work, and controlling it, cannot the novelist throw himself into it and be carried along to some goal that he does not foresee?" (96–97). This supports my view of the narrator as actor, placed alongside his characters. Forster says about Gide's narrator: "Edouard is not just a chronicler. He is an actor too" (98). The penultimate movement of *Aspects* is the work on Fantasy and Prophecy, later fully realized by Northrop Frye:[7] it is a legitimization of aspects of the novel not contained in the traditional comedy of manners novel, so that works like *Tristram Shandy* or *Wuthering Heights* or *Moby Dick* (the same works Frye discusses with a more elaborate set of terms) become part of an eclectic novelistic, or prose, tradition. The climax to *Aspects* is Forster's well-known choice of rhythm over pattern, which allows his conclusion: "Not completion. Not rounding off but opening out" (169). What is at stake in every aspect of the novel is not a naïve realism or a copy theory of truth, but a sophisticated series of techniques that produce what Forster approvingly quotes Nietzsche as requesting, "formidable erosions of contour" (101).

The sign, at the stylistic level, that Forster finds for this opening out in his own novel "isn't in words at all" (*PI,* 320), as one of his characters says. Forster finds a sign beyond the tentative "perhaps" with which he punctuates sentence after sentence. In fact it is, quite literally, in punctuation that he finds a stylistic correlative to what he calls opening out. I refer here to his use of ellipsis. It is obvious first, and abundantly, in the dialogue of the characters. Quite naturally (though Forster's use grows obsessive) it suggests hesitation, tentativeness, even a lack of information or understanding, sometimes a failure in speech. In addition, there is the novel's most famous elliptical sentence: "Beyond the sky must not there be something that overarches all the skies, more impartial even than they? Beyond which again . . ." (40; all ellipses in reference to *Passage,* for the remainder of the chapter, are not mine, but the text's). Here the ellipsis is connected to a question, which underlines in almost every case the basic quality of the elliptical thought. In the elliptical, or dialectical sentence, declarative sentences turn out to be, because of a crucial doubt at their source, questions in their own right, necessitating answers of their own ("question and answer" is of course the heart of the dialectical method and the crucial framework of dialogue). The doubt in the sentences is often answerable in two different, really opposite (or dialectical) ways. This syntactical form is, in its own way, "the architecture of Question and Answer" (70), but where, all too often, the answers are not forthcoming, and are sometimes indefinitely delayed. Mrs. Moore, puzzled herself, seeks retirement in a world "where no young people will come asking questions and expecting answers" (200). In any case, the elliptical sentence fails, at least immediately, to fulfill our expectation of answers, and supplies further questions. It is the analogue, on the level of syntax, to the series of narrative views, or what might better be called the series of unfinished views, or even the unfinished series of views. In each case, the elliptical sentence or elliptical narrative view is incomplete, and therefore engenders another related, often opposing, and usually delayed, sentence or view.

The elliptical sentence sometimes opens out because of a failure of words to suggest an infinite quality. The sentence on the arches beyond arches seems a case in point, as does the following phrase, where the Hindu god's divine effluence, never completely nameable or measurable, is seen "irradiating little mortals with His immortality. . . ." (*PI,* 289), an immortality that, like the series of arches, knows no bounds. But actually the ellipsis, already in these two examples, suggests a difference—the difference between doubt and faith, the emphasis changing from the writer's genuine wonderment over the existence of the infinite (this is why a question attends the ellipsis about the arches), to his linguistic inability to name and measure the infinite. Most often, the ellipsis underlines his doubt, a hesitancy that comes of an ignorance that has a tragic side, like the ignorance over what the caves are. In these cases it is often combined with its near-equivalent on the lexical level—"perhaps," a word that comes close to conveying the emptiness of the ellipsis. The two are combined, appropriately, in Adela's answer (notice it is no real answer) to Fielding's question about her being in the caves alone—"Perhaps . . . ." (239)—and suggest a hole in understanding that places the novel on the brink of tragedy. As we might expect, the conjunction of the ellipsis with "perhaps" is carried over into the narrator's description of the Marabar hills when, for the moment, all people have disappeared inside the caves: "Before man, with his itch for the seemly, had been born, the planet must have looked thu ;. The kite flapped away. . . . Before birds, perhaps. . . . And then the hole belched and humanity returned" (147). The hole seems to belch before our very eyes, to produce humanity's most generic sign, words themselves, amid the interstices of a bare page, amid the vast stretches of prehistoric time and a near-barren planet. The ellipses represent these bare places, and the words do battle with them in front of us, and look small, even precarious, mere impertinences, the way people do in this landscape. This description of the Marabar hills precedes Mrs. Moore's encounter with the echo, and leads to the literal hole in the novel, and the hole in man's reason, namely, the caves of ou-boum.

The ellipsis and "perhaps," it should be clear by now, come to symbolize, at least from one angle, the unseemly itself. They represent what reason and form and order have yet to settle or to fill up. I am suggesting that the emptiness of the caves, and their associated imagery of "pit" (*PI*, 163), "hole" (146), "abyss" (208), and "void" (264), is pictured literally in the novel's ellipses. If the cave is a topographical reification of the void, the ellipsis is its stylistic reification. The failure of the Word is enacted in "ou-boum" as well as in ". . .". Mrs. Moore's "God . . . is . . . love" (51) reveals less awe and reverence, in those pauses, than doubt (recalling "She must needs pronounce his name frequently as the greatest she knew, yet she had never found it less efficacious," 52). The ellipsis here conveys hesitation about the existence of God where the words "God . . . is . . . love" struggle desperately, and unsuccessfully, to fill the void that God is supposed to have filled. In this way "God . . . is . . . love" turns into the nonsensical "God si love"—"the singing went on even longer . . . ragged edges of religion . . . unsatisfactory and undramatic tangles. . . . 'God si love'" (316)—where the ellipses represent not the ineffable divine presence, but the ragged and formless ceremony and the tangle of words that tries to produce God's presence.

The ellipsis is the sign of a fractured world, where good and evil, order and chaos, meaning and meaninglessness, are unintelligibly mixed. Words, usually a safeguard against an overwhelming chaos (as they are in Wordsworth's dream of the deluge, for example), break down and become a strange Babel where, even while only one language is spoken, it is spoken in such fragments as to make little sense: "Was he in the cave or were you in the cave and on and on . . . and Unto us a Son is born, and unto us a Child is given . . . and am I good and is he bad and are we saved? . . . and ending everything the echo" (*PI,* 205). In such sentences we realize "the inarticulate world is closer at hand and readier to resume control" (114) than we usually expect, and we understand Mrs. Moore's cynicism over speech: " 'Say, say, say,' said the old lady bitterly. 'As if anything can be said!' " (200). Babel seems literally represented not only in the hierarchy of languages I have already discussed (enshrined most dramatically in the esoteric Sanskrit), but also in the everyday conversations between Fielding and Aziz. With Fielding amused and mildly annoyed at the way Aziz mistakes his words and intentions (another example of misinterpretation in the novel), the narrator writes, "Tangles like this still interrupted their intercourse. A pause in the wrong place, an intonation misunderstood, and a whole conversation went awry" (274). The pauses that are the novel's ellipses almost always seem in the wrong place, and come close again and again to tragic interruptions. It is ironically enough just such a pause, pictured once again by an ellipsis, that causes the temporary, but nonetheless tragic, misunderstanding between Aziz and Fielding: " 'Some news that will surprise you. I am to marry someone whom you know. . . .' He did not read further" (293).

If Forster's art in the end is elliptical, it is no surprise that the empty caves assume such a prominent position in the novel. I would have said "central position," but that would misrepresent the novel's most striking technical feature. Forster's elliptical style depends precisely on the absence of a center, or at least on a center that keeps being displaced. The special quality of the novel is an elliptical style of thinking that can now help to restate more fully, in line with the elliptical sentence, the entire narrative structure of the novel. Any single narrative view in the series I have described can be said to be elliptical for one of two reasons: either it is exploded by the next view and therefore is seen, in retrospect, as incomplete, or, to be more truly elliptical, it contains in its midst a hole (an interruption, a pause, an interval, an anticipation) that immediately marks it out as incomplete. This is the case where, in chapter 1, an elliptical (and proleptic—this punctuation is rhetorical) reference to the extraordinary caves anticipates and is fulfilled by a later chapter, or where distance, while the prevailing viewpoint, is devalued in the name of proximity, or where rumor and local report open up the geological view by anticipating the complications of vision that generally dominate "Caves." It is a method that can be called elliptical or dialectical, but if we call it the latter, we must distinguish it from Hegel's dialectics. It reaches no Hegelian synthesis, and thereby comes closer to what T. A. Adorno calls "negative dialectics": "Such thought therefore aims at maintaining contact with the concrete, painfully continuing a process of thinking about the world itself, at the same time that it rectifies its own inevitable falsifications at every moment, thus appearing to unravel everything it had been able to achieve. Yet not altogether: for the genuine content acquired remains, albeit in what Hegel would have called a canceled and transcended fashion; and negative dialectics does not result in an empty formalism, but rather in a thoroughgoing critique of forms, in a painstaking and well-nigh permanent destruction of every possible hypostasis of the various moments of thinking itself."[8]

The special elliptical quality of Forster's thought makes for what can be called an incomplete vision—the series of views that knows no end— and produces a series of altering categories, pictured geographically in the novel in a number of ways, both in the surprising claim about the ancient and apparently eternal hills ("Yet even they are altering," *PI*, 123) and in an early description of the moon's brightness on a sand bank: "The radiance was already altering, whether through shifting of the moon or of the sand; soon the bright sheaf would be gone, and a circlet, itself to alter, be burnished upon the streaming void" (32). Only the void is permanent, and upon it, as upon the blank page, pass alternatives, alterations too numerous to count or categorize. In the largest terms, the novel contains its own self-criticism just insofar as formlessness upsets form, evil upsets good, or nonlanguage upsets language. But just as important (in fact, part of its formlessness) is the shifting quality of even such apparently fixed and opposing categories, really of all the novel's categories. Underlying all along my argument about the narrator's position in the novel has been exactly such an alteration of categories and definitions, until we see the narrator as another actor in the novel. More dramatically, however, good and evil, apparently the opposite poles of the novel, meet and merge at curious points, becoming almost indistinguishable; both, for example, are represented by an echo and by an ellipsis. The echoing ellipsis suggests the infinite good of an immortal god (as I have shown) and also an evil that is limitless: "Evil was loose . . . she could even hear it entering the lives of others. . . ." (194). We hear about the vision of good what is true as well about the vision of evil (where "ou-boum" is only an approximation): "How can it be expressed in anything but itself?" (288). The evil the novel pictures is outside time ("Before time, it was before space also," 208), and so is the good: "Not only from the unbeliever are mysteries hid, but the adept himself cannot retain them. He may think, if he chooses, that he has been with God, but as soon as he thinks it, it becomes history, and falls under the rules of time" (288). Certain experiences (and both the visions of good and of evil seem to come under this heading) cannot be expressed in words, so an ellipsis or echo is used to represent them. Even modes of vision are mixed: Adela hallucinates Aziz's presence in the cave (evil), and Godbole hallucinates Mrs. Moore's presence in the temple (good).

The word reports history (since prehistory is defined by the absence of man and word), and ellipsis pantomimes all that is outside history. The echo is the elliptical sound that tries to signify the ahistorical, whether in ou-boum or in the Hindu chant. Both good and evil stop speech short, both flow out beyond the bounds of thought, reason, and language. An echo itself is an elliptical form, generating out of itself a further echo ("echoes generate echoes," *PI*, 147–48); every sound that is an echo is incomplete, and the echo seems to go on forever, never to finish, never to complete itself. For this reason the ellipsis is its proper sign. And with full ambiguity, as I have just suggested, the elliptical echo can stand either for good or evil, itself a mirror of "the echoing contradictory world" (117). In fact, it seems a void, or malleable sound, that can (like the plain ellipsis) take on any meaning, even diverse meanings. The novel presents the Marabar echo, whose "ou-boum," unchangeable, devalues all things; the "Radhakrishna Radhakrishna Radhakrishna Radhakrishna Krishnaradha" (313–14), or Hindu chant of love; and, most ambiguous of all, "Esmiss Esmoor / Esmiss Esmoor / Esmiss Esmoor / Esmiss Esmoor. . . ." (225), where the solemn invocation of Mrs. Moore is devalued when we learn that "people who did not know what the syllables meant repeated them like a charm" (225). The ellipsis, because it is a hole in thought, appropriately is fillable by diverse conjectures. What words manage to do, as is clear in Adela and Fielding's last conversation, is not to center the universe, not to find its order, but temporarily to displace the void in a series of gestures: "the words were followed by a curious backwash as though the universe had displaced itself to fill up a tiny void, or as though they had seen their own gestures from an immense height—dwarfs talking" (264). The only thing for certain is what lies behind the echo, namely, the grandest ellipsis of all, silence itself: "Outside the arch there seemed always an arch, beyond the remotest echo a silence" (52).

The reader feels scandalized in such a novel. He reads the warnings against interpretation, but in shrinking from interpretation he either reduces himself to a passivity and tranquillity that the novel clearly criticizes or he perceives a meaningless world of absurd connections, which is itself an interpretation—in fact, one of the crucial interpretations offered the reader of this novel. Not to act is as much an action as acting, and noninterpretation seems, or at least produces, interpretation. The reader realizes that to choose a single character as one's guide is to fail to learn the book's lesson. It is equally impossible to find a simple embodiment of evil in the novel: Forster decries evil in the guise of a villain, a Lovelace or Uriah Heep. The reader also learns that to choose a single narrative view is like choosing a single character. He must see the novel as a series of complicated and shifting relationships, and in Forster's description of "a highly organized novel" there is at least the first step (even though it seems the last) in the reader's task in *Passage:* "The facts in a highly organized novel (like *The Egoist*) are often of the nature of cross-correspondences and the ideal spectator cannot expect to view them properly until he is sitting up on a hill at the end" (*AN,* 87). But even this view of the novel is held in dialectical tension with another; even this secure position on the hilltop overlooks an abyss, a fall, just as Forster topples the writer's similar position, "poised above his work" (96). Forster insists on the value of first readings, and in music, first hearings: "We forget that Beethoven intended his Symphony to be heard always for the first time" (*T,* 119). The position at the end is at times inauthentic—it often betrays the essential quality of the experience of reading and listening by transforming this process into a message or a fixed set of categories and motifs. A work of art "presents itself as eternally virgin. It expects always to be heard or read or seen for the first time, always to cause surprise" (118). To give up the experience of a work of art is to become a critic and enter the perils of translation, not unlike the artist when he tries to translate life into art (reminiscent of Forster's warning about double mistranslation, from life into art into lectures): "It does not expect to be studied, still less does it present itself as a crossword puzzle, only to be solved after much re-examination. If it does that, if it parades a mystifying element, it is, to that extent, not a work of art, not an immortal Muse but a Sphinx who dies as soon as her riddles are answered" (118). These facts explain how the work of art is "recalcitrant to criticism" (118). While to be situated inside the work of art at any single point is inauthentic, because the novel's elliptical style means one is always in transit and in the midst of a developing notion, to be situated outside the work of art is to have that distanced view that the novel itself questions: "For we ought really to read the book in two ways at once," "to perform a miracle" (119) that is hardly possible. The critic "ought to know everything inside out, and yet be surprised" (119).

The form of *A Passage to India* is constituted out of disagreement, where each particular form is disputed. It is a form built around formlessness, an elliptical or negatively dialectical form, or finally, to come to terms with the geological metaphor that haunts the novel, an eroded form. Forster's acceptance of Nietzsche's request in art for "formidable erosions in contour" directs every aspect of *Aspects of the Novel*. Moreover, this notion of geological erosion suggests a connection between text and topography that is, in hermeneutics, a guiding metaphor: it can be seen in Freud's topographical model of psychoanalysis and more recently in a series of books by Michel Foucault that bear, as title or subtitle, the idea of the archeology of human knowledge.[9] This geological or archeological view of the lost land mass or civilization is used by historians, psychoanalysts, theologians, and, not least of all, literary critics, as the model for certain kinds of texts, and it gives to the opening chapter of "Caves," I believe, a special status.

Forster's version of the geological vision turns around our expectations. It only seems to suggest the conventional solution to the problem, namely, that once we strip the surface layer, we reach the truth. What the geological vision does suggest, however, is that every layer is both true and false; there is no final discovery of a single level of truth. Truth is multidimensional: it is seen only through many eyes, and because it is always shifting (the way the land itself is) it cannot be grasped and held still. In fact, it travels toward a future that is never precisely identifiable, that is elliptical—"It may be that in aeons to come an ocean will flow here too" (*PI*, 123)—and has a past that stretches out beyond recorded history to prehistory and surmises (the narrator surmises how "the planet must have looked," 147). This absence of Truth is mirrored in the absence of viewpoint (this is the phrase Forster uses about *Bleak House*), the absence of style (ellipsis), the absence of a central character (despite critics' attempts to find one), the absence of plot (the central action in the novel, the event in the caves, is never explained), and the absence of central symbols (the echo itself denotes absence and incompleteness, as does the cave; like the unknown green bird, such symbols represent uninterpretability itself). What Forster says of that other great novel of evil, *Moby Dick,* seems equally true of *Passage*. Ever hesitant of interpretation, Forster's commentary on *Moby Dick* seems more a warning against interpretation than interpretation itself. He characterizes the kind of dialectical tension I have attempted to show in *Passage*—"The essential in *Moby Dick,* its prophetic song, flows athwart the action and the surface morality like an undercurrent. It lies outside words" (*AN*, 138)—and he warns against (a perfect warning for his own novel, which I have tried to heed) "harmonizing the incidents, and so losing their roughness and richness. . . . There has been stress, with intervals: but no explicable solution, certainly no reaching back into universal pity and love" (138-39). The intervals in Forster's novel, perhaps even more dramatic than in Melville's, are the ellipses that interrupt all aspects of its form, warning against the interpretative act of harmonizing. This is the kind of text Forster attempted in *A Passage to India,* one whose erosions in contour may make it, if more difficult for certain kinds of readers, somewhat more congenial for the reader with Nietzsche's requirements in mind: "to be able to read off a text as a text without interposing an interpretation is the last developed form of 'inner experience'—perhaps one that is hardly possible—".[10]

8
D. H. LAWRENCE

THE NEW VOCABULARY OF *WOMEN IN LOVE*:
SPEECH AND ART-SPEECH

> *Conversation is not a search after knowledge, but an endeavor at effect.*
>
> Keats to Haydon

> *I have been long, long convinced of the paltry subterfuges of conversation.*
>
> Haydon to Keats

> Marriage as a long conversation. *When marrying, one should ask oneself this question: Do you believe that you will be able to converse well with this woman into your old age? Everything else in marriage is transitory, but the most time during the association belongs to conversation.*
>
> Nietzsche

The argument over philosophy and literature that caused Keats so much torment is taken up again by Lawrence. "Lamia" is Keats's most fully articulated poem on the subject; what Eliot christened the dissociation of sensibility, and judged more than two centuries of poetic technique by, is treated here as the subject of a tragic allegory in which man is divided between beauty and truth, between poetry and philosophy. It is perhaps the natural aftermath of the youthful and impulsive choice of a world of sensations over thoughts. The mature Keats is, like Lycius, torn between two apparently irreconcilable lives, and when he comes round to seeing philosophy's value he is already on the point of giving up poetry: poetry, he believes, is not so fine a thing as philosophy for the same reason an eagle is not so fine as a truth. It is only for isolated and unsure moments that Keats reconciles these differences, and can claim that a fine writer is the most genuine being in the world, excepting the human friend Philosopher (but even here the two seem in competition). The marriage to the beautiful and alluring Lamia is questioned, and

172

Keats is surprised that philosophy (that is, Milton's divine philosophy) is not harsh and crabbed, but has charms of her own.

In Lawrence there is very little of this equivocation, and his role as matchmaker (rather than bridegroom, or should I say bigamist, wooing and marrying one after the other) is clear from the start. Lawrence declares that philosophy and the novel (it is on this change of emphasis, from poetry to novel, that much of the difference between Keats and Lawrence rests) were married, like our first parents, from the beginning of time, and he bewails their separation: "It seems to me it was the greatest pity in the world, when philosophy and fiction got split. They used to be one, right from the days of myth. Then they went and parted, like a nagging married couple, with Aristotle and Thomas Aquinas and that beastly Kant" (*PP,* 520). For Lawrence the separation is never, as it often is with Keats, inherent in the nature of the profound differences between literature and philosophy, nor does Lawrence see himself as hopelessly torn between them (like a fickle lover). Quite the contrary, they become the constituents that compose the healthy and whole person (if that person is smart enough to get *them* back together). What turns the tragic and insurmountable divorce in Keats to the music of hopeful nuptials in Lawrence is clearly the latter's concept of the novel. While for Keats, at his most skeptical, both poetry and philosophy deny aspects of experience, and a writer his wholeness (poetry becomes a covert and coquettish demon obsessing him, making him subject to a kind of intoxication that often is illuminating, but often blinding, while philosophy represents a kind of truth that is bloodless, withering all human value into nothingness, and missing all beauty and joy), the novel, as Lawrence conceives it, is capable of a truth adequate to experience, in fact a truth that pushes experience to its richest limits.

Keats and Lawrence seem most similar in their characteristic gestures of dismissal, disavowing the truth of their speculations: "I have not one Idea of the truth of any of my speculations" (*L,* 1, 243), and "Don't ever mind what I say. I am a great bosher, and full of fancies that interest me. Only these are my speculations" (*CL,* 179). But whereas Keats rarely feels he finds the literary medium to explore and test these speculations, and has to give up poems like the Hyperions because he cannot make the proper division between false art and true feeling, Lawrence sees in the novel the great opportunity to test speculations, whether they are the mere flights of emotive fancy or the probings of the philosophic mind. He believes in the novel's powers of inquisition and irony, in its unfailing truthfulness to experience. The novel then becomes protection against what Keats feared, and thought he saw in Wordsworth, namely, the writer who so peacocks and broods over his speculations that he produces a false coinage and deceives himself: "The novel is the highest

form of human expression . . . because it is so incapable of the absolute,"
"It won't *let* you tell didactic lies, and put them over" (*R*, 106). So,
while Lawrence likes to think that "Plato's Dialogues are queer little
novels" (*PP*, 520), in the end he must criticize them because of their insufficient irony and their lack of the stuff of everyday life: "If, in
Plato's *Dialogues,* somebody had suddenly stood on his head and given
smooth Plato a kick in the wind, and set the whole school in an uproar,
then Plato would have been put into a much truer relation to the universe. Or if, in the midst of the Timaeus, Plato had only paused to say:
'And now, my dear Cleon—(or whoever it was)—I have a belly-ache, and
must retreat to the privy: this too is part of the Eternal Idea of man',
then we never need have fallen so low as Freud" (*R*, 107).

It is clear that what the novel has to offer philosophy is a way out
of "the algebraical tack: Let X stand for sheep and Y for goats: then
X minus Y equals Heaven," and so on. But philosophy offers speculations that stretch the imagination, propositions that lead to new realms
of thought and experience: "The novel has a future. It's got to have the
courage to tackle new propositions without using abstractions" (*PP*,
520). This knowledge of how fruitful the two may be together is the
reason behind Lawrence's role as matchmaker: "They went and parted.
. . . So the novel went sloppy, and philosophy went abstract-dry. The
two should come together again—in the novel" (520). As the highest
form of human expression, the novel is the right context for philosophy
to come to truth in. In fact, it becomes a special way of testing ideas
because, to use an appropriate phrase of Keats's, "axioms in philosophy
are not axioms until they are proved upon our pulses" (*L*, 1, 249). The
complicated way the novel allows theory, and tests it on the pulse of
experience, is my subject: the only solution to their divorce is for
philosophy to be taken over once again in a nuptial (if somewhat quiz-
zical) embrace by the novel.

For Lawrence, the typical artist upholds the outworn ideologies of
a culture; the examples are legion, from the classic American writers'
repressive Protestant ethics to Tolstoy's Christianity to Hardy's choice
of the community over the aristocrat or individual. In *Women in Love,*
Lawrence proposes a different kind of artist—not the artist who masks
his passions in ideas, but the artist who gives himself away. It is somewhat ironic (given that Lawrence learned from Nietzsche to beware of
moral interests) that his simplest strategy against subterfuge is directed
against Nietzsche's view of the artist: "And in so many things, I have
made myself well. I was a very queer and nervous girl. And by learning
to use my will, simply by using my will, I *made* myself right" (*WL*, 131).
Hermione's doctoring of herself is a criticism of Nietzsche's view of the
artist curing himself, though here it has become nothing more than the

Nietzschean will supporting certain aspects of the personality while it masks others. It allows Hermione finally to become an artist of sorts— "She had a true static impressiveness, she was a social artist in some ways" (292). It is, for Lawrence, a deadly prescription, a cure that kills rather than saves. Unlike Yeats, Lawrence will have no part of the Nietzschean mask, and in fact suggests that the artist's health lies in just the opposite direction. The point is made, perhaps somewhat obliquely, in Birkin's wise understanding of Gudrun's art. If Lawrence warns, in the example of Tolstoy, that art is a "cover" (*PP,* 479) for inner failure and fault, Gudrun's art (like Hermione's) is surely of this kind because, like the clothes she wears (a literal cover that disguises and protects), it is a masquerade, and one that keeps the world at a distance. Birkin explains: "She drops her art if anything else catches her. Her contrariness prevents her taking it seriously—she must never be too serious, she feels she might give herself away. And she won't give herself away—she's always on the defensive" (*WL,* 87). This notion of giving oneself away defines personality in general, the artist's personality, and even the problem of sexual relations in the novel. Art and love both are methods of communication (Lawrence, for example, explains that passion is at the source of both writing and kissing, *CL,* 171), and both allow the subject to give himself away, or if put to perverse uses, to defend his singularity and shut himself up in a noncommunicative envelope.

All the characters, in one way or another, either give themselves away or refuse to. When, for example, we see Hermione as "social artist," in perfect and willful control of herself and the social situation, we discover that Ursula "gave herself away to the other woman" (*WL,* 293)—a fine clue that giving oneself away is defined as what the artist, social or otherwise, does not do. In the opposite vein, Birkin amazes the characters of the novel with "the way he can give himself to things" (255). He tells Ursula, "in coming to you, I am without reserves or defenses" (138); he is "giving himself away" (136) to her. Gerald, on the other hand, "was not going to give himself away" (196), and his relationship with Birkin fails to develop for this reason. But it is Gudrun, not Gerald, who figures centrally as the opposite of Birkin's generosity of spirit, profligacy (as Ursula sometimes sees it), call it what you will. When she thinks Gerald has talked intimately to Ursula about her, we learn that "she could not *bear* it that Gerald gave her away" (370). In art and in love, she refuses what, in the end, she mockingly accuses Gerald of, "You give yourself away by that last" (447). Birkin, when he hears how Gudrun has slapped Gerald, laughingly thinks, "Poor Gudrun, wouldn't she suffer afterwards for having given herself away!" (195).

Gudrun and Birkin are shown at the most opposite extremes on this issue in Gudrun's reaction at the Pompadour to the reading of Birkin's letter. Birkin has expressed his deepest feelings, only to be publicly mocked by his readers—an anticipation of the reception of Lawrence's own words in print. Gudrun reacts typically: "Why does he give himself away to such canaille?" (*WL,* 377). To give oneself away is clearly an act of sympathy and love, a letting go of what Lawrence called the ego or the achieved self; the phrase also implies the revelation of a secret, usually an embarrassing one, a glimpse behind the armor of the self. Giving oneself away, then, in love and in art means unmasking oneself, allowing at once the deepest passions and thoughts, and any guile, to be shown. It is a dressing down that Gudrun, on the defensive (her clothes act as a challenge to the world, and put her equally on the offensive), never permits in love or art. As opposed to Loerke's and Gudrun's disclaimers about the intimate relation of art to life, Lawrence himself openly admits that this book is his life: it is "a record of the writer's own desires, aspirations, struggles" (viii). In fact, this central idea figures in Ursula's accusation that the bronze statue is really a portrait of the artist as a young man. Loerke, it seems, has unwittingly given himself away to the shrewd eye of Ursula, but it is Ursula who is criticized, by Gudrun, predictably enough, for her "foolish persistence in giving herself away" (421). Gudrun is quick to cover for her fellow artist, and she and Loerke fight from atop, and attempt to secure, "the height of esoteric art" (421), while she sees Ursula in the embarrassingly obvious position the artist is never in. Birkin gives himself away in his letter, as he does in his life, and Ursula does the same in her argument about art—in fact, in giving herself away, she provides in her own behavior a lesson that the artist should know best of all.

The view of the self-corrective capacities of language that I briefly introduced in my first chapter must be scrutinized in *Women in Love:* how does language allow Lawrence to give himself away? how does it stretch out imaginative life and ironically cry down mere theory? how can it avoid both the abstract symbolism of X minus Y (where no passion exists) and the free association of psychoanalysis (where reason seems to have lapsed completely)? But first I must explain that this view of language's self-corrective capacities forces on Lawrence something of a double view of the reader. On the simplest level, the reader is to save the text of *Anna Karenina* or *The Scarlet Letter* almost the way the psychoanalyst does. For a text like *Women in Love,* however, his role is somewhat different. He is still to save the text; just as a text is always potentially true (in spite of its surface morality), a text also is always potentially made up of lies. Lawrence, after Nietzsche, sees the simple truth (if such a thing exists) always threatening to become the Truth, lying writ large. It is in the nature of almost all discourse, not simply art or dreams, to have equivocity of meaning, even lies and truth in a complicated mix. If we miss the contextuality of any statement or event it begins to assume the proportions of a lie, and the problem of lying becomes equally the reader's and the writer's.

The reader of *Women in Love,* then, is asked not to let the text lapse (as so many readers do) into lies. He is asked, almost the way Reynolds is asked by Keats, to help separate the false and artificial from the true voice of feeling, to help the artist in his task. In this activity the reader is not so much set up in opposition to the artist (as he would be in the case of Tolstoy), but in a similar position. Artist and reader are engaged together in this test of meaning, detecting the point at which speculations turn abstract and untrue, measuring where the emotions rise to an ecstatic rhapsody that is false (Lawrence claims that "ecstasy achieves itself by virtue of exclusion. All vital truth contains the memory of all that for which it is not true," *CL,* 300). The reader then provides a double check against the subterfuge of art: he is to back up the artist's own self-critical gesture. Rightly measured, the text grows into a fabric larger than its parts, and both artist and reader are saved by seeing that "out of a pattern of lies art weaves the truth" (*CAL,* 2). The foreword to *Women in Love* is in the nature of an afterword, the author self-taught and self-cured. It is retrospective for Lawrence, though prospective for the reader, warning him that, if correctly read, these words are "not superimposition of a theory" (*WL,* viii). There is in *Women in Love,* then, a double dialectic, one within the work, and the other reaching beyond it. In the first, ideas and emotions, theory and experience, clash and interrogate each other, often through the dialogue and interactions between characters. In the second, novelist and reader engage in the dialectics of art-speech, and of a new vocabulary and a conventional vocabulary. It is these two aspects of the novel that need exploration, and I propose to begin with an analysis of what I call the novel's new vocabulary, moving from particular words to the sentences they make up, to the dialogue such sentences participate in, and to the actions such dialogue engenders and bestows value on (much the way words, in Wordsworth, bestow on things a glory not their own).

Birkin, as the novel's major spokesman, provides its major theories. The necessary translation of these theories into words—whether written to, and mocked by, the Pompadour crowd, or spoken to Ursula, and in turn criticized and misunderstood by her—is a major source of the novel's irony: "There was always confusion in speech" (*WL,* 178). A typical example of this kind of irony is the dialogue between Ursula and Birkin in which this idea of the confusion of speech is the narrator's concluding gloss. Birkin explains that he wants "love that is like sleep," even "like death," and Ursula objects to these similes: " 'But,' she said gravely,

'didn't you say you wanted something that was *not* love—something beyond love?' He turned in confusion" (178). Ursula's objections begin to
reveal a kind of linguistic irony at the heart of the novel. Similes, perhaps even metaphors, are not a radical enough means to allow Birkin to
escape the term "love." In fact, all his descriptions and definitions of the
relationship he wants are measured against, and therefore haunted by,
the word "love," and eventually, of course, he uses the word (though it
now is supposed to carry with it the accumulated meanings of all his
talks with Ursula). What Birkin complains of in Gerald, namely, that all
of Gerald's activity is really a reaction against something, seems at least
partially true about himself. The deadly action-reaction syndrome seems
a characteristic of Birkin's linguistic attempt to taboo the word "love"
and start from scratch with a new concept and word to replace it. The
elaborate redefinitions of "love" become a linguistic version of repetition compulsion, and people seem, even in the words they speak, com-
pelled to react and repeat rather than to act and originate. Language
seems like those Alps in the end, a cul-de-sac out of which Birkin cannot escape; in naming how he wants to be beyond love, love remains the
central principle. Birkin's description of other people seems an adequate
description of himself and his words: "They were all essentially alike,
the differences were only variations on a theme. None of them transcended the given terms" (296). The lack of true otherness in people is
expressed linguistically: the staleness of language seems also to name the
staleness of all human contacts. There is only a set of given terms available, and people, the expression of these words (rather than vice versa),
speak and act only according to the given terminology. People can transcend neither their own limited lives nor the words that are the sign of
their limitations.

   The basic ironic characteristic of language in the novel is its repetition, that deadly "repetition of repetitions" (*WL*, 184) that Birkin and
Ursula want to avoid. If Birkin seems always to repeat the word "love"
in trying to escape it, more ironic still is the way in which his central
formulations are repeated in and by such characters as Gerald, Gudrun,
Loerke, and Winifred. There is a large group of words, by no means
ordinary or casual, that is developed by Birkin in the novel as a crucial
and prominent new vocabulary, and these words seem inevitably to link
him and his hypotheses with their ironic counterparts. It is another example of those ironic variations on a theme. There is an insidious echo
in the novel that, if it does not devalue all meaning, like Forster's echo,
does couple Birkin and his hypotheses with what they try to escape. This
basic confusion in language is at once the novel's texture and text. When
Birkin claims, for example, that he wants a relationship that is based on
something "inhuman" (138), what are we to make of the fact that it is

precisely on an "inhuman principle" (220) that Gerald establishes his industry? These words, it must be insisted, are not used casually, nor are they an indication of careless writing. Just the opposite, they show a kind of rhetorical irony we rarely expect in Lawrence.[1] Again and again, "inhuman" and then "impersonal" characterize Birkin's and Gerald's goals. In fact, "impersonal," which at first might seem an elaboration of one of the kinds of "inhuman" and therefore a means of discriminating between them, is used neutrally in both cases, only adding to our confused sense that Gerald's scheme in some way does repeat Birkin's.

Women in Love constructs a new vocabulary, so that when the reader first sees these words he realizes that he is to learn their meaning and to proceed. What is baffling about this novel's vocabulary is that it seems deliberately to defy our educative powers. The reader is more surprised, not when he sees a fairly common word like "inhuman" used in a special way, but rather when the word is repeated later and he realizes that it now has an additional, and sometimes antithetical, meaning. It is, in short, a vocabulary that seems not to respect our understanding of vocabulary. Where, one asks, in these schemes and their vocabularies, does Gudrun's feeling that there was "this awful, inhuman distance which would be always interposed between her and the other being" (*WL*, 339) fit? Is this the "inhuman" quality that prevents meeting and merging in Birkin's theory, but gone awry so that it allows no relationship at all? Even inhuman or impersonal passion seems to be distinguished, indistinctly, from Birkin's inhuman relatedness: "His passion was awful to her, tense and ghastly, and impersonal" (435). Finally (though this in no way exhausts the uses of the word in the text), the "pure inhuman otherness of death" (186) in Ursula's Birkin-derived meditation on death in "Sunday Evening" is certainly the opposite of the inhuman principle of Gerald's system: the first leads into a new world of otherness, the latter into the world of mechanical repetition.

My last sentence has just shown how the reader can begin to discriminate between uses of the same word. But I do not mean to imply that this is always a simple task, one he can perform with little trouble or anxiety. If it is easy to distinguish between two uses of the same word, as the uses begin to multiply easy discriminations begin to diminish. The narrator is showing that the inhuman principle behind Birkin's theory can be expressed in Gerald's system as an inhuman mechanicalness, and in this way that terms and concepts take on a dangerous efficacy, a deadly reality when applied to life. The inhuman quality Birkin desires with Ursula, or that Ursula imagines in death, is realized, but with darker consequences, in Gerald's industry and in Gudrun's failure at relationship and in the passion of Gerald and Gudrun. The word turns sour, it seems, in the mouth of experience. In fact, experience seems to deny simple

definitions and consistent and universal meanings. Its complexity will
not allow such simplicities, and the word becomes, as it appears again
and again, the desecration of theory, the kind of marriage between
ideas and experience I spoke of earlier. Only a pure metaphysic, and not
its criticism, depends on singularity of meaning: "For not to signify one
thing is to signify nothing" (Aristotle, *Metaphysics,* 1006b). The novel's
value exists only in the opposite direction, for when "its meaning is
fixed and established, it is dead" (*Ap,* 5); and what Lawrence says about
the whole work is true of its parts, particularly of its vocabulary.

So, we see that Birkin's insistence on momentariness, and on a state
in which the individual is "responsible for nothing" (*WL,* 138), begins
to suggest a kind of ironic childishness when seen, for example, in Winifred. Birkin's changeableness is repeated in the girl who, "like a soulless
bird flits on its own will, without attachment or responsibility, beyond
the moment" (212). A cornerstone of Birkin's understanding of the
new relationship he wants with Ursula, "singleness," is echoed in Loerke's
"fine adjustment and singleness" (396), "an uncanny singleness, a quality
of being by himself" (412), as well as in Winifred, who is "quite single
and by herself, deriving from nobody" (212). Is it that Birkin and Loerke,
for example, share this quality, but other qualities differentiate them?
Or is it that singleness, like "inhuman," has more than one meaning, in
fact two different, even antithetical meanings? Further echoes begin to
make up a network of associations that baffle the reader, at least the
new reader. We must remember Forster's wise admonition never to lose
the sense of the first experience of a novel: simply to make up one's
mind that Birkin and Loerke are different, and to translate *a priori* for
the same word different meanings, is to miss the most distinctive quality
of the novel's rhetoric. The meanings of these words may be, if we take
Maurice Merleau-Ponty's advice about words in general, less easily defined than we usually assume: "what gives its meaning to each word is
the sentence. It is because it has been used in various contexts that the
word gradually accumulates a significance which it is impossible to
establish absolutely."[2] If Lawrence means the reader simply to see an
easy contrast (as readers sometimes suppose) between Birkin and Loerke,
or between Birkin and Gerald, he unnecessarily complicates matters by
this repetitive vocabulary. Instead, his vocabulary becomes a linguistic
test to discover the real other and measure it against the variations on a
theme. Lawrence seems at every turn to counter Birkin's attempt at a
new idea by making it invariably, at least at first, a variation on the given
terms. Gudrun's question to Ursula at the end of the novel seems to close
in on Birkin and Ursula's ideas of escape and transcendence: " 'And what
will happen when you find yourself in space?' she cried in derision. 'After
all, the great ideas of the world are the same there!' " (429). Even space

seems a claustrophobic prison-house, with the same repetition of repetitions as here on earth.

What I have called the new vocabulary of *Women in Love* is not confined to the few words I have looked at. A chapter like "Class-Room," organized around the idea of education, becomes a veritable vocabulary lesson for the reader. There is a fine escalation of idea as, first, Ursula instructs her students; second, Birkin instructs Ursula on pedagogical method; and finally, Birkin, Ursula, and Hermione engage in a pursuit of learning that transcends theories of childhood education. What is finally at stake here, for adults and children alike, is a knowledge of knowledge itself, how and what one learns. With Birkin's discourse on the different kinds of knowledge, Ursula, who is "concerned now only with solving her own problems, in the light of his words" (*WL*, 36), becomes less the teacher than the student problem-solver, and the reader is put in a parallel situation. Ursula and reader alike attend to a definition of a kind of knowledge that seems, paradoxically, to contradict any previous concept of knowledge. Ursula points to the novelty in Birkin's definition when she asks, "How can you have knowledge not in your head?" (36). Birkin coins the term "dark knowledge," eschewing all traditional associations, from Plato on, of light with knowledge and truth. Birkin's dark knowledge is not mental, or as Ursula (good student that she is) puts it later, at its most paradoxical, it is "the knowledge that is death of knowledge" (311). The point is made, with the same thrust toward the reader's education in language, when Lawrence declares, "that's as far as our education goes, in the direction of feelings. We have no language for the feelings, because our feelings do not even exist for us" (*PP*, 757). "Dark knowledge" is an attempt to name a feeling, to educate ourselves in the feelings. But if, having learned this vocabulary lesson, we keep in mind that Birkin means two things by knowledge (mental knowledge and a "dark knowledge" that he here defines), the reward seems scant as we are halted again and again by the subtle and contradictory uses of this word: (*1*) "There is no new movement now, without the breaking through of the old body, deliberately, in knowledge, in the struggle to get out" (*WL*, 178–79); and (2) " 'You can only have knowledge, strictly,' he replied, 'of things concluded, in the past' " (79). The two examples show the word used with deliberately opposite meanings in mind, and the good student of "Class-Room" might begin to feel self-satisfied, rushing in where he should fear to tread, reading for (*1*), dark knowledge, and for (2), mind knowledge. He would be dead wrong. The first quotation describes the necessity of speech, and certainly cannot be equated with simple dark knowledge; it becomes in fact another kind of knowledge (about which I will have much to say later), neither dark nor mental, and one for which Lawrence gives no further adjective (like "dark") in qualification. Moreover, mental knowledge is praised in the novel, even in "Class-Room," where Birkin argues with Hermione that the pupils need more, not less knowledge: they are dead "not because they have too much mind, but too little" (34). His act of turning on the electric lights to facilitate the lesson on reproduction is a symbolic act acknowledging his faith in clear and rational understanding, in mind knowledge. This makes us wonder if the kind of knowledge represented by (2), so criticized by Birkin, is different from the student's botanical lesson. In any case, freed from the adjective "dark," "knowledge" lives an independent life. Even the ground-breaking education received in "Class-Room," where we learn to see a word like "knowledge" in a new light (actually, through the dark) with a new meaning, cannot keep us apace with the word's active life in the text.

One or two final examples will show the wide range of the novel's new vocabulary. Again I start with one of Birkin's hypotheses, for they seem to be the verbal seeds out of which the whole of *Women in Love* grows: he wants Ursula and himself, in the novel's most famous formulation, to be "two single equal stars balanced in conjunction" (142). The important word here is "equal," because it receives from Birkin a rather full definition that makes it absolutely inappropriate to his hypothesis. Earlier in the novel Birkin listens with disdain to Hermione's claim that men are "all equal in the spirit," and contradicts her: "We are all different and unequal in spirit—it is only the *social* differences that are based on accidental material conditions. We are all abstractly or mathematically equal, if you like. . . . But I, myself, who am myself, what have I to do with equality with any other man or woman? In the spirit, I am as separate as one star is from another, as different in quality and quantity" (96–97). The last sentence here makes clear that "two single equal stars balanced in conjunction" is a false, contradictory statement. The qualities of "different" and "separate" become, through these passages, defined as the opposite of "equal." Now Birkin is led into this contradiction in a somewhat extenuating circumstance through a misunderstanding of words on Ursula's part. He explains his notion of relationship to Ursula with the simile, "like a star in its orbit," but for orbit she understands "satellite" (142). Trying to convince her that he does not want her subservience, he declares her equality to him, and thereby contradicts the central tenet of his belief. Moreover, it is interesting that one of the central terms of his hypothesis, namely, "equilibrium," shares the same Latin root with "equal," and is generally understood to have a similar meaning. But by "star-equilibrium" Birkin hopes to mean a balance that transcends the mathematical notion of equality.

This antithetical use of words derived from the same root, whether in standard usage or in the special vocabulary of *Women in Love,* occurs frequently. Birkin corrects Ursula, for example, by insisting on the distinction between "sensuous" and "sensual" (*WL,* 38). And then there is the following implicit discrimination by the narrator: "It was the first great step in undoing, the first great phase of chaos, the substitution of the mechanical principle for the organic, the destruction of the organic purpose, the organic unity, and the subordination of every organic unit to the great mechanical purpose. It was pure organic disintegration and pure mechanical organisation" (223). It is at once an extraordinary piece of prose, and a typical way that words are used by Lawrence. The reader is offered no direct and discursive definitions of words here, and the notion of etymological similitude becomes a fiction by the time the passage ends. The words seem to define themselves through context, through their associations with other words, but not necessarily through etymological association. Underlying the whole passage is the slow and deliberate repetition of the term "organic"—once, twice, three times, four times— with a fifth mention of the word that seems in a sudden, unexpected, and almost unrecognizable metamorphosis to become the final word, "organisation." "Organic" and "organisation," formed from the same root, mean entirely different things for Lawrence: the first has the Romantically endowed meaning that is so popular today, natural and whole, while "organisation" means the opposite, something mechanical. Lawrence, in such texts, gives a Saussurian test of difference, suggesting that words attain meaning, not through the notion of similarity, but difference.[3] The reader is put in the position of discovering those minute differences that will allow the word, and the sentence it is in, to have meaning. Lawrence dramatizes the point by denying such conventions as the etymological similarities between words. He will choose the same word ("inhuman"), or two words made from the same root ("equal/ equilibrium," "organic/organisation"), and make us see that we can understand these words, or more precisely, their use, only through their difference. Here the variations on a theme that seemed no different make all the difference, and the ostensible similarity between all things gives way to a world of authentic variety. The given terms are never transcended, if we mean by this, tabooed and replaced by a totally new language (what Birkin seems to expect at times); they are transcended as they are given new meanings.

There can be little doubt that the new vocabulary of *Women in Love* arises, at least at first, through the new and different meanings Birkin's speech accords to a conventional vocabulary. And over the course of the novel, new meanings are given to "love," "marriage," "knowledge," and "death" by Birkin's conversations with the other characters. His understanding of this process of revitalization, however, is problematic. Sometimes he seems to think that his new meanings can be consistent, and can adequately name the single idea he intends for them, but like all theorists he forgets that these words live a life beyond his system. Actually it is this very notion of systematic ideas that is ironically examined by Lawrence through Birkin's relationship to the other characters, and ultimately to the narrator. Birkin is the character who, in all of Lawrence's fiction, comes closest to a self-portrait, and it is no accident that he is also in danger of simple theorizing, of doing what the novelist is in danger of doing, namely, applying his metaphysic to the world. Gudrun in fact criticizes Birkin's mind for "its lack of self-criticism" (*WL*, 256). There is what Ursula more correctly detects in Birkin, however, as a "duality": "There was a certain priggish Sunday-school stiffness over him, priggish and detestable. And yet, at the same time, the moulding of him was so quick and attractive, it gave such a great sense of freedom" (122). Birkin actually notices this same duality in himself, and chides himself and his theorizing: "But he too had his idea and his will. He wanted only gentle communion, no other, no passion now. . . . Perhaps he had been wrong to go to her with an idea of what he wanted. Was it really only an idea, or was it the interpretation of a profound yearning? If the latter, how was it he was always talking about sensual fulfillment? The two didn't agree very well" (245). Birkin conducts a fight within his own soul to make his ideas the natural expression of his own feelings and experiences in life. In this way he epitomizes the exact opposite of the systematic thinker. He is Keats's chameleon poet: "Mr. Birkin, he is a changer," "He is not a man, he is a chameleon, a creature of change" (85). And he is unfair to his words when he imagines for them a fixed meaning. Words live a promiscuous life (I mean this as an oblique reference to Birkin's theories on love); they refuse no relationship and seem to owe no single allegiance or loyalty. Ursula complains about Birkin in similar terms: "He would behave in the same way, say the same things, give himself as completely to anybody who came along, anybody and everybody who liked to appeal to him. It was despicable, a very insidious form of prostitution" (121). The life of the man is like the life of his words—both are changers. If Ursula complains of his "word-twisting" (297), and that "he says one thing one day, and another the next" (286), the reader finds these turns in meaning ultimately a refreshing (if at first dizzying) escape from a dry singleness of idea, or from what Ursula herself decries as "too picturesque and final" (11) in his speeches.

While Ursula's mockery certainly deflates Birkin's tendencies toward the picturesque, I have been attempting to show as well that the vocabulary of the novel—or to put it another way, the complicated relation between Birkin's and the narrator's vocabulary—shows the reader, for example, that the individual who is beyond responsibility, or whose life is based on singleness or momentariness, may also be beyond any

authentic relationship; or that the inhuman principle can become
mechanical rather than vital and impersonal in a natural way; or that
equilibrium can lapse into mechanical and chaotic equality. The novel
is a warning that all hypotheses, like the words that are their signs, may
fall from the single meaning the theorizer intends for them. There is a
delicate line, in life as in language, that differentiates one concept or
word from another (or, for that matter, the different senses of a single
word), and he who dares cross it enters a confusion of universal proportions, a chaos that is his, and his world's, undoing. My vocabulary here
may seem hyperbolic, but in the case of Gerald (which I will now look
at) it seems appropriate.

The novel, perhaps more than any other genre, is the creation of a
world, one so powerful in fact that it may dwarf the world it seeks to
represent. It is no accident that Lawrence sees, like Wordsworth, the
Word behind his creation; but for Lawrence, the novel, if it is more
easily the representer of a full-blown world, has within it also a richer
kind of irony than any other genre, and he delights in the Word's tenuous
life in the dangerous stalking ground of the novel: "Now in a novel there's
always a tom-cat, a black tom-cat that pounces on the white dove of the
Word, if the dove doesn't watch it." The novel, in other words, will not
"let the human Word fly a bit too freely" (*R*, 106). The narrator of the
novel (if we can temporarily forget Mino) is its black tomcat, ensnaring
Birkin's words, or for that matter any of the characters' verbal hypotheses,
and making them live a rich, varied, albeit ironic, life.

While Birkin is clearly the author's spokesman, this has sometimes
obscured the fact that characters like Gudrun and Loerke, actual artists,
are self-reflections, while a character like Gerald, the industrial magnate,
seems to bear no relation whatsoever to Lawrence or the artist's enterprise. But *Women in Love* is a ghostly hall of mirrors (the author insists
that it is only a record of his own desires, aspirations, and struggles), like
the London cafe where the Bohemian artists, "reflected more dimly, and
repeated ad infinitum in the great mirrors on the walls" (54), can see
themselves if they dare look. Gerald, not even least of all, becomes the
reflection, from a particular angle, of Lawrence. Gerald is a theorizer of
a system in whose employ is a vocabulary ("inhuman," "equal," and
"impersonal") similar to Birkin's. Gerald is the classic example of the
man who fits the world to his metaphysic and seems to represent, in another sphere, Lawrence's claim that the novelist has everything to fear
from his metaphysic: "In his travels, and in his accompanying readings,
he had come to the conclusion that the essential secret of life was harmony. He did not define to himself at all clearly what harmony was. The
word pleased him, he felt he had come to his own conclusions. And he
proceeded to put his philosophy into practice by forcing order into the

established world, translating the mystic word harmony into the practical word organisation" (220). Like the novelist, Gerald seems to start
with words: "the terms were given" (220), and his mistakes are defined
linguistically, first through a mistaken definition, and second through a
mistranslation (Lawrence is insistent here, and underscores the linguistic
element in Gerald's "desire to translate the Godhead into pure mechanism," 221).

Gerald is a theorizer who fails to understand how words work. But
the point is sharper than this. He shuttles carelessly between worlds,
from theory to practice, and fails to realize one of the major ideas of the
novel, namely, that words owe their meaning to context. Gerald's mistranslation, then, is the novelist's own translation—a linguistic explanation of language's contextuality that at the same time marks out a
dangerous space between theory/ideology/metaphysic and life. It is a
criticism of Hegel that is stated rather baldly, and stands next to Gerald's
mistranslation in "Industrial Magnate": "The idea flew through them:
'All men are equal on earth,' and they would carry the idea to its material fulfillment. After all, is it not the teaching of Christ? And what is an
idea, if not the germ of action in the material world" (WL, 217). The
point is made (with "equal" taking on a linguistic edge, suggesting that
words, and the spheres they are drawn from, are unequal) through the
important word "equal": "Mystic equality lies in abstraction, not in
having or in doing, which are processes. In function and process, one
man, one part, must of necessity be subordinate to another" (218). This
last statement further clarifies the distinction between idea and practice,
and the untranslatability and intransigent contextuality of words, at the
same time that it reveals Birkin's "star-equilibrium" through a glass
darkly by making us ask what sphere "love" belongs to. "Equality" (the
passage goes on to call it, for further clarification, "mechanical equality")
is the wrong word for Birkin's new love, but if love does not exist in the
world of abstraction, is it a "function and process" (notice the characteristic periphrastic doubling in Lawrence's definition, where "process" produces both "function" and the easier "having" and "doing" as contextual
definitions), and if so, does it require what Ursula fears, subordination?
"Star-equilibrium" seems a balance almost unimaginable, neither in this
world of having and doing, nor in the world of abstract ideas.

In any case, Gerald's systematic thinking develops into a brilliantly
complicated network of associations that reaches at once the novelist's
own enterprise and that of Birkin and Ursula's love. Finally, the problem
may be stated semiotically: all theories are systems of signs, and whether
they take practical form as Gerald's economic system or as the contract
that Birkin imagines binding himself and Ursula—"Best to read the terms
of the contract, before we sign" (WL, 139)—there is always a danger that

the translation of concept into sign, and sign into real-life situation, will distort the original intention or meaning. The idea has its most extravagant demonstration in the view of Gerald as a God who has not fully understood his creative capacity, who seems to contract a world without understanding the terms of the contract. Gerald's system is modelled on a Cartesian God's: it is to be "a productive spinning, as the revolving of the universe may be called a productive spinning, a productive repetition through eternity, to infinity" (220), and it does in fact create "a new world, a new order," but one that turns out to be more "chaos" (223) than universe. Gerald's linguistic command—the "Gerald says" (222) that both his father and the miners obey like the law—creates not an organic or harmonious, but rather an organized world, and the God of the machine seems an ironic reflection on the myth of the ultimate artist, God. Jesus, in carrying the word (the Word) "equal" to all men, becomes the literal representation of God's linguistic mistakes, making us question if indeed the Word can be made flesh. The final chaos of the industrial system, then, owes two linguistic debts: first, to Gerald's confusion over "harmony" and "organisation," and related mistranslations, and second, to God's mistaken idea of "equality," and its translatability to the real world of working men. Lawrence's poetry overflows with examples, both comic and tragic, of a malaprop God, and he finally insists that the universe comes into being not through words at all:

> If ever there was a beginning
> there was no god in it
> there was no Verb
> no Voice
> no Word.

> There was nothing to say:
> Let there be light!
> All that story of Mr God switching on day
> is just conceit.

(C, 2, 681)

Finally, these examples of the Word's unhappy life in the novel are, in one sense, Lawrence's reflections on the world of artistic creation, and while there is no denying the word in the world of the novel, still that ironic tomcat signals the danger of the white dove of the Word flying too freely, and moreover, of the trouble that ensues when it represents itself as a common fowl. The Word makes an uneasy transit to the real world, and to that mirror of everyday life, the novel.

Gerald's understanding (or misunderstanding) of words requires of him the kind of mistranslation I have looked at. When Birkin asks him if everything is "all right" between him and Gudrun, Gerald answers: "I never know what those common words mean. All right and all wrong, don't they become synonymous, somewhere?" (*WL*, 430). But Gerald's lack of linguistic discrimination goes beyond common words, and is in fact at the heart of his character. He seems to stand in an opposite position to Ursula: if she argues, with the word "love" as her prime example, that its meaning is single, absolute, and unchangeable, Gerald's understanding of words is that they are perfectly interchangeable, synonymous with countless other words, "harmony" and "organisation" being his most representative example. Gerald's understanding of the interchangeability of words is a mistaken corollary based on the novel's crucial insight: if a single word (or clearly related words) can have antithetical meanings, then words normally taken as different ("all right" and "all wrong") may mean the same thing. Gerald's is a partial insight: it is true, for example, that Birkin sees "love" and "hate" often with the same meaning, but while the novel seeks a language of value through discriminations, even discriminations of usage for the same word, Gerald lapses into an easy interchangeability of words. Curiously enough, Ursula's and Gerald's understanding of words can be seen as analogous. Both are posited on a translatability of words that is playfully mocked in a little scene in "Breadalby" that is generally overlooked: " 'There is a most beautiful thing in my book,' suddenly piped the little Italian woman. 'It says the man came to the door and threw his eyes down the street' " (79). We learn, of course, that the Contessa is reading an old American edition of *Fathers and Sons*, translated from the French: "Bazarov ouvra la porte et jeta les yeux dans la rue" (79). The company reconstructs this sentence, but the Russian original seems just beyond their purview. The Contessa's triple translation shows something about language in general, as well as revealing that Ursula's and Gerald's understanding of language, apparently at opposite poles, converges. If each word is given an absolute meaning—just as we might translate single English equivalents for single French words in translating a French Turgenev—we produce a meaningless sentence. While we have substituted for all the words of the original some equivalent, some "equal" (to give a linguistic turn to Lawrence's notion of equality that I think he intends), we do not have the relationship of the words, the idiomatic sense of the language. This passage belies the sense that every word has a consistent meaning, or a single equivalent, and that when Lawrence, for example, writes "inhuman," we learn what it means, and translate this meaning for the word the next time it appears. The view of language that believes words have absolute meanings that are consistent and easily identifiable (Ursula) can believe in the easy interchangeability of words (Gerald).

Lawrence complains that the vocabulary he inherits is often too precise. If Keats wants English to be kept up, and most writers complain that language is not precise enough, Lawrence takes a stab at the precision of the Northern languages while explaining that Italian cannot be easily translated into English: "it is almost impossible to reproduce in the more cut-and-dried northern languages, where every word has its fixed value and meaning, like so much coinage. A language can be killed by over-precision, killed especially as an effective medium for the conveyance of instinctive passion and instinctive emotion" (*PP*, 266). A closer look at the typical mode of definition in the novel suggests Lawrence's way out of definition, at least cut-and-dried definition. A new vocabulary, if it is to be understood at all, must be defined, but the reader begins to see that when Birkin thinks he is giving Ursula definitions—he wants love like sleep, he wants love like death, he wants star-equilibrium—his definitions are in need of definition. Birkin's famous description of the "river of darkness" in "Water-Party" is a case in point. The passage is characterized by an insistent series of appositive phrases, where grammar becomes a rhetorical device. "A river of darkness" and "the black river," terms for the same river, both engender more elaborate periphrases—"that dark river of dissolution" and "the black river of corruption," respectively. These two phrases then seem grouped under "destructive creation," which is opposed to "the stream of synthetic creation." No reliance on simple conventional meanings for "dissolution," "corruption," or "synthetic creation" provides the passage with its meaning, and in fact an apparent contradiction like "destructive creation" signals at first not meaning, but a new vocabulary for which the traditional meanings no longer hold. "Synthetic creation" seems more like a tautology than a helpful discrimination to measure "destructive creation" against. Finally, there is an associative development in the passage where prefixes seem to mark out major distinctions: the reader expects, for example, that the "dis/des" words represent "dissolution/ destruction" and the "pro" words ("progress/process/production") represent "synthetic creation." This expectation is reversed, however, in a passage like the following: "Dissolution rolls on, just as production does. . . . It is a progessive process—and it ends in universal nothing." It is like the case in which "organisation" and "disintegration," normally antithetical as their prefixes imply, become almost synonymous, with "organic" a genuine antonym for both. The phrase "progressive devolution" (*WL*, 196), used later in the novel, nicely suggests Lawrence's coupling of pro/de words. What the marsh seems to spawn, then, is not so much the lotus and snakes, but a viscous and oblique vocabulary that, as definition, seems impossibly periphrastic. Finally, when the passage flowers quickly into symbols—"the snakes and swans and lotus—marsh flowers" on the one side, and "roses, warm and flamy" (163–64) on the other—the reader begins to feel mocked, realizing this is less the final flowering of a carefully articulated sign system than just so many further terms. The symbols do not represent a signified and comprehended idea, but are only part of the ever-elaborating definition by periphrasis—in fact, just further terms with no special status at all.

Michael Riffaterre, in another context, has defined two kinds of periphrasis that can be helpful here: "one in which the kernel word is given (the periphrasis is then a descriptive expansion); one in which the word has to be guessed from a circuitous description."[4] Both forms of periphrasis are apparent in Lawrence. Despite Birkin's desire to taboo "love," there can be little doubt that it becomes a kernel word, like "death" or "marriage" or "knowledge," for which there are countless elaborate periphrases. Common words, then, those of a conventional vocabulary, remain in the new vocabulary but are redefined through periphrasis: a simple extension like "sort of ultimate marriage" (*WL*, 53) attempts to give the kernel word new meaning and latitude, first by the adjective that marks it off as more profound than we normally see it, and then by "sort of," which is vague enough to allow almost endless elaboration. The passage I have just looked at, on the other hand, is striking because of the absence of any center. There is no single word that stands out, and the reader, by adding or subtracting (there are phrases meant to supplement each other, and others to oppose each other) words and meanings, tries to name the crucial term not given. Here meaning seems at once undetermined and overdetermined, with a plenitude of terms and apparent definitions vying for central significance. This second form of periphrasis suggests a refusal to coin (to use Lawrence's metaphor of value) a new word for fear that it, like "love," will simply become a lie, a fixed meaning like so much coinage.

Lawrence's famous characterization of art as subterfuge—"Truly art is a sort of subterfuge"—is linked to his notion of the impeccable truth of literature as art-speech: "Art-speech is the only truth" (*CAL*, 2). I am interested here in this idea of art as art-speech and its relation to narrative structure. The narrative technique of *Women in Love* can be seen as a complicated series of dialogues, or speech acts, based on something like Saussure's "circuit of discourse," where the *parole* of the speaker is distinguished from the *langue* of the person who understands him.[5] On one level a character like Birkin, in his talks with Ursula or Gerald, introduces an idiosyncratic vocabulary that is understood against the backdrop of his, and these other characters', more conventional terms. The new terms of his that are understood—"dark knowledge," "star-equilibrium"— can be understood at least partially only through their relationship to a common stock of words and meanings already understood. On another level, narrator and reader can be seen as engaged in a kind of dialogue, in which the new vocabulary of the narrative (far more complicated than

Birkin's, because it introduces three and four and five different uses of a word like "inhuman") meets the conventional vocabulary of the reader. It was Merleau-Ponty who brilliantly moved the "circuit of discourse" between speaker and listener into the domain of writer and reader: "Sedimented language is the language the reader brings with him, the stock of accepted relations between signs and familiar significations without which he could never have begun to read. . . . But speech is the book's call to the unprejudiced reader. Speech is the operation through which a certain arrangement of already available signs and significations alters and then transfigures each of them, so that in the end a new signification is secreted."[6]

The words in the title *Women in Love* are familiar enough to the prospective reader; they announce a subject of interest, one that he feels he already has some understanding of. It is only in the course of reading the novel that he begins to realize he did not understand the title at all. Not only "love," but even "women" begins to take on further meaning in a chapter like "Woman to Woman," which sets out, through its difficult discriminations between "female" and "woman," its complicated notion of the different roles of women, and its description of Hermione as a man, to measure the extent of the pendulum-wide swing from woman to woman. The book allows the reader to read it through its use of common terms, but it educates him, most deliberately in a chapter like "Class-Room," by making him see new terms and new meanings for old words. To relinquish language because of its conventional meanings was a step Nietzsche always seemed on the point of taking, because for him language seemed nothing more than vulgarization: "the speaker has already vulgarized himself by speaking;" language represents our "social or herd nature;" "words make the uncommon common."[7] Lawrence moves beyond this position (as does Nietzsche himself, if truth be told, in the kind of discriminations he makes between words like "bad" and "evil") through the notion of speech, a dialectic able to bear new meanings. Lawrence understands that the word, once understood, is of course in danger of becoming part of that sedimented language, or herd language, that Merleau-Ponty and Nietzsche respectively describe. As Merleau-Ponty puts it, "a signifying intention . . . exhausts itself to the extent that it is fulfilled. For its aim to be realized, it must not be completely realized, and for something to be said, it must not be said absolutely."[8] For this reason Lawrence's new vocabulary never stops bearing new meanings, and its periphrastic mode of definition often leaves out the kernel word.

I have shown how the reader's education is never finished in *Women in Love*. On the lexical level the redefinition of words never seems completed, and even on the syntactic level there is redefinition occuring. This is true even of a word like "will," which I at first saw as an exception to the fluidity of meaning of the text's other words; it always seemed an overworked word, with a predictable enough meaning because of Lawrence's critique of Nietzsche. While it certainly does not attain the complexity of many of the other words used, still Birkin attempts to give it a new meaning through a change in syntactic function, one that sets up a fluidity of meaning between "will" and "power" for much of the novel. Arguing that "the Wille zur Macht is a base and petty thing," he tells Ursula about the Mino's action: "It is a volonté de pouvoir, if you like, a will to ability, taking pouvoir as a verb" (*WL,* 142).[9] The process of syntactic redefinition makes Birkin's apparently incorrect reference to declining a verb (48) seem less like a mistake than part of these syntactic changes he imagines for the conventional language, with verbs like nouns and nouns like verbs. And certainly the new definitions of the personal pronouns "me" and "you," with the well-known argument against "I," give new meanings for these standard syntactic entities.

We begin to see that the individual speech act is the only one that confers meaning: "Humanity is a huge aggregate lie, and a huge lie is less than a small truth. Humanity is less, far less than the individual, because the individual may sometimes be capable of truth, and humanity is a tree of lies" (*WL,* 118–19). Traditional meanings of love, after all, are hypocritical, and what love actually means is hate: "It's the lie that kills. If we want hate, let us have it—death, torture, violent destruction—let us have it: but not in the name of love" (119). So the venture into the individual speech act commits us to no unnecessary confusion: indeed the conventional vocabulary, if we look at it closely, is filled not simply with confusion but with lies, and words like "love" are empty masks for the opposite feeling. The individual speech act, at first committing us to confusion, eventually rewards us with genuine meaning. A word's meaning, then, is not governed by preestablished rules, by humanity or the herd, and Ursula's explanation of the meaning of "Whom" to Billy—"It's the accusative of who" (188)—is part of the closed-circuit language system Lawrence is devaluing. To say that words are defined only through their function is to show how Lawrence once again undermines pure theory. If a word like "equal" seems a mathematical abstraction and not of the world of "function and process," then Lawrence is defining not only "equal," but all words and the way they work. To understand a language, one must see a distinction between the theoretical set of rules that govern it (an ideal realm of grammatical rules and lexical definitions) and the new language that can be created from it through the flexible functions words can actually have. It is the difference between theory and practice.

To say that the meaning of words depends on their use finally means for Lawrence a relationship between words and deeds. A word's use with other words eventually leads to its use as part of action. If words are "a gesture" (*WL,* 178), as Lawrence says, they are further defined through the further gestures, or actions, one performs. Birkin's and Loerke's activities, for example, as well as the words that they use and that are used about them, help to discriminate in what sense both are "single." It is for this reason that Birkin sees words not as separated from action, but as partially defined by action. Words and actions, or to use the terms that belong to the Biblical passages Birkin paraphrases,[10] words and works, are parallel activities whereby people make themselves known, if not to God, then to other people: "By their works ye shall know them, for dirty liars and cowards, who daren't stand by their own actions, much less by their own words" (119). Love means hate, then, precisely because the actions performed in the name of love are in fact "death, murder, torture, violent destruction" (119). Ursula claims that actions do not alter the meaning of words—"What they *do* doesn't alter the truth of what they say, does it?"—while Birkin retorts: "Completely, because if what they say *were* true, then they couldn't help fulfilling it" (119). If Birkin is in danger of becoming a "word-bag" (180), it is not so much because he speaks too much, but because his speeches often are unsupported by his actions. If Ursula sees a word as inviolable against the actions committed in its name, still it is she who provokes Birkin to support his words with acts: "You don't fully believe yourself what you are saying. You don't really want this conjunction, otherwise you wouldn't talk so much about it, you'd get it" (144). The Hamletizing (179) on which Birkin is always verging is not only a soliloquizing but a dangerous procrastination and inability to act. The novel seeks a marriage of words and actions, in which each, by itself only a gesture, helps to define the other.[11]

The practical uses to which language is put in the text—either through the simple repetition of conventional meanings or the experimentation with new meanings that is the rebirth into a new world—surface as a major theme. Birkin institutes, for the novel as a whole, an ambiguous terminology that will describe, through a linguistic metaphor, the most essential nature of the characters. Birkin, in the chapter "In the Train," explains to Gerald about their present life, "We've got to bust it completely, or shrivel inside it, as in a tight skin," and in an oblique elaboration of this idea, declares that "life is a blotch of labour, like insects scurrying in filth" (*WL,* 47). The web of associations this imagery spins is complicated. Both Hermione and Gudrun, for example, are earlier characterized by this insect imagery; Hermione is "like an insect in its skin" (36) and Gudrun is "like a beetle toiling in the dust" (5). The latter clearly anticipates Birkin's declaration by combining the image of the insect with some sort of labor ("scurrying," "toiling"). Further-more, these images of the insect, connected with the "tight skin," are really an indirect reference, through antithesis, to a different meaning for labor. For example, the early description of Ursula—"If she only could break through the last integuments. She seemed to try and put her hands out, like an infant in the womb" (3)—suggests that labor, as childbirth, is a breaking through that tight skin (or "last integuments") that seems to enclose the insect. Like so much of the vocabulary of the novel, then, labor develops a double meaning. Its two meanings are more conventional than those accorded to many words in the novel; in fact, they are dictionary meanings. But the two meanings of labor become eccentrically antithetical in this novel because of the rather specialized meanings that the processes of work and birth take on.

If "In the Train" establishes labor as work, the two succeeding chapters, "Creme de Menthe" and "Totem," describe that totem in which the woman's "labour" (WL, 67, 71) is childbirth. In "Moony," however, this same totem is insistently described through beetle imagery, thus linking it to the scurrying insects of mere work—"her face was crushed tiny like a beetle's," "her diminished, beetle face," "knowledge such as the beetles have," "her face looked like a beetle's" (245–46). This is a typical example of the way the novel reverses its own hypo-theses, its own vocabulary, its own train of associations. We are led to believe that the opposite of labor as repetitive work is the labor of dark physical sensation, pictured in the woman's childbirth, but this becomes too simple a meaning for the novel to bear, and is criticized. The totemic woman in labor, used effectively to suggest the pun, now seems to reduce labor once again to the meaning it had in "In the Train," namely, mere work.

The novel's growing awareness of a deeper kind of labor, one that is genuinely creative, is realized in "Water-Party" through the idea of speech as labor, supporting the technical aspects of language I have been remark-ing in the text:

> There was always confusion in speech. Yet it must be spoken. Which-ever way one moved, if one were to move forwards, one must break a way through. And to know, to give utterance, was to break a way through the walls of the prison as the infant in labour strives through the walls of the womb. There is no new movement now, without the breaking through of the old body, deliberately, in knowledge, in the struggle to get out. (WL, 178–79)

Language as birth is at once technique and theme in the novel. "To know" and "to give utterance" are placed in apposition, and the new meaning for "knowledge," from "Class-Room," now seems obsolete. Birkin's declaration in "Breadalby" that "you can only have knowledge . . . of things concluded, in the past" (79), is now emphatically denied by a definition of knowledge as movement into the future, "forwards," "through," and "out." Such adverbs and prepositions increase the sense of the activity of knowing and uttering, as does a verb like "give" in "to give utterance" (a suggestive echo of "to give birth"). The subjects of the passage—both the confusion of language and its process as birth or re-birth—are mirrored in the style. The supreme circuitousness of the mode of definition suggests this confusion, a groping after the right word. There is a winding list of phrases that may bear a new meaning or may only be a confused tangle. Because both knowing and uttering take on new meanings in the passage, the definition is two-sided, not with an original, problematic word and its more easily understood definition, but with two words and two definitions: knowing is defined as uttering, and vice versa.

Since the conventional vocabulary always seems disappearing before our very eyes, we have in Lawrence these two-sided definitions where there is almost no conventional starting point. It is a perfect example of the pure contextuality of words, where each word helps define the other and where definition is defined by the word it is defining. It is like look-ing up a word in the dictionary, and then having to look up a central word in the definition, ad infinitum. To this I must add the explicit part of the definition: to know and to give utterance are "to break a way through the walls of the prison," where this metaphor is further defined by a simile, "as the infant in labour breaks a way through the walls of the womb." The apparent equality of words and phrases—words stand in apposition to each other, and then are defined with a metaphor that is further defined by a simile—makes us ask, using Lawrence's insidious linguistic categories, if we are to see the words as "equal," or as transla-tions of each other, or as representative of parallel activities. We begin to see that the confusion in speech may sometimes be a virtue, actually the process of rebirth itself, where appositions, metaphors, and similes deliberately confuse different spheres of activity.

The novel's foreword also defines language as labor, and introduces the definition with the new term "verbal consciousness": "The people that can bring forth the new passion, the new idea, this people will en-dure. Those others, that fix themselves in the old idea, will perish with the new life strangled unborn within them. Men must speak out to one another" (*WL*, viii). Verbal consciousness as labor, the central new idea of *Women in Love,* surpasses the conventional Lawrencean categories of blood- and mind-consciousness because its very purpose is to define a way out of this tragic division. As "the passionate struggle into conscious being" (viii), it is an attempt to articulate, and live by, the most profound

thoughts and emotions. *Women in Love* marks the high point in Lawrence's search for the reconciliation of the two great ways of knowing.
I have shown how Birkin hopes to come to Ursula, not with a mere idea,
but "the interpretation of a profound yearning" (245), and Lawrence
in *Phoenix* solicits "not a bare idea or an opinion or a didactic statement, but a true thought, which comes as much from the heart and the
genitals as from the head" (*PP*, 279). The language of the foreword—
"the new passion, the new idea"—makes this clear, and suggests Lawrence's place in a long tradition of redefining the logos: John made it
the Word, and in the tradition I am following, from Milton to the modern day, it often appears as Reason, and sometimes as Idea, variously
coupled with Imagination (Wordsworth) and even passion (Lawrence,
not to mention Wordsworth, as I showed in my second chapter).
Lawrence defines it somewhat traditionally as "divine reason" and
"mystic reason." In any case, his erotic coupling of passion and idea
(like the union of deed and word) is his way out of the problem of
theory, and this is why he insists that verbal consciousness "is not superimposition of a theory" (*WL*, viii). Speech in fact becomes a coupling
that knows no bounds. It is a bridge between people (like love itself),
and also between the individual's at first inarticulate passions and his
conscious, expressive being.

Language can be said to be a creative labor (as well as hard work) in
precisely this way: it gives birth to one's relationship with the world,
and to one's relationship with oneself. The failure to give birth to oneself is the failure to "speak out," whose consequence is strangulation
("the new life strangled unborn within them").[12] The novel's imagery
of general restraint—the tight skin, the last integuments, the need to bust
this life—becomes pinpointed, as in Keats's Hyperions, as the restraint
on speech. In this light people are bid not simply to speak, but to speak
out, as if the adverb describes at once speech's essential power to make
external and available to all people one's innermost thoughts and feelings, as well as one's actual delivery out of the womb. Again, the adverb
makes speech a genuine activity, in the same way that Keats begins to
compare writing and doing. This adverbial thrust to the activity of
speech occurs again when Birkin attributes the failure of the African
culture to the fact that "the relation between the senses and the *outspoken* mind had broken, leaving the experience all in one sort, mystically sensual" (*WL*, 245, emphasis added). Hence the totem as beetle, the
meaningless toiler in the dust.

Finally, the novel's motif of strangulation suggests how people in
fact are not speaking out to one another. Gerald's ecstatic meditation
on, and final action toward, Gudrun is "to strangle her, to strangle every
spark of life out of her" (*WL*, 452). In one of their last dialogues to-

gether, Gerald seems "strangled" and Gudrun's heart is "beating to suf-
focate her" (433). Hermione, "speechless, like a stricken pythoness"
(35), ironically wants to wreack a similar vengeance on fate, "to grip the
hours by the throat" (91). Gudrun, thinking of the baby Gerald is,
wants only "to stifle and bury it, as Hetty Sorrell did" (457). Mrs. Crich
rages at her children with a similar threat: "If I thought that the children
I bore would lie looking like that in death, I'd strangle them when they
were infants" (327). These last two examples suggestively combine the
idea of suffocation with the infant whose life is cut short. The child not
allowed to reach maturity is the one, like Wordsworth's Boy of Winander,
whose speech is silenced.

SILENCE IN *WOMEN IN LOVE*

"Excurse" is more than a turning point in the novel, it seems a turn-
around. At first the chapter title names only the motorcar trip that
Birkin and Ursula take, but as the chapter comes to a close we realize
that it suggests their excurse out of the known world into a new world
of sensual reality. In fact, with this chapter's description of a perfect
state beyond language, the title indicates, in light of the novel's central
meanings up to this point, almost a journey outside the world of the
novel. As the title richly suggests, this may be an excurse that is also a
thematic digression.

This chapter insistently describes a perfect silence that, nevertheless,
is dramatized as communication. It tells over and over again of the
silence the lovers experience: they find "the living silence," "this pure
living silence," the "living, subtle silence," and they are "fulfilled in
silence" (*WL*, 310-11). Finally, "She had her desire of him, she touched,
she received the maximum of unspeakable communication in touch,
dark, subtle, positively silent" (312). The central linguistic metaphor of
translation is denied here in a reality that seems untranslatable because
it is unlinguistic—"the being never to be revealed," "never to be translated," "the suave, pure, untranslatable reality" (311). The word "still"
occurs again and again, as it does in Keats's Hyperion poems, carrying
the double force of silence and immobility. And as in Keats, the immobility is a "rest" (311), but one that brings "riches" (used seven times
on pages 305-8), an ironic inversion of Gerald's busy world of work.
Rest (not work) rewards the lovers with riches, in contrast to the hollow
wealth of Gerald, really "poor Gerald" (457, 458), and of Hermione,
really "poor Hermione" (284). Birkin and Ursula, in the midst of their
new-found rest and riches, appropriately "write their resignations from
the world of work" (308).

There is a crucial moment, however, in the lovers' shared silence that helps to place it in the context of the novel's developing meanings:

> He stood on the hearth-rug looking at her, at her face that was up-turned exactly like a flower, a fresh, luminous flower, glinting faint-ly golden with the dew of the first light. And he was smiling faintly as if there were no speech in the world, save the silent delight of flowers in each other. Smilingly they delighted in each other's presence, pure presence, not to be thought of, even known. But his eyes had a faintly ironical contraction. (*WL*, 304–5)

This is, of course, the central romantic formula for which Wordsworth is celebrated, and that reappears in Keats, Yeats, Forster, and all the major writers of the tradition: it is the loss of consciousness (and speech—the two, as in Nietzsche, are practically synonymous for these writers) through identification with nature. Keats's lines in the "Ode to a Nightingale" declare it most directly, when the speaker desires "the ease" (a synonym Lawrence uses for the lovers' "rest;" see, for example, 302, 303, 306) of the nightingale, but recognizes that man lives in a world where even to think is to be full of sorrow. Wordsworth's more oblique formulation is closer to Lawrence's in its emphasis on the state of silence; it is quintessentially enacted in the Boy of Winander episode (and again in the Lucy poems), where the child is subsumed in the natural world's silence. The image of the "delight of flowers in each other," which I explained in Yeats's Shepherd poems (via Blake and Shelley), describes a simple natural world that seems to shun us the more we try to enter it. It is permanently self-enclosed in silence the way human relationships never can be.

The two suggestions of irony that unsettle the passage actually stem from this discrimination. Already Birkin seems to be of the scene and beyond it, possessing that double consciousness that is the heart of irony, an irony all too human. The silent delight of the flowers suggests "their pure presence, not to be thought of, even known," while the "faintly ironical contraction" of Birkin's eyes suggests a singleness and knowledge that is intransigently human. The contraction of his eyes even suggests a slight withdrawal into the singularity that is human. The passage, reaching out toward a radical simplicity, is complicated by the sophistication of Birkin's unexplained irony, which must stem from his consciousness of the fact that this state of perfect silence comes, even here in "Excurse," only after one of the lovers' most heated verbal dis-agreements. In other words, the state beyond language is, paradoxically, wed to language. This point is doubly made, both on the level of event and through the literary discourse that describes it; that is, while Birkin's and Ursula's actual silence seems to depend on the words that precede it, it is also enacted and described for the reader only through the narrator's verbal abilities, which are at this moment, ironically enough, far more verbose than usual. Birkin and Ursula everywhere in the passage seem out of place, contradistinguished from that to which they are being compared. For humanity alone there is no reaching the perfect silence without language. This is the full power of the passage's hypothetical slant—"as if there were no speech in the world."

Moreover, the scene indirectly makes one of those unsettling, but by now characteristic, connections with what it stands in opposition to. The word "knowledge" comes back to haunt us again, and seems used in an impossibly contradictory way. How can we distinguish between, on the one hand, the "mindless progressive knowledge through the senses" (*WL*, 245) that is criticized in the African culture and, on the other hand, the "unthinkable knowledge" (310) of Ursula and Birkin that continually insists, like the African knowledge, on its separation from everything mental? Lawrence writes of a "mindless silence" (312), a "sensual reality that can never be transmuted into mind content" (312), and finally that "she must lightly, mindlessly connect with him" (311). Going back to the passage on the African process of dissolution, or ahead to Birkin's Pompadour letter decrying the attempt "to *lose* ourselves in some ultimate black sensation, mindless and infinite" (376), this positive mindlessness that Birkin and Ursula experience is difficult to justify. The central clue to the death of the African culture is its lack of speaking out. If the passage on Birkin and Ursula reaches toward a simple sensual experience that is at once mindless and silent—mindless and silent as the flowers—the reader can distinguish it from the deadly African experience only by explaining that it is prepared for through language, through the use of the outspoken mind. The "unspeakable communication" becomes valuable communication because it is sustained by the words that become silent, go underground if you will, for this short-lived moment. The speech that has fed and nurtured this silence, that comes before and after it, supports and sustains it. Words themselves speak of silence in the passage through a patterned series of apparent contradictions, almost in an attempt to cancel each other out and attain a special kind of silence, a silence everywhere underscored by words. Words continually seem to work at cross purposes, as in the following: "the knowledge which is death of knowledge," or "the reality of surety in not knowing" (311). There are passages built on apparently contradictory uses of words: "for her to take this knowledge of him as he had taken it of her," and "He knew her darkly, with the fullness of dark knowledge," and "she would know him," are temporarily contradicted by a phrase like "the reality of that which can never be known," finally boiling down to, in the last sentence of the chapter, "They hid away the remembrance and the knowledge" (311–13). "The being never to be revealed," the "unrevealed touch," and "her unrevealed nudity" all become, in the end, "known as a palpable revelation of living otherness" (311–12). The unknown becomes known, the unrevealed revealed.

There is a parallel movement of revelation, then: the nonverbal communication of the lovers reveals the unrevealable, while the verbal communication between narrator and reader translates the untranslatable, where words, because of the fine pitch of meaning they have acquired, are revelatory of all experience. Love and speech are in fact seen as parallel activities by that crucial passage on speech as labor: first Lawrence describes "love that is like sleep, like being born again," and then he proceeds to describe two other activities that are compared to the way "the infant in labour strives through the walls of the womb," adding to "to know" and "to give utterance" the further implicit apposition "to love" (WL, 178). The silent and mindless love of Birkin and Ursula in "Excurse" is in fact an enactment of what their speech has described. This is not to say that the speech itself is not a form of enactment as well, or that silent touch is merely a substitute for speech; the dialogues Birkin and Ursula engage in are themselves a version of star-equilibrium, a crucial step in the encounter with real otherness.

Later, in "Flitting," the reader discovers the only other major moment in the novel that apparently praises silence. The passages are connected at first through the description of Ursula as a flower: "Now, washed all clean by her tears, she was new and frail like a flower just unfolded, a flower so new, so tender" (WL, 360). The moment comes to speech with Birkin's articulation of three words, perhaps the most important words in the novel:

> "I love you," he whispered as he kissed her, and trembled with pure hope, like a man who is born again to a wonderful, lively hope far exceeding the bounds of death.
>
> She could not know how much it meant to him, how much he meant by the few words. Almost childish, she wanted proof, and statement, even over-statement, for everything seemed still uncertain, unfixed to her. (361)

It is the most tenderly ironic moment in the novel. Ursula has waited, sometimes with patience and sometimes without, for Birkin's pronouncement of these words, but now it is she who finds them inadequate and meaningless. Ursula has also waited for Birkin to move beyond words, for the kind of silent relationship enacted in "Excurse," but now she wants "statement, even over-statement" from the man she earlier accused of being a word-bag. The reader discovers a new silence, assailing rather than supporting the lovers' relationship, and far different from the silence of bliss in "Excurse": "There were infinite distances of silence between them" (361), distances Ursula wants filled up with words. Ursula may be new and frail as a flower, but there is a world of difference between the silent delight of flowers in each other and the silent and alienating distance between lovers here.

Oddly enough, the passage takes an unaccountable turn in praise of silence:

> He said, "Your nose is beautiful, your chin is adorable." But it sounded like lies, and she was disappointed, hurt. Even when he said, whispering with truth, "I love you, I love you," it was not the real truth. It was something beyond love, such a gladness of having surpassed oneself, of having transcended the old existence. How could he say "I" when he was something new, unknown, not himself at all? This I, this old formula of the age, was a dead letter. . . .
>
> When everything is silent, because there is nothing to answer, all is perfect and at one. Speech travels between the separate parts. But in the perfect One there is perfect silence of bliss. (*WL,* 361–62)

The reader may feel here, as Ursula often does, drawn along by mere word-force: "She was always frightened of words, because she knew that mere word-force could always make her believe what she did not believe" (428–29). The passage, in its entirety, goes in two directions, contradicting itself, offering a summary statement that seems false to the passage as a whole. There is in fact the kind of tension I mentioned as characteristic of Wordsworth's poetry between the discursive, apparently summary statement at the conclusion and the actual narrative event preceding it. The "infinite distances of silence between them" unexpectedly are transformed into "the perfect silence of bliss." Birkin's criticism of the word "love" now extends to the personal pronouns on either side of it. The contradictions within the passage aside, this notion of "the perfect One" is a contradiction of Birkin's impassioned plea for individuality and of his criticism of "meeting and mingling" (139). In fact, the difference between "I" and "you" is based on the very difference star-equilibrium is founded on, and the essential quality of language—of minute differences between even what is apparently "equal," or the same—is, Lawrence shows, the allowance of star-equilibrium.[13]

The thrust of the passage, then, suggests not language's inadequacy for star-equilibrium, but rather a new, and in fact the most extravagant theory of the novel so far. "The perfect One" of silence overturns the notion of star-equilibrium by rejecting the valuable presence of "real otherness." The testing of theory becomes for Lawrence a never-ending process. Rather than settle with a single idea, like star-equilibrium, he must always push each idea a step further to mark precisely at what point it becomes inauthentic. It is a notion of balance in the novel not unlike that which he imagines between individuals. Star-equilibrium, after all, is an idea of balance applicable to all individual things, and the truth of the novel as a genre depends on its truth to the balance of life: "Morality in the novel is the trembling instability of the balance. When the novelist puts his thumb in the scale, to pull down the balance to his own predilection, that is immorality" (PP, 528). Both the balance of star-equilibrium and of the novel are upset when we realize that "the perfect One" seems a hypothesis based on what Birkin earlier criticizes as this attempt "to absorb, or melt, or merge," this "fusion" (WL, 301), not to mention an ironic fulfillment of Ursula's earlier fear: "You want me to be your thing, never to criticize you or to have anything to say for myself. You want me to be a mere *thing* for you" (243). The state beyond personhood, beyond personal pronouns, is a state of thingness. The inhuman quality Birkin desires is coming dangerously close to mere insentience. The thingness of silence does not seem to be the perfect bliss of the flowers—or if it is, this now seems a dumb materiality (and a subtle foreshadowing of Gerald and Gudrun's fate!). In other words, the mindlessness of Birkin and Ursula's experience in "Excurse," carried to its extreme conclusion, becomes the silence of "the perfect One," a state not simply beyond egotism, but beyond all that is human. But Birkin's latest theory must be tested more fully, both against what I have already pointed out as true in the novel, and what there is to learn in the novel's remaining chapters.

Birkin has been at these crossroads before, in fact with the very word that stands between "I" and "you." With the word "love," he eventually realizes that he has two alternatives—to have the word "prescribed, tabooed from utterance," that is to "ban" it (WL, 122), or to redefine it. And the same two alternatives exist here. In fact, the inadequacies of language and of silence seem akin, and "Flitting," rather than simply proselytizing for silence, is one of the most ironic moments in the novel in its undervaluing of both silence and speech. Neither "I love you" nor the silence that exists before and after the words satisfies the lovers, and Ursula opts for "statement, even over-statement" (the general movement of the novel all along), while Birkin wants to leap into a new silence, "the perfect One." Through their talk, the word "love" takes on a fuller meaning, but the pronouns used with it also alter. There is, for example, Birkin's understanding that there is "a naked kind of isolation, an isolated me that does not meet and mingle" (137), "a final me" and "a final you" (137), "the you your common self denies," (139), or his discrimination— "It isn't even you, it is your mere female quality" (243). In these phrases, "me" and "you," through these qualifications, in every case do seem adequately to name the lovers, and not some egotistical entity, suggesting language's flexibility, its capacity to name what perhaps has never been named before. Birkin does the same in trying to identify his love for Gerald, where "a relationship in the ultimate of me and him" (355) echoes his general reassessment of the pronouns and his successful naming of the other. These elaborations may become laborious, and may lead Birkin to the brink of desiring a pure silence, but there is always a return to language. So, after all these discriminations and redefinitions, Birkin tells Ursula he wants a relationship where "there can be no calling to book" (138), and then, "Best to read the terms of the contract, before we sign" (139). The ultimate evidence of their love seems their talk: "Isn't it strange . . . how we always talk like this! I suppose we do love each other, in some way" (179).

What is particularly ironic about Birkin's desire to taboo "I" and "you" is that these pronouns, of all words, are the most flexible. Termed "shifters" by Jesperson and Jakobson, personal pronouns constitute a code about a message; in other words, they are a kind of metalanguage that is deeply instructive about how language works. Jakobson, criticizing the Humboldtian tradition, which sees personal pronouns as a primitive aspect of language, shows that they are one of its most complex features. He explains, for example, that pronouns are only lately acquired in a child's language, and they belong to the early losses in aphasia.[14] Winifred provides a clever instance of this first point. Not expressing any childishness on her part, but rather as motherly pampering and condescension to her pets, she uses personal pronouns in the following way: "Look at his portrait, darling, look at his portrait, that his mother has done of him" (*WL*, 228); "Let its mother stroke its fur then, darling, because it is so mysterious—" (236). Billy's quandary over whether or not Ursula will hear his prayers is genuinely deepened by her answer, "Whom you like," because it seems inexact in its identification of audience:

> "Who'll hear us say our prayers?" asked Billy anxiously.
> "Whom you like."
> "Won't you?"
> "Yes, I will."
> "Ursula?"
> "Well, Billy?"
> "Is it *whom* you like?"
> "That's it."
> "Well, what is *whom*?"
> "It's the accusative of who."

There was a moment's contemplative silence, then the confiding: "Is it?" (188)

The insecure child, in need of the comfort of his older sister, is temporarily excluded from communication with her as her answer points to a complicated set of linguistic rules he cannot participate in. She may be the audience for his childish prayers, but he is an inadequate audience for her communication. He remains anxious precisely because the pronoun does not refer to a single individual. And Lawrence comically suggests the wide range of meanings for these pronouns with Birkin's response to hearing Brangwen call Ursula "she": " 'She,' thought Birkin to himself, remembering his childhood's corrections, 'is the cat's mother' " (249).

Pronoun shifters, as these examples from the text suggest, are explained through a duplicity of meaning. For example, on the one hand, by a conventional rule, I consistently designates the addresser of the message. On the other hand, I designates the addresser only by being existentially related to this address; that is, I shifts in the normal course of any conversation to name two, or more, different speakers. Shifters then epitomize language's contextuality, changing their meaning depending on who speaks them and to whom they are spoken. They seem in this light to describe perfectly the delicate and fluctuating balance between individual and relationship that characterizes star-equilibrium. The perfect moment of silence in "Excurse," for example, is managed by the narrator through an eloquent balancing of personal pronouns: "For she was to him what he was to her, the immemorial magnificence of mystic, palpable, real otherness" (WL, 312). The copulas suggest an interchangeability of roles, while the difference between the pronouns "he" and "she" names the "otherness" of value. Here is the best proof that the pronounless "perfect One" is antithetical to star-equilibrium and the previous silence the lovers enjoyed. Even in Hermione's description of Birkin as "a neuter" (36—a linguistic definition of him that carries with it Lawrence's understanding that "only the machine is absolved from vital relation. It is based on the mystery of neuters," R, 235), Lawrence's sense of the personal pronoun's bestowal of personhood on the individual is opposed to a mechanical materiality.

Finally, if I have understood the talk between Birkin and Ursula all along, the pronouns "I" and "you" are its very symbols. In a passage that could be a brilliant gloss on the text in "Flitting," Ernst Cassirer explains the necessity of such pronouns:

This yearning for a direct contemplation in thought and feeling, which could dispense with all symbolism and mediation, rests on a self-deception. It would only be justified if the world of the "I" were a given, finished, and enduring entity, if words and images had no other task than to *transport* this givenness from one subject to another.

But the true relation is quite otherwise. In speech and art the individuals not only share what they already possess; it is only by virtue of this sharing process in speech and art that individuals have attained what they possess. This can be observed in any living and meaningful conversation. It is never simply a question of imparting information, but of statement and response.[15]

Nothing could be truer to Lawrence's meaning, for language in *Women in Love* is anything but the simple transfer of established meaning. The passage in "Flitting" on "the perfect One," then, can be seen as a double-barrelled criticism of star-equilibrium and verbal consciousness. It is itself a loss of all balance, a leap into a theory that cannot be supported, at least by what we have learned so far in the novel. In Lawrence's terms, verbal consciousness as "the passionate struggle into conscious being" stands in opposition to "those that fix themselves in the old idea" or, for that matter, in the old self. Those that do not speak out seem destined, then, to epitomize the dead letter, the old I, while verbal consciousness allows the birth of the new self by verbally redefining it. The danger the novel sees all along—of stasis, thingness, and materiality—hovers around all such decisions not to speak out, not to use "I" and "you."

Finally, what I have been attempting to identify as the most significant aspect of the narrative structure of *Women in Love*—the discriminations between narrator and characters—would be lost if Birkin's ban on personal pronouns took effect. Just as "I" and "you" can be fully understood only in terms of the person who speaks them, all the words of the novel can be understood only in so far as they are attached to a person. This is the farthest meaning of the contextuality of words, namely, that they do not simply exist neutrally in the context of all the book's other words, but that they need to be discriminated between on the basis of person. If, as I have shown, actions help define words, it is the actions of individuals that give individual meanings to words. And the important distinctions between two characters when they talk to each other, sounded in the difference between "I" and "you," are reproduced on the narrative level when an implicit, unstated "I" interacts with, but remains differentiated from, the "he" and "she" of the characters. Lawrence is a master of the use of these pronouns, and this use becomes part of a crucial fluctuation of authorial sympathy and distance. A chapter like "Sunday Evening," for example, is a meditation on death by Ursula in which her thoughts are described by Lawrence's playing all stops on the pronominal scale. The technical oddity of the meditation is how little Lawrence uses the conventional mode of reporting a character's thoughts. Far less than might be expected does he use quotations that mark out the clear space that is the character's own, not to merge or be confused with the narrator's; nor does he consistently report her thoughts with the simple use of "she," clearly demarcating the difference between character and narrator. What is personal, and limited to Ursula (that is, to "she"), waxes into the universal and the philosophical. The pronoun "one" designates this change by its universal reference, extending the validity of the thought to all men: "one might fulfill one's development to the end, must carry the adventure to its conclusion" (*WL,* 183). Such cavalier philosophizing is punctuated by questions that usually bring the philosophy home to the self, to a more personal base, but to one that nonetheless includes more than just Ursula. This philosophizing "one" turns to the somewhat more personal "we": "Why should we ask what comes after the experience, when the experience is still unknown to us?" This "we" is still a step beyond the conventional "she." Particularly when used in the form of a question, as in the above example, it suggests the idea of dialogue between an unstated "I" and an unnamed other, perhaps the narrator or reader. I can say at least that the narrator chooses to make no differentiation between himself and Ursula. In any case, "one" and "we" fluctuate as they seem to identify thoughts that are shared, that is, thoughts no longer located, or at least applicable, to a single self. This changes momentarily to "he," which, like "one," distances the narrative's base: "If a man can see the next step to be taken, why should he fear the next but one?" (184). The meditation fluctuates again between "one" and "she," finally turning to the use of quotation that allows the novelist to use "I," that is, Ursula clearly talking to herself. This modulates into the most important practice, the pronounless sentence—"To die is to move on with the invisible" or "Death is a great consummation" (183-84)—where there is a curious confusion in which the reader does not know whether this is Ursula's thought or the narrator's, or both.

The complicated display of personal pronouns shows how the single individual can be identified differently again and again: singly, or as part of an unspoken dialogue ("we," in which reader or narrator implicitly joins), or as part of a larger group ("he" standing for man). This is Lawrence's continual probing of the relationship of individual to group, of self to other. It is also a testing of the bounds of truth, an experiment in how flexible and inclusive it is and what generalizations it will stand. The reader is enlisted to discriminate between author and character, and to judge if such discriminations are necessary. Is this the narrator's thought, he asks, as well as, is this thought acceptable to me, am I part of "one," of "man," of "we," or do I baulk at these inclusions? So while there is an apparently growing sympathy between author and character in these passages, this often unsettles the reader who may be less willing to lose himself. Of course the act of reading, as in Forster, is just such a losing of oneself, but these kinds of passages are provoking in the apparent assumptions they make about the reader's selflessness and his willingness to agree with Ursula. All of this culminates in the passage's pronounless sentences, which seem to issue vatically from no source at all, general truths that, while they are the natural outcome of these pronominal fluctuations, are perhaps most provoking of all. Here is the technical importance of the passage, crucial to the structure of the entire novel. Here, where the pronouns drop out completely, we realize the delicate balance that holds the whole narrative together, namely, the distinction (sometimes growing dimmer and dimmer) between character and narrator. Clearly, the most puzzling sentences in this passage, or in any other in the novel, are those that possess no clear pronoun to identify whether the thought is the character's or the narrator's. It is the perfect example of language's becoming nearly uncontextual, that is, words still contain the context of the words that surround them, but are indistinctly related to an authorial source. In fact, the only way the words become fully meaningful is by the reader's sometimes frustrated attempt to identify their source, especially if it is not given.

Such passages become less an expression of the blissful silence of the perfect One—we feel unsettled, and rightly so, by assuming a perfect union between narrator and character, or reader and character, on any point—than of a puzzling and unnerving silence. They enact, in fact, an imperfect One, where the thought of the passage begins to flow indiscriminately outward: it is first simply Ursula's thought, then attributable to every man, but finally to no one. If there is confusion in speech, there is also confusion in silence, especially that silent lacuna that fails to identify the author of a thought. Finally, it is no accident that the passage on the silence of the perfect One functions in precisely the same way. "I" is used without quotation marks, almost as if the author himself is now speaking, or at least is merged (a linguistic "merging" like the meeting and merging in love Birkin earlier denounces) with his character, and the dictum, "in the perfect One there is perfect silence of bliss," has an ambiguous source that the reader struggles to identify. It is a pronominal silence that confuses, and the reader, like Ursula, wants statement, even overstatement, to clarify this important point.

"Excurse" and "Flitting," whether describing deliberate excursion or harum-scarum flitting, are important thresholds in the novel's developing meaning. One could express the novel's development, thus far, through a series of grammatical permutations, halfway houses in the novel's journey through meaning. There is, first, Birkin's plea to be allowed to use only the first person singular: "Why should every man decline the whole verb? First person singular is enough for me" (WL, 48). It is a declaration of selfhood, at whose farthest point all action disappears, and the verb becomes merely a copulative (a true declining of the verb) because all activity is subsumed under the divine presence of the pronominal self—"I, myself, who am myself" (96), he says, echoing God's statement of pure presence in Exodus 3.14. Second, with this relaxation in conjugation—Birkin is freed to say only "I" instead of "thou, he, we, you, they"—comes a similar relaxation, now in the use of the verb itself. When Birkin is ready to couple "I" with an active verb, that verb must be understood not to be a desiderative: "Love isn't a desideratum—it is an emotion you feel or you don't feel, according to circumstance" (122), with the grammatical thrust that love does not belong to that verbal category in which the verb is derived from, and ruled by, another verb ("I wish to love," or "I must love," for example). Third, with the discovery in Ursula of the proper object of his love, comes the complicated interplay of self and other, the "final me" and "final you," beyond the simple singularity of "I, myself, who am myself" (a state that, prolonged too long, becomes mere solipsism). This discourse between self and other, with shifting and balancing roles, occurs through dialogue; it brings the novel's meaning to the point of "Excurse," where, after all these changes in the lovers' discourse are realized, the "gift and give again" (312) of Birkin and Ursula's silent communication rests firmly upon the dialogue that has preceded it: both their dialogue and their silent touch are versions of star-equilibrium. But "Excurse," with its introduction of the possibility of this silent communication, sets the stage for "Flitting," and the dramatic break with the growing interaction between self and other, spoken and otherwise. The random, flitting movement of the chapter is epitomized in the two untypical moves Ursula and Birkin make on this point, the often reticent Ursula opting for statement, even overstatement, and the generally loquacious Birkin opting for the blissful silence of the perfect One. This latter hypothesis breaks with the novel's developing meaning because it describes a state beyond grammar, beyond personal pronouns, beyond language altogether. "Flitting" becomes the final plateau of meaning before the novel's ascent to ultimate meaning in the last three Alpine chapters. In fact, it really gives no meaning, only two alternatives, talk and silence. It allows the novel's final chapters, and another excursion, this time continental, to elaborate further, and in unexpected ways, on the relative merits of speech and silence. Here, in the last three chapters, there is an enactment of the silence of "the perfect One," and of silence in general, a last ironic series of enactments of theory.

The last three chapters of *Women in Love* are written with a gripping logic whose hold on the characters and on the stream of meaning in the novel is so tight and relentless that it is comparable to "the great cul-de-sac of snow and mountain peaks" (391) in the Alps themselves, a point beyond which no further excursion can be made. By this I mean that these chapters are a categorically precise climax to a lengthily elaborated idea, and they leave little choice but to conclude against the hypothesis of silence. The reader finds in them a reaffirmation of the need for words through a vital distinction between the silence of union and the mere silence of isolation. The frozen Alps are an ironic, even tragic, reversal of "the living silence" (311), and they warn of the fate of those who live without the struggle for verbal communication: "It was a silence and a sheer whiteness exhilarating to madness. But the perfect silence was most terrifying, isolating the soul, surrounding the heart with frozen air" (389). Again and again the central characteristic of the Alps is silence—a "snow-silence" (399), "the eternal, infinite silence" (400), the "deep and silent snow" (388), a "terrible waste of whiteness and silence" (390). Once more, then, a crucial word in the novel's developing vocabulary goes in two opposite directions, and doubles back to unsettle a previous hypothesis. Linguistically "the perfect silence of bliss" in "Flitting" depends solely on the climactic prepositional phrase to distinguish it from "the perfect silence" that, in the Alps, is maddening and terrifying. And this emphasis on silence even causes a shift in the basic process of the narrative; these three chapters proceed, unlike any other section, predominantly through indirect discourse, the power of words seeming to reside at last with only the author himself. Finally, if I have made it seem as if the vocabulary of silence gathers positively in "Excurse" and "Flitting" and negatively only in the Alps chapters, I have simplified the case. The necessity of speech, expressed in the way I have already suggested, is also emphasized throughout the novel by a consistent (except for "Excurse" and "Flitting") association of silence with emptiness, isolation, and death: silence again and again seems interposed between people, separating them, so that there are "blank silences" (315), or "spaces of silence" (265), or "dead stillness" (326), or the "infinite distances of silence between them" (361) of "Flitting" itself; "complete silence" is defined by "utter failure in mutual understanding" (250); the silence of Mr. Crich describes an excursion, not into a new life, but into death—"He only withdrew . . . into the silence" (222), "more and more a silence came over him" (205); and in the empty Brangwen house there is "a silence like death" (358). The Alps chapters, however, solidify this negative meaning of silence, making out of it a full-fledged criticism of the hypothesis of the blissful silence.

In these last chapters, "a dead silence" (*WL,* 422) smothers all, and
the Alps become at once a "cradle of silent snow" (390) for the infant
and a burial ground for the man. Infant and dead man merge (as in the
images of the stifled infant, used both by Mrs. Crich for her husband
and by Gudrun for Gerald) to describe the individual who has not broken
out of the womb, who has failed to bring forth the new idea and the
new passion, and who has been unable to give utterance. The novel's
evolutionary scheme, then, matches mastodon and ichthyosaur with the
man who is unable to "embody the utterance of the incomprehensible"
(52). In fact, Birkin's fear of the Alps appropriately combines a fear of
inarticulateness with an evolutionary regression: "Birkin said they would
all lose their faculties, and begin to utter themselves in cries and shrieks,
like some strange, unknown species of snow creatures" (412). The silent
flowers of "Excurse" are replaced by a frightening dumbness; Wordsworth's and Lawrence's romantic hypothesis about the language of
nature is turned into a nightmare, and in the novel's evolutionary
scheme man does seem headed, finally, backward to an extinction like
that suffered by the mastodon and ichthyosaur precisely because of his
failure to speak out. The stifled infant is a microscopic, and individual,
version of the race become extinct. The need to move forward, to break
a way through, now seems antithetical to the excurse into silence. In
fact, Gudrun deliberately desires the silence of nature, here the ultimate
and deadly silence of the Alps that devalues Birkin's simple choice (in
"Flitting") of the One over the different parts, of the perfect silence
over speech: "she would be a oneness with all, she would be herself the
eternal, infinite silence, the sleeping, timeless, frozen centre of the All"
(400). The oneness of "Flitting," its speechlessness, is subsumed here in
a frozen world outside life, in a sleep near death (like the sleep that becomes Gerald's death in the Alps). And Ursula, in a central image of the
novel, "felt the cold was slowly strangling her soul" (425). Her realization that "this utterly silent, frozen world of the mountain-tops was not
universal" (425) is a life-giving breath of air. She understands finally that
silence, for these two lovers whose relationship all along has been built
upon speech, is a strangulation of their most essential being, a final death
blow to everything they have meant to each other. In any case, as the
Alps show man's failure at embodying the utterance of the incomprehensible, in fact a frozen silence that will make him some day extinct,
they become an oblique reference to a classical tradition, the ancient
seat where the incomprehensible once was uttered. The Alps are "the
navel of the earth" (390, 391, 400), a reference to the ancient "Omphalos"
at Delphi.[16] But here they are an oracle gone silent, refusing to utter the
sacred language that connects man and God. Man's failure at communication seems to have lost him the ability to speak with God, and in the end

he learns, through God's silence, how "God can do without man" (470).

This idea of the ancient Omphalos gone silent is foreshadowed, curiously enough, through the character of Hermione. She is "speechless, like a stricken pythoness of the Greek oracle" (*WL*, 35), and when not speechless, there is an ironic break in her speech between that which is inspired and oracular on the one hand, and that which is empty on the other: "There was a break, as if the pythoness had uttered the oracle, and now the woman went on, in a rhapsody-wearied voice" (287). Hermione, representing at once two traditional sources of knowledge— the ancient Greek oracle and the Old Testament tree of knowledge—is, however, "a priestess without belief;" she is the pythoness struck dumb and "a leaf of the old great tree of knowledge that was withering now." Like the traditions that filter through the mists of Keats's Hyperion poems and point indistinctly to forgotten hieroglyphics, such references in Lawrence speak of traditions that were once alive and true. With a historicism in the vein of Keats, Lawrence writes that "the old great truths *had* been true." But in Lawrence these traditions are now the ones that must be broken through, and it is evident that Hermione works within these traditions even while she disbelieves: "Hermione, who brooded and brooded till she was exhausted with the ache of her effort at consciousness, spent and ashen in her body . . . gained so slowly and with such effort her final and barren conclusions of knowledge" (284). This "mother superior" (291) is herself "suckled in a creed outworn" (284) (she speaks soon after, without irony, of her mother's death), and this may account for her abortive brooding, which, in a fine pun, is a mental labor that hatches no significant idea, merely "barren conclusions." It is a brooding that has lost all connection with its sexual procreative functions, not to mention that divine brooding whose idea (or logos or Word) creates the world out of the dark abyss in Milton (*Paradise Lost*, 1.21; 7.234). Her brooding not only does not transform the abyss, it is the source of a veritable abyss within her. As a meaningless and purely mental work, though exhausting, it repays her not with riches, but makes of her who "believed in Mammon" "poor Hermione," all "spent" (*WL*, 284) in the attempt to earn a significant place in the marketplace of ideas.

While we never see Hermione at the Alps, descriptions of her early in the novel suggest the meaning of this landscape and, significantly, Gerald's place in it. In the first chapter the narrator says of Hermione, "there was a terrible void, a lack, a deficiency of being within her . . . she was established on the sand, built over a chasm . . . any common maid-servant . . . could fling her down this bottomless pit of insufficiency . . . she could never stop up the terrible gap of insufficiency" (*WL*, 11). The imagery of emptiness—void, chasm, pit, and gap—points to the failure of a divine kind of brooding, and is used to describe an inner quality of Hermione's that, as the novel proceeds, is externalized in the empty landscape of the Alps.

The same terminology and technique characterizes, far more consistently and meaningfully, Gerald, who, in an insightful marriage of inner and outer worlds, thinks to himself, "You seem to be clutching at the void—and at the same time you are the void yourself" (*WL*, 317). This sense of emptiness in Gerald is first, before it becomes externalized in the Alps, an ironic inversion of his work. He feels, for example, "as if the very middle of him were a vacuum, and outside were an awful tension" (225)—an adequate description of the mines themselves. After all, he himself declares he has no other life than his work, so he becomes not only the master of the mines, but the mines themselves, the product of his own work. Gerald's inner life, or lack of it, then, is appropriately and consistently described as something about to collapse, or to cave in: "The whole of everything, and yourself included, is just on the point of caving in, and you are just holding it up with your hands. Well, it's a situation that obviously can't continue. You can't stand holding the roof up with your hands forever" (317). Gerald, "agonistes" (427), is a collapsing Samson: destruction is dealt both to Milton's and Lawrence's Samson by a wily female (in fact, Gerald's description of the effect Gudrun has on him is close to Milton's account of Samson—love "blasts your soul's eye . . . and leaves you sightless," "your brain . . . charred as rags," 431) and both are, to use Milton's description of Samson, "overlabor'd" (*Paradise Lost*, 1327). In fact, again and again in Lawrence's essays Samson is the type (to use the language of the novel) who fails to break a way through, and instead is toppled in the midst of a ruined world, often of his own building: "For we shall be like Samson, buried among the ruins" (*R*, 98). If the death of Milton's Samson in the end is for some divine purpose, Gerald's destruction is precisely because he has no divine purpose. The structure he has built seems to topple him; the false temple to a false God—namely, himself—falls on the Deus ex Machina who (in the special case of Gerald) is unable to escape in divine flight beyond the tragic circumstances of earth, the earth he has ruined.

Lawrence describes the lack of divine purpose in Gerald in a traditional terminology: "His mind was very active. But it was like a bubble floating in the darkness. At any moment it might burst and leave him in chaos. He would not die. He knew that. He would go on living, but the meaning would have collapsed out of him, his divine reason would be gone" (*WL*, 225). Like Wordsworth, Lawrence uses Miltonic terms, and describes Gerald and his created world without "divine reason," without "mystic reason" (225), and therefore on the point of collapse. Bereft of the logos to order it, this world must return to its primitive origins, to a state before unity existed, to "chaos." Gerald, as god of the machine, in those mistranslations of the mystic words of creation (like "harmony"), has succeeded not in creating a world, but in creating a chaos that is his own undoing as well: "His eyes were blue and keen as ever, and as firm in their sockets. Yet he was not sure that they were not blue false bubbles that would burst in a moment and leave clear annihilation. He could see the darkness in them, as if they were only bubbles of darkness. He was afraid that one day he would break down and be a purely meaningless babble lapping round a darkness" (225). The "bubble," in a nice wordplay, turns into "a purely meaningless babble." Gerald the machine will "break down" and become the antithesis of the ordering logos, just a meaningless and mechanical babbling, the Babel that is an ironic representation of the dispersion from God. In a final ironic undercutting of the Wordsworthian tradition, for Gerald "life was a hollow shell all round him, roaring and clattering like the sound of the sea . . . and inside this hollow shell was all the darkness and fearful space of death" (314). Wordsworth's shell of poetic inspiration turns out to be hollow and meaningless, and what is left is just the skeleton of a life. Yeats's roaring inarticulate sea is here the "noise" that is at once the chaotic sea around Gerald and a perfect expression of the babbling man himself. The great dark void that circles at the center of his soul becomes, as the novel proceeds, the Alps. If the Alps are an oracle gone silent, they are also, to follow this latest association of images, the void that the absent divine reason or logos leaves untransformed. The Germanic Alps, the empty and silent burial ground of the Nordic races, where the characters feel "deserted in the waste of snow, like a dream" (389-90), are Lawrence's version of Wordsworth's dreamlike Arabian desert, or, for that matter, the Biblical and Miltonic abyss, or Keats's rocky Scottish highlands become the Titans' stony hell, or Yeats's heaven, itself become desolate and void, or Forster's primitive Indian caves.

The complicated confusion of internal and external landscape that all modern writers learned from Milton—when Satan realizes, "Myself am Hell" (*Paradise Lost*, 4.75), or when Samson understands, "Thou art become (O worst imprisonment!) / The Dungeon of thyself" (154-55)—becomes in Lawrence, finally, a description of pure externality: Gerald becomes the hollow shell, and the human, because without inner life, becomes the merely material. If Gerald can break down like the machines he uses, if he can collapse and cave in like the mines he builds, then in the end he is like the cold inert matter he sets his will against. Birkin notices in the dead body of Gerald, for example, a "last terrible look of cold, mute Matter" (*WL*, 472). It is difficult for Birkin to realize because he wanted to exchange with Gerald the gift of words, but Gerald (in the midst of the passage on his babbling collapse) forsakes words: "words were futilities. He had to keep himself in reckoning with the world of work and material life" (225). The final image of Gerald as "mute Matter" is particularly ironic because Gerald's whole enterprise takes steam from his distinction between man and Matter: "for was not mankind mystically contradistinguished against inanimate Matter, was not the history of mankind just the history of the conquest of the one by the other?" (221). Moreover, this Matter with a capital M (the "Matter he had to subjugate;" see 216, 220, 221) is like the Miltonic Matter that the Word transforms—"Thus God the Heav'n created, thus the Earth, / Matter unformed and void" (*Paradise Lost*, 7.232-33). The hollow shell without inspiring words, then, prefigures this "mute Matter," and these two words become "mute material" (*WL*, 471), repeated three times on a single page, a phonetic articulation (in the manner of "mimes" and "Minette") of the juncture of silence and matter. As "the life breath was frozen into a block of ice beneath the *silent nostrils*" (468-69, emphasis mine), it is evident that speech is connected to the very lifebreath that we draw and that makes us alive.

In a startling connection to Keats's stony Titans, Gerald's muteness is prefigured through the mythic representation of Gudrun as "a vivid Medusa" (*WL*, 440), turning Gerald to stoniness and muteness. The sculptress works her last work of art in Gerald, who becomes "like a statue" (459), with "the face of a statue" (441), worked by her hands. This image of the stone also plays a part in the picture of Gerald as Samson: "Gerald is so limited, there is a dead end to him. He would grind on at the old mills for ever. And really, there is no corn between the millstones any more. They grind on and on, when there is nothing to grind— saying the same things, believing the same things, acting the same things" (455). Gerald, like Milton's Samson at the mill and Keats's Titans, epitomizes the meaningless labor that turns out to be no movement, no production, divorced at once from his own "ethics of productivity" (49) and Birkin's "productive happiness" (245). If he thinks his work will reproduce, in a vision of linguistic labor, "so many wagons, *bearing* his initial" (214, emphasis added), we know work and words are often at odds. Likewise, if gleefully "at last he saw his own name written on the wall" (214), it may be the writing Daniel once interpreted, which told of a powerful despot destroyed, with words used against the work of the tyrant-master. (Gudrun, in fact, does read the Old Testament words on the wall: "It was as if she had seen some new *Mene! Mene!* upon the wall," 403.)

That eternal repetition that says and does nothing now becomes no motion at all, certainly not the "productive spinning" (*WL*, 220) Gerald imagines at the heart of his industry. Rather, it becomes a circularity that whirls him, as if in the game children play, into an unmoving statue. The picture of Gerald as a "dead end" who would "grind on" with no result surely is a description of Gerald and Gudrun's sexual relationship, now reduced to mere work. Birkin, telling Gerald to end the relationship, warns him not to "work on an old wound," but Gerald seems grotesquely exhilarated by the very destructiveness of this new kind of work, sexual labor. He says, "It blasts your soul's eye" (both an ecstatic exclamation of excitement and a description of a mechanical destructiveness particularly appropriate to the master of the mines), "you're shrivelled as if struck by electricity," "every stroke and bit cuts hot" (where "stroke" and "bit" denote mechanical parts and functions as well as the lovers' caresses, 430–31). Finally, that their sexual relationship is work, and not labor in the creative sense, becomes clear not only through Gudrun's declaration that Gerald's grinding produces no corn, but in her mad declaration that Gerald himself is an infant, one that she would gladly stifle and bury. It is another grotesque version of producing oneself: Gerald the lover fathers only himself, an "infant crying in the night" (457), one that his mistress-mother (like his real mother before her) threatens with suffocation.

Gudrun and Gerald are, to use Birkin's phrase, perfect snow creatures who inhabit this landscape, and their few words approximate the "cries and shrieks" (*WL,* 412) Birkin imagines in such creatures. In these final chapters Gerald and Gudrun move between stifled, inarticulate words and stony silence, in a landscape that bears at once the signs of sculptress and industrial magnate: the lovers seem stranded "in a valley of pure concrete heaven" lost amid "banks of snow" (388). The single most important dialogue between them ironically repeats the many arguments over love that precede Birkin and Ursula's marriage. For Gerald and Gudrun, however, it is a retrospective look back at what has been wanting, a dialogue held too late and almost forced out of its two victims. Gudrun questions Gerald on how much he loves her, and Gerald pleads, "I don't know what you mean by the word 'love' " (433). In the end, after Gudrun forces Gerald to admit he has never loved her, we read:

> "Say you love me," she pleaded. "Say you will love me for ever—won't you—won't you?"
>
> But it was her voice only that coaxed him. Her senses were entirely apart from him, cold and destructive of him. It was her overbearing *will* that insisted.
>
> "Won't you say you'll love me always?" she coaxed. "Say it, even if it isn't true—say it Gerald, do."
>
> "I will love you always," he repeated, in real agony, forcing the words out. (434)

The distinction between her "voice" and her "senses" is telling; it is the ultimate failure of verbal consciousness, where language is simply a deliberate act of will, an act of aggression committed against the enemy, neither the union of one's thoughts and passions, nor the reaching out to the other person in love. She evidently responds in the same way: "only her will was set for him to speak to her" (435). That Gudrun can beg for lies from Gerald, and that Gerald can give them, is a description of what words have been to them all along. These lovers, who want hate in the name of love, are the perfect example of those liars Birkin earlier cries down.

Actually, such dialogues become rare in the Alps, and dialogue turns to monologue as the characters' words go unanswered and even unheard: " 'I shall always love you,' he said, looking at her. But she did not hear him. She lay, looking at him as at something she could never understand, never. . . . But she only lay silent and childlike and remote" (WL, 392). It is interesting that silence here suggests a regressive childishness. Lawrence, unlike Wordsworth, has no myth of the transcendent innocence of childhood,[17] and instead associates the child with what he calls a reduction backward, perhaps another ironic note on the "silent delight of flowers" and the evolutionary regression—what he terms "devolution" (196)—such an image begins to suggest. It is in this sense that the Alps are indeed a perfect cradle, not only for Gerald, who, in death, is fetally "curled up as if for sleep" (468), but also for Gudrun, who resents Gerald's infantile need for sleep because she herself wants "this perfect enfolded sleep" (457). In "The Crown" Lawrence explains childishness as a regression that modern man, in pursuit of progress, ironically falls prey to: "With all our talk of advance, progress, we are all the time working backwards . . . to the *corruptive* state of childishness" (notice how "working" is not progress, but regression, R, 60). In this essay he associates this childishness with "sentimentality," and the same association is made through Gudrun and Loerke: "they took a sentimental, childish delight in the achieved perfections of the past" (WL, 444). Loerke is also "like a child" (395), with a "boyish figure" (395), and is called by Gerald "that little brat" (418). He is a "mud-child" (417), an image that combines the child with Birkin's terminology, in the Pompadour letter, of "flowers of mud" as a sign of "the great retrogression, the reducing back" (375). In any case, these proposals and rehearsals of "I love you" are mock ceremonies that repeat Birkin and Ursula's meaningful dialogues, with one partner either lying or not hearing.

Finally, all words turn to silence. If the Alps themselves seem a silent covering that prevents all communication, the very room Gerald and Gudrun share seems to put a ban on conversation. They are "in a bare, smallish, close-shut room," which Gudrun appropriately says is "like being inside a nut," the image of enclosure used earlier to describe Hermione's mental bondage. Lawrence brilliantly combines, in a pun, this sense of restraint with their silence through a verb and adverb opposing the foreword's "speak out": "Here they were shut up together in this cell of golden-coloured wood" (*WL*, 390). It is a phrase that is repeated in the description of Gudrun after the tragedy of Gerald's death, and one that is connected there with several images of her silence in the face of the tragedy: "When they brought the body home the next morning, Gudrun was shut up in her room" (466). Birkin's questions to Gudrun intuitively circle around the idea of speech:

> "Loerke says that Gerald came to you when you were sitting on the sledge at the bottom of the Rudelbahn, that you had words, and Gerald walked away. What were the words about . . . ?"
> Gudrun looked up at him, white, childlike, mute with trouble. "There weren't even any words," she said. (468)

In the attempted strangulation, and in the association of childlike again with "mute" (the same word used to describe Gerald, in connection with "matter"), we feel the full force of Gerald and Gudrun's tragedy: "There weren't even any words." The tragedy has three linguistic signs: first, the dialogue of lies; second, the monologues in which one person hears not; and finally and most dramatically, interior monologues in which no words are spoken aloud to the other person. Example after example suggests how Gerald and Gudrun fail to fulfill the foreword's requirement to speak out:

> And to herself she was saying (405)
> she screamed in silence to herself (406)
> She leaned over Gerald and said in her heart (409)
> she repeated to herself (435)
> she said to herself (436)
> he said to himself (436)
> he asked himself (436)
> He was only talking to himself, saying (452)
> So he talked to himself (453)
> To himself he was saying (453)
> she said to herself (454)

These speeches to the self are the ultimate undermining of the basic grammatical form that Birkin, in a hasty longing after silence, wants to leave behind: "I love you" establishes communication between self and other, between subject and direct object, while the form "he said to himself / she said to herself" joins subject and object in what Lawrence elsewhere calls "a monologue of self-analysis" (*R*, 60)—the self not making contact with anything beyond itself. It is the grammatical sign for the kind of narcissism Freud found in children, where the sexual instinct in childhood is without an object; it accords perfectly with the images of

Gerald and Gudrun as children, and deepens the sense of their regression. Their movement away from speech, away from the other, is a movement toward a narcissistic infancy. This grammatical form is an explanation of that curious identity between "craftsman" and "creature" (*WL*, 443): the world is shrunk through a pure solipsism, and one becomes at once the activator and the object of activity. It is appropriate, in this sense, that Gudrun does not play the simple Medusa to Gerald's stoniness, but is seen by her new companion in precisely the same terms when she is complimented by Loerke "as he would say a piece of sculpture was remarkable" (449). We know about Gudrun that "her pity was as cold as stone" (434), becoming at last the artwork of her own hands. Both Gerald and Gudrun, then, are associated with the matter and stone that are supposed to be merely the objects of their work. Finally the evolutionary reductionism, the "devolution" that the novel describes, associates loss of speech with the reduction backward. If the tortured dialogues and monologues suggest a regression back to some kind of primitive snow creature, or to the muteness of childhood, the silence of the interior monologue leads, it would seem, to a stony materiality from which all signs of life, human and otherwise, have departed.

In the silence of the Alps a voice rings out: it is Loerke's. His verbal accomplishments are a last turn in the novel's developing logic. Formally, Loerke's talk teases us into comparisons with the novel's hypothesis of verbal consciousness. His use of language, "full of odd, fantastic expression, of double meanings, of evasions, of suggestive vagueness" (*WL*, 445), surely matches at least at certain points Birkin's, and even the narrator's, verbal techniques. Loerke locates his most essential being within language, and even echoes with Gudrun the I-you foundation of Birkin and Ursula's talk: " 'Do not ask me to be strong and handsome, then. But it is the *me*'—he put his fingers to his mouth oddly—'it is the *me* that is looking for a mistress, and my *me* is waiting for the *thee* of the mistress, for the match to my particular intelligence' " (450-51). Furthermore, the earlier disassociation of Gudrun's "voice" and "senses," which seemed to contradict the hypothesis that verbal consciousness could link mind and body, seems reestablished in Loerke and Gudrun's talk: "She took a peculiar delight in this conversation. It was a real physical pleasure to her to make this thread of conversation out of the different-coloured strands of three languages" (445).

Backed into a corner where the discriminations grow subtler and finer, the reader now distinguishes not simply between talk and silence, or between two kinds of silence, but between two kinds of talk. The physical pleasure Gudrun derives from conversation is not language's bridge between the traditional dualism of mind and body, but a substitute for bodily pleasure. Loerke and Gudrun cavalierly use language to dismiss, in fact, the central concern of the novel, and theirs is a discourse that is not, at the same time, intercourse: "Pah—l'amour. I detest it. L'amour, l'amore, die Liebe—I detest it in every language. Women and love, there is no greater tedium" (*WL,* 450). Loerke's voice is not the expression of a full-bodied man, not the articulation that joins the new idea and the new passion: "His body was slight and unformed, like a boy's, but his voice was mature, sardonic, its movement had the flexibility of essential energy, and of a mocking penetrating understanding" (396). And the strands of language that Gudrun seems to weave into a colorful pattern—almost as if the sculptress is as adept in the art of weaving, "she skillfully wove herself to her end" (445), a dying generation in which the artist once again seems his own deadly product—describe language as cover, as mask. Like her bold stockings, language is a garment, a mask, an elegant gesture that defines Gudrun against the world and keeps it at arms' (and legs') distance. It is the end of the tradition's long flirtation with language as the gauzy garment through which we catch glimpses of the divine thought or idea, and works perfectly with Lawrence's understanding of exposure: Gudrun's ultimate refusal to give herself away, and her delight in exposing others, has its corollary in her dressy words.

Gudrun uses language to finish communication, not to start it. Her "pronouncements" (*WL,* 15) are verdicts handed down from the artist who sees through the wrong end of the opera glasses: "She saw each one as a complete figure, like a character in a book, or a subject in a picture, or a marionette in a theatre, a finished creation. . . . She knew them, they were finished, sealed and stamped and finished with, for her" (8). This is a criticism of artistic vision, the artist's reduction of the life around her into the simplicities of fiction, the parasitic tendency to feed on life simply to transform it into the stuff of art. Also, Gudrun seems to be an aloof god who sees her creation and, without judging it good, judges it finished. Here Gerald's pun about Gudrun's drawing the rabbit is right on target—"Draw him and quarter him and dish him up" (230). Gudrun's pronouncements epitomize the "dead letter" that, according to Birkin, is humanity; her understanding of someone does not invite the free flow of vital communication and exchange, but becomes a "sealed" and "stamped" dead letter, sent without direction and without expectation of response. With an irony that cuts deep, Gudrun fades out of the reader's ken at the end of the novel when we learn, finally, the consequences of the dead letter: "Gudrun went to Dresden. She wrote no particulars of herself" (472). In the same way her new companion, Loerke, seems "isolated in his own complete envelope" (442), epitomizing how their discourse becomes a kind of "correspondence" (439)—letters of wit and double meaning, requiring no answer, gratuitous verbal displays in the midst of the Alpine silence. The first glimpse of Loerke, appropriately, is during his recitation of a Cologne dialect. It is a "monologue," and its effects are strangely silencing, as his audience is "strangled in ultimate, silent spasms of laughter" (396). Already Loerke's words are addressed to an audience that is supposed to make no articulate answer, and the effect of the words combines the novel's association of strangulation and speechlessness—words in the employ of silence. The monologue is the ultimate form of what Birkin earlier accuses himself of, Hamletizing, and the letters are monologues written rather than spoken.

Gudrun and Loerke are the deadly doubles of Ursula and Birkin, even of the narrator, devaluing at every turn the meaning the novel has slowly accorded to language. This new argument is similar to what I have called the skeptical underthought about language in the Hyperions. In *Women in Love* the position of this argument is, of course, particularly strategic. Like the pledges of Keats and Yeats to incompleteness, here in Lawrence the undercutting of language's value at the conclusion of the work seems a final way out of theory, out of easy solution, out of the artistic lie. That Lawrence has taken pains to tease us into analogies, that he deliberately expects us even for a moment to confuse Loerke and Gudrun's talk with the verbal consciousness of Birkin and Ursula, suggests the ironic function of this pattern. And finally, that it is the two artists of the novel who use this false language is the clearest indication that in some sense Gudrun and Loerke are a frightening look in the mirror, that they reflect the danger to which the writer in particular may succumb.

It is the artist in Gudrun and Loerke that Lawrence aims his irony at, especially in a group of descriptions, shot through with apparent contradictions, that seem determined to place these two on the great chain of being or on the evolutionary scale the novel develops. Gudrun and Loerke (like Gerald) play God: "They played with the past, and with the great figures of the past, a sort of little game of chess, or marionettes, all to please themselves. They had all the great men for their marionettes, and they two were the God of the show, working it all" (*WL*, 444). It is at once Lawrence's criticism of the Protestant work ethic, with God as the divine worker whom Gudrun and Loerke must match, and of romanticism's model of the artist as god. As in everything with these two, work infects even its opposite. Loerke explains earlier how, at the fair in his frieze (and, I could add, in the Alpine skiing, tobogganing, sleighing, and skating the couples engage in), there is simply "serving a machine, or enjoying the motion of a machine" (415). Here Loerke and Gudrun's play, their "little game," is just such a version of work. In fact, their whole correspondence—that is, every aspect of a relationship that seems verbally directed—is described as such a game:

> Their whole correspondence was in a strange, barely comprehensible
> suggestivity, they kindled themselves at the subtle lust of the
> Egyptians or the Mexicans. The whole game was one of subtle inter-
> suggestivity, and they wanted to keep it on the plane of suggestion.
> From their verbal and physical nuances they got the highest satisfac-
> tion in the nerves, from a queer interchange of half-suggested ideas,
> looks, expressions and gestures, which were quite intolerable,
> though incomprehensible, to Gerald. He had no terms in which to
> think of their commerce, his terms were much too gross. (439)

Gudrun and Loerke's correspondence, then, is a form of "commerce,"
one too subtle (in its terminology) even for the industrial magnate. And
at the heart of all their play is the game of language: they are always
"laughing in an endless sequence of quips and jests and polyglot fancies.
The fancies were the reality to both of them, they were both so happy,
tossing about the little coloured balls of verbal humour and whimsicality.
Their natures seemed to sparkle in full interplay, they were enjoying a
pure game. And they wanted to keep it on the level of a game, their relationship: *such* a fine game" (*WL,* 460). Language as game—a traditional
association in modern linguistics, found, for example, in Saussure and
Wittgenstein—suggests that for all its evasions and suggestivity, for all its
complicated double meanings, what Loerke and Gudrun's language
amounts to is an eccentric game whose rules are mastered by them, and
not by Gerald. In this sense the disagreement between Loerke and Gerald
is "a contest of words" (440). These games have a consistent "ground-
work" (445) that is little more than work, making them epitomize the
laborious game described earlier in the novel: "how known it all was,
like a game with the figures set out, the same figures, the Queen of chess,
the knights, the pawns, the same now as they were hundreds of years ago,
the same figures moving round in one of the innumerable permutations
that make up the game. But the game is known, its going on is like a
madness, it is so exhausted" (92). The novel, with its prolific multiplica-
tion of meanings, suggests another meaning for game in Birkin's vision of
creative evolution: "If humanity ran into a cul-de-sac, and expended itself,
the timeless creative mystery would bring forth some other being, finer,
more wonderful, some new, more lovely race, to carry on the embodiment
of creation. The game was never up. The mystery of creation was fathom-
less, infallible, inexhaustible" (470). Birkin's final hypothesis is a translation of Oceanus's first-in-beauty, first-in-might speech in "Hyperion." Its
language—"expended," "inexhaustible" (contradicting the "exhausted"
chess game)—suggests a human world "expending itself" the way
Hermione is "spent," as opposed to a labor that never tires of creation,

implicit in Birkin's earlier hope that humanity will once again find that creative language able to embody the incomprehensible.

Gudrun and Loerke may play God, but in their perfect representation of mankind's predicament, whether it is humanity as a dead letter or as the mechanical player of a game of circular permutations, they begin to epitomize the quality that dooms humanity to something less than human. If they seem to speak a complicated language that makes them seem like a replacement of the stricken pythoness (that is, if not gods themselves, interpreters of the gods), their language really is the opposite of the prophetic oracle's; it is in fact a glorification of the ancient Babel that isolates man from man and race from race. The crucial clue to Lawrence's definition of work—that it is repetitive rather than progressive—characterizes the language play of Loerke and Gudrun: "Apart from these stories [of the destruction of the world by a ridiculous catastrophe of man's invention], they never talked of the future" (*WL*, 445); "They praised the bygone things, they took a sentimental, childish delight in the achievements of the past" (444). Finally, the exclusive orientation of their language to the past and its resistance to change ("they preferred to stay in the eighteenth and the nineteenth centuries," 445) suggest a literal regression in time, down the chain of being. Their games, then, are another sign of their childishness. In this light Loerke is not so much the god of creation as one of its creatures: "She [Gudrun] too was fascinated by him, fascinated, as if some strange creature, a rabbit or a bat, or a brown-seal, had begun to talk to her" (417). There is no clearer statement of how far language can fall short of bridging body and mind. Loerke's words, for all their sophistication, seem to activate only a half-man. Among the menagerie he represents is the "magpie" (412), a noisy and mischievous bird that, like the parrot, mimics and confuses the speech of others. His is a doubly regressive speech, then. By parroting words already spoken, he creates an ironic "new" vocabulary that is barely comprehensible and ultimately confused. This mimicry (which his monologue consists of) may be the ultimate fate of all words; Halliday's comical intoning of Birkin's words, which stands for the hostile audience's reception of every new vocabulary, is an example.

Loerke is a grotesque version, to use the words Lawrence often paraphrases, of the Word made flesh—the Word, God's instrument, stuck in the body of a lower creature. Words and nothing more are as much a regression as the material silence of Gerald's physical perfection. It is in this sense that Gudrun recognizes in Loerke "the creature, the final craftsman" (*WL*, 443), and in which the apparent contradictions describing his evolutionary position come to rest. He is a god who produces only himself. In fact, he is a god whose creation has gone awry, producing in himself that which it grotesquely delights in admiring. If he admires "a confusion in nature" (439), and like Gudrun sees "the world as distorted, horrific" (442), he is the best representative of these confusions and distortions, a god who finally creates himself in the distorted world's image —the rabbit or bat that speaks, the insect sealed in an envelope of words.

Lawrence faces a final set of alternatives—to lie or to remain silent. He translates the terms of painting into literature, and vice versa: the blank is a visual image in the painting of Cézanne that begins to stand not merely for emptiness, but for silence, a deliberate silence the artist chooses. Lawrence's understanding of Cézanne reveals a drama that can be extended to most great artists, and is certainly a covert reading of his own struggle as a writer; he names it the fight with the cliché. In *Women in Love* this fight is well-known. The old language must be broken through, but the new language is always on the verge of becoming sedimented, of becoming cliché. The Lawrence we inherited after his death (and in some corners he is still alive)—not too different from the Pompadour crowd's portrait of him—was nothing but cliché, a string of prophetic utterances from a flatulent guru. Lawrence knows, like Cézanne, that he is always in danger of the cliché, whether his audience reduces him to it or he falls prey to its easy temptation himself. The Pompadour letter suggests both: we are suddenly put in the position of a hostile audience, and we hear excerpts, "choice bits," words and phrases out of context; they ring with a sense of absurd foolishness as they are read in a mocking tone ("he read in the sing-song, slow, distinct voice of a clergyman reading the Scriptures," *WL,* 374) amidst hiccups and giggles. The words seem as traitorous as the false friends who read and listen to them. They exist as a small text—a letter, really Birkin's "dead letter" now literally before our eyes—that is unable to tell with complexity and completeness what the lengthy novel has told. The words are divorced from action, even from the personality and voice that originated them. They seem like words spoken in a hostile vacuum to an audience who fails to understand them; the difficult vocabulary, the new vocabulary, is like a foreign language, always slightly ridiculous to the audience of another tongue. These words, then, have at once the ring of the cliché and the foreignness of phrases of another language. They have been heard over and over until they seem like clichés, and are in this letter proselytizing like clichés, but they still appear strange to the Halliday group because they are not fully comprehended. This letter stands on the brink of the novel's conclusion; it is almost an experiment in the way language becomes sedimented, a final reduction, before the startling silence of the Alps, of the novel's complex language and meaning into a single, short, metaphysical text. Lawrence knew, I think, that his audience would make of *Women in Love* something like the Pompadour letter, that is, they would reduce it to choice bits, losing the crucial senses of contextuality that I have noted all along, and make it the butt of laughter. It is the artist giving himself away flagrantly, cynically (for he knows he will be taken in any case).

Lawrence's remarks on Cézanne, however, suggest the artist's way out, and one of the strategies against subterfuge Lawrence himself uses at the end of *Women in Love:* "Then again, in the pictures he seems to be saying: Landscape is not like this and not like this and not like this and not . . . etc.—and every *not* is a little blank space in the canvas, defined by the remains of an assertion. Sometimes Cézanne builds up a landscape essentially out of omissions. He put fringes on the complicated vacuum of the cliché, so to speak, and offers us that. It is interesting in a *repudiative* fashion, but it is not the new thing" (*PP,* 581). This is of course a description of the action-reaction syndrome in *Women in Love:* the painter unable to produce a new landscape, or the writer unable to produce a new vocabulary, falls back upon blankness, with the consolation that at least he has not produced the cliché. It is the reason behind Lawrence's hesitation to create a new vocabulary, and stands behind what I have called the missing kernel word in so much of his prose. "The blank is vacuum, which was Cézanne's last word against the cliché. It is a vacuum, and the edges are there to assert the vacuity" (581). Keats and Lawrence are like Cézanne in this: the skeptical undertone that rumbles language's failure finally is represented in the great empty places of their works—the rocky and vacant place of the fallen gods, and the Alps of the fallen god of the machine—and even in these writers' open-ended endings. The literal fragmentariness of Keats's poems amounts to approximately the same thing in *Women in Love,* a non-ending: I mean for us to see literally at the end of the novel a blank, a white space of emptiness and silence, like the white wall of the Alps, like an unpainted spot in Cézanne's canvas, like the missing kernel word suddenly materializing as a glaring emptiness on the page otherwise filled. The blank white page at the end of Lawrence's novel seems to eat into Birkin and Ursula's conversation, and just as Birkin is on the threshold of the full articulation of a new idea, what Ursula christens "a theory, a perversity" (*WL,* 437), it is aborted by the white space that rushes in to silence the lovers, a white space like the deadly cradle that puts Gerald to sleep.

The novel's final conversation, in fact, seems to precipitate the void, a chasm which cannot be crossed. In this way it is like the conversation that opens the novel, in which Gudrun and Ursula, locked in a terminology unable to express their feelings, try to discuss marriage. This opening conversation proceeds as a series of questions (Gudrun) and answers (Ursula), but the answers become further questions precisely because Ursula does not understand Gudrun's terms. Already we are in the midst of troubled meanings, and definitions for "marriage" and "experience" are slow in coming. There is a "blank pause" (*WL,* 3) in the conversation, a momentary blank in their speech that anticipates its close: "and the conversation was really at an end. The sisters found themselves confronted by a void, a terrifying chasm, as if they had looked over the edge" (4). The sisters are "working and talking" (an association that becomes ironic as the novel proceeds), and the tasks they perform—sewing and drawing—are conventional, if unconscious, attempts at filling the void. The blank pause that interrupts their talk is like the blank each is filling, whether with thread, or crayon, or talk; it is all a working "embroidery" (1) to hide the abyss that inevitably stares at them from just behind their work and talk. This is the void pictured at the end of the novel, both in the Alps and in the blankness of the last page.

While in each case the void frustrates the characters' attempts at communication, it becomes a deliberate strategy for Lawrence: it is the final safeguard against subterfuge, mere embroidery, and countless new theories. This is what he terms in Cézanne the assertion of vacuity. In *Women in Love* Birkin puts it this way: "There wouldn't have to be any truth, if there weren't any lies. Then one needn't assert anything—" (238). To assert nothing is finally not to be betrayed into the perilous seas of truth and falsehood. When the novelist does choose the silence he obviously finds alluring in "Excurse," he comes up with the blank silence at the end of the novel. This is no mythic silence, no plenitude of meaning; it is an escape from meaning, an uncommunicative silence that teases us into a desire for more words, for more knowledge about Birkin and Ursula. In perhaps the most outrageous doubling of all, we see that work ends in nothing, whether it be the chaotic nothing Gudrun, Loerke, and Gerald produce or the simple nothingness that Lawrence chooses in the end. "You can't make art out of nothingness. *Ex nihil nihil fit!*" (*PP,* 763). Lawrence compares the virgin to the blank page— "virginity, like a blank white sheet on which nothing is written" (*SLC,* 85)—and we begin to see that for Lawrence, as for Keats (who looked upon fine phrases like a lover, and trod the path of love and poesy in "Endymion"), no matter how many times we defile the virgin page with our pen(is),[18] it shows up shortly again blank and chaste as ever. In fact, writing may be more like kissing (and Lawrence draws this analogy) than like intercourse: it is an outlet for one's passion, but it may produce nothing. Or, the *logos spermatikos*[19] may be infertile, the labor only work—the work, in fact, of art. Birkin complains to Ursula, "one seems always to be bumping one's nose against a blank wall ahead" (*WL,* 117), an image that, with Lawrence's own Freudian notion of erotic undermeanings in mind, describes both the lover's and the writer's frustrations. For the writer it is, as well, a partial comfort: simple vacuity is always his first and last protection against the lie. Only nothing seems assertable in the end.

9 EPILOGUE

THE WORD

Wordsworth, in the last book of *The Prelude,* explains in divine fashion, "I rose / As if on wings, and saw beneath me stretched / Vast prospect of the world which I had been / And was" (14.379–82). It is a world granted only to those divine minds who win, mirrorlike, a world in which "the consciousness / Of Whom they are [is] habitually infused / Through every image and through every thought" (14.114–16). Lawrence, in the same autobiographical vein, reacts with horror to a world that is at the same time himself:

> because I was the author and the result
> I was the God and the creation at once;
> creator, I looked at my creation;
> created, I looked at myself, the creator:
> it was a maniacal horror in the end.
>
> (*C,* 1, 258)

Loerke, Gudrun, and Gerald all epitomize this confusion of craftsman and creature. Lawrence criticizes the romantic model of the artist as God until it becomes just another picture of the worker, producing and reproducing himself: "It is an inherent passion, this will to work, it is a craving to produce, to create, to be as God. Man turns his back on the unknown, on that which is yet to be, he turns his face towards that which has been and he sees, he rediscovers, he becomes again that which has been before" (*PP,* 429). Such a God fails at genuine creation, however, and Loerke seems to betray this failure unwittingly in his description of art's relation to nothing: "It is a work of art, it is a picture of nothing, of absolutely nothing. It has nothing to do with anything but itself" (*WL,* 421). The god-artist who seems to aim at creation comes up with the opposite, nothing (like Gerald's chaos or the end Gudrun weaves herself to). In the artwork's exclusive self-reflexiveness is that loss of object (or other) that was in the grammatical constructions at the heart of Gerald and Gudrun's relationship; as in the poem above, it is God's creation "in the end" (not in the beginning), on the verge of annihilation, nothingness. In this way the common phrase "work of art" begins to ring with new meanings. Loerke, of course, is insistent in his praise of work: "the acts of labour are extremely, maddeningly beautiful" (414). Lawrence's novel ends with the realization that the work of art can lapse into mere mechanicalness, another warning Lawrence provides for himself, and a meaning Wordsworth (calling his world in the end "a Work that shall endure," *P*, 14.311) never imagined for the work of art. It is, for Lawrence, a nightmare vision, a version of the Coleridgean imagination become the Marxist goal—the worker reproducing himself, objectifying himself to himself, in work.[1] In my first chapter I suggested how the language act might be seen as analogous to the deed, making words and deeds (or work) similar activities. Lawrence makes the ultimate criticism of God as the worker, and the Word as mere work.

If Lawrence eschews God as a model for the artist, then the Word no longer can be a model for the writer's language. In Lawrence's devaluation of the Word can best be seen the tradition's final moment. We can measure the distance we have come by realizing that the passage I quoted in my second chapter from St. Augustine on Isaiah 40:8, which seemed appropriate enough to Wordsworth, is Lawrence's point of departure for the criticism of the Word:

> I don't believe in any dazzling revelation, or in any supreme Word. "The grass withereth, the flower fadeth, but the Word of the Lord shall stand for ever!" That's the kind of stuff we've drugged ourselves with. As a matter of fact, the grass withereth but comes up all the greener for that reason, after the rains. The flower fadeth, and therefore the bud opens. But the Word of the Lord, being man-uttered and a mere vibration on the ether, becomes staler and staler, more and more boring, till at last we turn a deaf ear and it ceases to exist, far more finally than any withered grass. It is grass that renews youth like the eagle, not any Word. (*PP*, 536)

Wordsworth's dream of the algorithm of language that finds its parallel in geometric symbols (while both Yeats and Lawrence devalue algebraic language) suggests a permanent and stable language, based on the Word of God, or at least on the men who hold daily communion with nature (Nature as God's Book). This is not to say that Wordsworth had no sense of the arbitrary associations words build up; indeed, perhaps no poet had a better sense, and his poetic theory, as Josephine Miles has shown in her pioneering study of Wordsworth's vocabulary, is presented as a solution to the problems of associationism: "the solution of the problem was to use in poetry those words which meant the same to the greatest number of persons over the greatest length of time. They composed the real language of real men because they were common in meaning to all common men; they had not the petty versatility of specialized speech: *Tree, mountain, shepherd,* would be such words; and *love, joy, fear, tear, heart,* and *nature, heaven, good, duty*; they are names of familiar phenomena, not deeply analyzed but taken in their general aspects."

It is, of course, just such a vocabulary that Lawrence criticizes: he claims that "the individual may sometimes be capable of truth, and humanity is a tree of lies" (*WL,* 118-19). "Love," the single word used more than any other by Wordsworth,[2] stands out in these lists of common words for obvious reasons: Wordsworth uses it with apparent ease, over and over again, to name a familiar phenomenon, while Lawrence devotes a novel to its definition. Now few critics have advanced Miles's work, and while I still may remain suspicious as to how unrevolutionary Wordsworth's vocabulary is—she concedes only that a word like "imagination," for example, is given in Wordsworth's poetry a "wider meaning" than before, and William Empson's elaborate attempt to show that "sense" is redefined in Wordsworth ends unsuccessfully with his throwing his hands up at what he sees as the muddle of Wordsworth's vocabulary[3]—I can agree that Wordsworth's poetic theory is plainly based on the belief in, and search after, a permanent language; the logocentric Arab dream and the preface make that much clear. For Lawrence such a language is a lie. In Lawrence's provocative understanding of lying, the lie becomes not any inconsistency or self-contradiction, but just the opposite. The lie is the Word, the absolute language that has no context. Lawrence can say, "My yea! of today is oddly different from my yea! of yesterday" (*PP,* 536), and know that this is not lying. He seeks, not a permanent language that is based on the unchanging, but a language that is capable of being perpetually renewed because it lives a life as active and contradictory as that of nature itself.

What I have shown as characteristic of Lawrence's vocabulary all along is also true of his understanding of the Word. There is no stable definition of the Word for Lawrence. The devaluation of the traditional Word is managed, first, through direct criticism, as in the passage just quoted on the rich life of the grass and the Word's staleness, and second, through the more typical Lawrencean mode of redefinition. In *Twilight in Italy,* for example, Lawrence first uses the term in the way we might expect: it is defined periphrastically in its conjunction with "the self-abnegation and the abstraction of Christ," "towards the elimination of the flesh," and "pure abstraction": "the Word was absolute" (34). Later, in the same volume, it epitomizes the exact opposite, the Blakean tiger rather than the meek dove: "The Word of the tiger is: my senses are supremely Me, and my senses are God in me" (39). These changes that Lawrence makes the unchanging Word undergo must be the most symbolic transformation of language—the unmoving Word that moves all things into life and harmony becomes, in Lawrence's vocabulary, not the *primum mobile,* but itself a moving vehicle carrying whatever meaning Lawrence chooses.

Lawrence is puzzled by the fact that humanity's word, unlike the tiger's, seems a rejection of the flesh. Having in mind the Fourth Gospel's concept of the Word made Flesh, he writes: "Myself, I am mystified at this horror over a mere word, a plain simple word that stands for a plain simple thing. 'In the beginning was the Word, and the Word was God and the Word was with God.' If that is true, then we are very far from the beginning. When did the Word 'fall': when did the Word become unclean below the navel?" (*PP,* 280). In fact, Lawrence takes the idea in a direction away from the New Testament. In an oblique reference to the Stoic terminology of the *logos spermatikos,*[4] Lawrence writes: "I lie in the womb of my times, to receive the quickening, the impetus, I send forth all my calls and call hither and thither, asking for the Word, the Word which is the spermatozoon which shall come and fertilize me and set me free. And it may be the word, the idea exists which shall bring me forth, give me birth. But it may also be that the word, the idea, has never been uttered" (433–34). The word as spermatozoon is Lawrence's clearest indication of the dual nature of intercourse—as discourse and love.

Finally, the old Word is redefined into the new word (significantly uncapitalized, but bearing the creative power of the traditional Word) that is a call to the flesh:

> Shall I tell you again the new word,
> the new word of the unborn day?
> It is Resurrection.
> The resurrection of the flesh.
>
> For our flesh is dead
> only egoistically we assert ourselves.
>
> And the new word means nothing to us,
> it is such an old word,
> till we admit how dead we are,
> till we actually feel as blank as we really are.

(*C,* 1, 513)

I have already shown, however, that even the Word decapitated, made a call to the flesh, is a foolproof protection against neither insidious lies nor an ineluctable blankness.

THE ECHO

The Word dwindles into the echo; actually the echo becomes its criticism. Kierkegaard, for example, seems to invoke this critical aspect of the echo as a positive power: "Echo, yes Echo, thou great master of irony! You who parody in yourself the highest and deepest on earth: the Word which created the world, since you merely give the contour not the fullness."[5] Another way of surveying the tradition that is the subject of this book is to examine briefly the trope of the echo, both as a devaluation of the Word and as a masterful form of irony.

The echo, by its very nature, must always stand in comparison to something else (in Kierkegaard's example, for instance, it stands next to the Word). I want to make a similar comparison—to see Echo as a Muse, placed beside Milton's Muse. Urania is invoked by Milton at the opening of the seventh book of *Paradise Lost* to give divine instruction, but the invocation has a subtler, more technical function in the structure of the book: the central action of book 7, the creation, is anticipated by Milton's addresses to Urania: "Voice divine," "Thou with Eternal Wisdom didst converse," "Say Goddess." In this way the reader is prepared to see the creation take place through the Word by recognizing the Muse's verbal powers, and thereby he is prepared to see Milton's authorship in the light of the "Author . . . of all things" (even Milton's choice of the seventh book in which to tell of the six days of work and the seventh day of rest reminds the reader, of course, of the meaningful coincidence of verbal authorship).[6] The Muse then is the power of the Word; she is the gift not only of divine inspiration, but also of divine creation.

I emphasize Urania's role here because, after all, this seventh book of *Paradise Lost* is, appropriately, the book that has stood behind what I have called the common topography from Wordsworth to Lawrence, and if a divine Urania has been less in evidence in these writers than Milton's text might lead one to expect, something like the voice of Echo has been heard. Ovid reveals that it is precisely this kind of landscape that Echo haunts: I think of the empty places I have described—Forster's caves, Lawrence's Alps, the seascapes of Wordsworth's Arab dream and of Yeats's early Shepherd poems, the rocky caverns of Keats's Hyperions. I wish to see Echo as another kind of Muse, not like Urania, the representation of the Word, but rather a Muse who represents, ironically, some devaluation of the Word. She sits, less grand than Urania, mourning absence. No guide herself to heavenly heights, she inhabits all lonely and desert places, and is a sign of the poet's isolation, of the self's desire for the other. She seems to represent, for these reasons, verbal power gone awry: hers is a (case)history that shows the juncture between madness and impaired speech. Keats describes her this way in "Endymion":

Or 'tis the cell of Echo, where she sits,
And babbles thorough silence, till her wits
Are gone in tender madness, and anon,
Faints into sleep, with many a dying tone
Of sadness.

(PW, 78)

Here she is no cure for madness, but is madness itself, readable through
a distorted language: her babbling (clearly the mythic sign of the tragedy
of language, namely, the Tower of Babel) seems at once to echo through
a silence it cannot fill (it is not the creative Word able to fill the blank
world) and to be that very silence (precisely because it is no language).
One must remember that the myth of Echo and Narcissus (like that of
Pan and Syrinx, for example, or any number of other myths of unhappy
love) is a consistent thread through "Endymion." A reading of the poem
could show that the young poet sought a personal myth in these classical
stories, and that Echo and Narcissus was an alternative to Endymion and
Cynthia, and in fact might have been chosen by the more mature poet.
The narrator of the poem, travelling the paths of love and poesy, always
sees these lovers from classical mythology as doubles for himself. In this
happy romance, Endymion's winning of Cynthia reproduces the poet's
access to the Word; the winning of Cynthia, "that completed form of
all completeness" (70), is, after all, analogous to the poet's winning
his 4,000 lines. It will not be long, however, before the myth of Echo
becomes the poet's model.

I am suggesting, then, that as early as "Endymion" the figure of
Echo is contemplated by Keats as a figure for the poet, or the poet's
Muse. In fact, he does picture the echo, in "Sleep and Poetry," as the
only poetic act the young poet is perhaps capable of:

O Poesy! for thee I hold my pen
That am not yet a glorious denizen
Of thy wide heaven—Should I rather kneel
Upon some mountain-top until I feel
A glowing splendour round about me hung,
And echo back the voice of thine own tongue?

(PW, 43)

Echo here is depicted as the echo of Poesy, and thereby becomes also
an echo of the current view of literary history as anxiety over influence,
over priority. The young poet seems dwarfed by his poetic inheritance,
and is about to shrink into mere (verbal) echoes of his masters. Echo
provides a mimetic function, but once removed: she is Poesy's poor
relation, and does not copy life, but copies the copy. She is a weak and
slavish Muse: Ovid describes how the young nymph wastes away until

she is nothing but a voice, and Yeats describes, as I have shown, the infirmity of the young poet's Muse. She does not, like Urania, take the poet into originality, into things yet unattempted in prose or rhyme, but into the shadowy cave of copies. In this way she appropriately sings, not for the triumphant God of *Paradise Lost,* but for the fallen gods. In fact, Coelus's plaint in "Hyperion," "I am but a voice" (*PW,* 229), is, of course, Echo's cry. God's Word, or at least this fallen god's Word, turns out to be just an echo, and Echo becomes the Muse of a poet who lives in a godless world where, in the desert void, his words quite naturally produce echo after echo.

The story of Echo and Narcissus, however, is neither just the mournful story of tragic love, nor even the desperate representation of the Word's inadequacy—indeed, already in Kierkegaard's brief depiction of Echo there is some delight in a form of irony yet to be uncovered. There is, then, another way of looking at Echo in which she does become a Muse of more powerful gifts. We must realize that, for a tradition based on the kind of ironic self-reflection I have been describing in this book, the myth of Echo and Narcissus is a complicated meditation on the relationship between self and other, where Narcissus takes his own words for another's (Ovid is careful to explain that Echo's words are, of course, only Narcissus's, and that the young boy mistakes them for another's, for the Other's); where Narcissus takes for another's his own image; and where Echo's own words are necessarily always another's. Echo comes as a warning to all writers; she knows full well the dangers of narcissism, having directly suffered its consequences herself, and therefore she is the spirit of critique, a muse of irony. She shows a self-consciousness that is barren (Narcissus), but at the same time she prepares the way for a self-consciousness that is a healthy self-criticism: Narcissus ironically represents the tragedy both of knowing oneself too well and of not knowing oneself at all, of having too little distance on oneself and having too much. Indeed, in these very opposites—or in the basic opposition between Echo and Narcissus themselves, where he is all self and she all other—lies the most potent aspect of echo, namely, the power of dialectic, of criticism, of self-criticism. Echo is like the spirit of error (in Hegel) that already seems the first step to truth: she is the spirit of negation—the spirit of the slave, of desire, of error—and she becomes, in this way, the power of irony. I am suggesting a Hegelian transformation of the notion of echo (even that the myth itself contains within it the seeds for such a metamorphosis) so that the idea of echo is at once canceled, preserved, and transcended. In this way Echo is invoked by Kierkegaard, and is the power that Nietzsche both fears and draws strength from: "Those who live alone do not speak too loud nor write too loud, for they fear the hollow echo—the critique of the nymph Echo."[7] She is a check on all writers, ready to find in them the hollow word, the vain and self-serving speech.

The echo is often too simply seen as a mere repetition, so that Echo becomes an exact replica, rather than a mirror image, if you will, of Narcissus (the myth itself contains echo within echo). But the kind of double consciousness that is the hallmark of Kierkegaard's philosophy depends on a different notion of repetition and on a different notion of the echo. As the spirit of irony, Echo's repetition always changes the intent or effect of the originating words. This can be seen in the myth itself, where Echo is able, through the repetition of Narcissus's words, to change the intent, and thereby the consequences, of his words. And it can be seen in Kierkegaard's example: "Yes, Echo, you whom I once heard chastize a nature lover when he exclaimed: 'Hear yonder, the lonesome flute tones of a lovelorn nightingale' [*Nattergal*]—and you answered: 'Mad' [*gal*]."[8] This power of irony in Echo, a power to move repetition (and a narcissistic fixation on the self) toward difference (and self-criticism), is in fact part of the verbal nature of the echo: it is clear, not only in Ovid's narrative or Kierkegaard's example, but also in such modern literary uses of the idea as Hopkins's "The Leaden Echo and the Golden Echo" or, perhaps more to the point because it shows the echo as the force of irony in the mind's reflection on itself, in Yeats's "The Man and the Echo." This latter poem shows how the idea of the echo becomes transcended in a writer's work: for the young poet of the Shepherd poems the echo was merely a solipsistic prison (and the poet himself, in his verbal echoes of such masters as Blake and Shelley, merely an echo of Poesy), while in this late poem the Echo has deeper and more powerful effects on the mind's dialogue with itself. By repeating the author, the echo turns his thought around, reconstitutes it, and shows him a second and third meaning in what he has said. The echo is a restless verbal form that does not cease to reflect back on itself; Forster explains that echoes engender echoes. The echo tolerates no final Hegelian synthesis. For this reason my chapters have refused to bring to a close the writer's conception of his strategy against the subterfuge of art. Just as a strategy is realized by an author, it must be criticized, opened to the critique of Echo, who institutes what I have called the skeptical underthought of the text, the echo in which any solution of the word's is questioned. "[T]he business of art is never to solve. . . ." (*PP*, 461). To quarrel with ourselves, to criticize our own speculations, is to learn a lesson from Echo, who reveals that the Truth is a fiction, and teaches a finer reading of the artist as liar.

NOTES

CHAPTER 1

1. Sigmund Freud, *The Origins of Psycho-Analysis,* ed. Marie Bonaparte, Anna Freud, and Ernst Kris, and trans. Eric Mosbacher and James Strachey (New York: Basic Books, Inc., 1954), pp. 165, 166.

2. Jacques Lacan, *The Language of the Self,* trans. Anthony Wilden (New York: Dell Publishing Co., 1968), p. 21. Also see Wilden's helpful commentary on this point, p. 109.

3. There is a wide divergence of opinion on Freud's view of art. Philip Rieff's popular position is that what the artist does is "regressive," "childish," and "escapist," and that "the work of art is something to see through; it is presumably best explained by something other than— even contradicting—itself" (introduction to *Delusion and Dream* [Boston: Beacon Press, 1965], pp. 10–11). This last statement is particularly interesting because, as we have seen, Lawrence defines art as the internalizing of this criticism, so that the artist becomes self-critical, but in Rieff's view of Freud "the artist, like the religious man, has no critical aptitude" (p. 14). Paul Ricoeur, on the other hand, makes the case for the work of art's being at once the symptom and the cure (*Freud and Philosophy,* trans. Denis Savage [New Haven: Yale University Press, 1970], p. 174).

4. Sigmund Freud, *The Standard Edition of the Complete Psychological Works of Sigmund Freud,* ed. and trans. James Strachey, 24 vols. (London: Hogarth Press, 1968), 5:548.

5. Ibid., 20:187–88.

6. Søren Kierkegaard, *Søren Kierkegaard's Journals and Papers,* ed. and trans. Howard V. Hong and Edna H. Hong, 4 vols. to date (Bloomington: Indiana University Press, 1967), 1:261.

7. Ludwig Wittgenstein, *Philosophical Investigations,* trans. G. E. M. Anscombe (New York: Macmillan Co., 1958), p. 146e.

8. Lacan, *The Language of the Self,* pp. 34–35.

9. Freud, *Complete Works of Freud,* 21:49.

10. See Freud, "Creative Writers and Day-Dreaming," in *Complete Works of Freud,* 9: 141–54.

11. Freud, *Complete Works of Freud,* 12:108.

12. Freud, *Complete Works of Freud,* 5:553.

13. Ibid., 5:548–49.

14. Ricoeur, *Freud and Philosophy,* p. 474.

15. Freud, *Complete Works of Freud,* 22:57.

16. Ibid., 16:435 and 13:176.

17. Ibid., 13:177.

18. See Freud's essay "Analysis Terminable and Interminable," in *Complete Works of Freud,* 23:209–53.

19. Søren Kierkegaard, *Kierkegaard's Concluding Unscientific Postscript,* trans. David. F. Swenson and Walter Lowrie (Princeton: Princeton University Press, 1963), p. 79.

20. Freud, *Complete Works of Freud,* 21:54.

CHAPTER 2

1. All references, if not otherwise designated, are to the 1850 text of the poem.

2. R. D. Havens, *The Mind of a Poet* (Baltimore: Johns Hopkins Press, 1941), p. 376.

3. See Joel Morkan, "Structure and Meaning in *The Prelude,* Book V," *PMLA* 87 (1972): 246-53; and Evelyn Shakir, "Books, Death, and Immortality: A Study of Book V of *The Prelude,"* *Studies in Romanticism* 8 (1969): 156-67.

4. Jane Worthington Smyser, "Wordsworth's Dream of Poetry and Science: *The Prelude,* V," *PMLA* 71 (1956): 269-75.

5. See *P,* p. 540.

6. Havens, *Mind of a Poet,* p. 375.

7. See sec. 23 of Plato's *Timaeus,* trans. H. D. P. Lee (Baltimore: Penguin Books, 1965), p. 35.

8. See John Milton, *Paradise Lost,* 7.211-12. This, and all other references to Milton, are to *John Milton: Complete Poems and Major Prose,* ed. Merritt Y. Hughes (New York: Odyssey Press, 1957). There are significant Miltonic echoes throughout book 5. See, for example, Wordsworth's description of modern educators as

> These mighty workmen of our later age,
> Who, with a broad highway have overbridged
> The froward chaos of futurity,
> Tamed to their bidding.
> (5.347-50)

The passage clearly echoes Milton's Argument to book 10, where Sin and Death build a similar bridge.

9. For an interesting account of the idea of the creative word in primitive myths, see Ernst Cassirer, *Language and Myth,* trans. Susanne K. Langer (New York: Dover Publications, 1946): "In the creation accounts of almost all great cultural religions, the Word appears in league with the highest Lord of creation; either as the tool which he employs or actually as the primary source from which he, like all other Being and order of Being, is derived" (pp. 45-46).

10. For a comprehensive survey of this trope, see Ernst Robert Curtius, *European Literature and the Latin Middle Ages,* trans. Willard R. Trask, Bollingen Series 36 (New York: Pantheon, 1953), pp. 319-26.

11. See, for example, Geoffrey Hartman, *Wordsworth's Poetry: 1787-1814* (New Haven: Yale University Press, 1967), p. 228. For a more general use of the concept, see W. G. Stobie, "A Reading of *The Prelude,* Book V," *Modern Language Quarterly* 24 (1963): 365-73.

12. See bk. XIII, sec. 15 of St. Augustine's *Confessions,* trans. R. S. Pine-Coffin (Baltimore: Penguin, 1961), p. 323. For a general account of Christianity's contribution to the trope of the book, see Curtius, *European Literature,* pp. 310-15.

13. I draw attention to the word "subsist" here not only because it is a significant thread that unites nature and books, but also because it carries with it the center of a well-known philosophical debate that Wordsworth was clearly aware of. Wordsworth seems to be altering the Lockean notion of "material substance" by arguing that an order of mind—variously defined by him as "love," a "deathless spirit," "the sovereign Intellect," and the Word—is the sustainer of all matter. See John Locke, *An Essay Concerning Human Understanding,* ed. Peter Nidditch (Oxford: Clarendon Press, 1975), bk. II, chaps. 23-24. Also see George Berkeley's argument against Locke, that all matter "must either have no existence at all or else *subsist* in the mind of some eternal spirit" (*The Principles of Human Knowledge and Three Dialogues,* G. J. Warnock [Cleveland: World Publishing Company, 1963], sec. 6, emphasis added; see also secs. 7-10 and 16-17).

14. For an excellent discussion of this, see Ernst Cassirer, *The Philosophy of Symbolic Forms,* trans. Ralph Manheim, 3 vols. (New Haven: Yale University Press, 1953), 1:127-32.

15. For examples, see Curtius, *European Literature,* p. 324.

16. On this idea of poetry as a primal or primitive language, the reader should see, under the "Noten und Ubhandlungen" to his *West-östlicher Divan* (*Goethes Werke,* 14 vols. [Hamburg: Christian Wegner Verlag, 1949]), Goethe's short note on "Orientalischer Poesie Urelemente," in which he describes, in terms remarkably close to Wordsworth's, the primordial elements of oriental poetry. He explains how the wandering Bedouin's language consists of relatively few stem words and root words unrelated to the small number of natural objects (camel and horse, mountain and desert, river and sea) that surround him, and how these primary expressions of

nature undergo a series of minor variations to become poetic language. Cf. Wordsworth's explanation, in the preface, that he has adopted the language of rural men "because such men hourly communicate with the best objects from which the best part of language is originally derived" (*WPW*, 735).

17. See Hartman, *Wordsworth's Poetry*, pp. 19-22, 231-32.

18. Modern language theory postulates a development very close to the one I am suggesting. See Cassirer: "In general, language can be shown to have passed through three stages in maturing to its specific form, in achieving its inner freedom. . . . The beginnings of phonetic language seem to be embedded in that sphere of mimetic representation and designation which lies at the base of sign language. Here the sound seeks to approach the sensory impression and reproduce its diversity as faithfully as possible. This striving plays an important part in the speech both of children and 'primitive' peoples" (*Symbolic Forms*, p. 190). Cassirer goes on to describe "analogical" expression (what I have called Wordsworth's attempt to reveal and describe, not simply mimic, the external order beyond him), and concludes by explaining how "mimetic or analogical expression gives way to purely symbolic expression, which, precisely in and by virtue of its otherness, becomes the vehicle of a new and deeper spiritual content" (p. 197).

19. See "I. A. Richards and the Dream of Communication," in Geoffrey Hartman, *The Fate of Reading and Other Essays* (Chicago: University of Chicago Press, 1975), pp. 20-40.

CHAPTER 3

On the epigraph to this chapter, see Robert Gittings, *The Mask of Keats: A Study of Problems* (Cambridge, Mass.: Harvard University Press, 1956), p. 156. Appendix A, devoted to Keats's markings in his copy of the *Inferno*, shows Keats consistently underlining, often with three and four lines, those passages in Dante that deal with speech and language.

1. Joseph Anthony Wittreich, Jr., *The Romantics on Milton* (Cleveland: Press of Case Western Reserve University, 1970), pp. 557-59.

2. Ibid., pp. 558, 553.

3. Ibid., p. 553.

4. Ibid., p. 560, on *Paradise Lost* 9.179-91.

5. This is quoted in Robert Gittings, *John Keats* (Boston: Little, Brown, and Co., 1968), p. 187, where he discusses Keats's attendance at the lecture "On Shakespeare and Milton," from which the quotation is taken.

6. John Milton, *Complete Poems and Major Prose*, p. 350.

7. Martin Heidegger, *Existence and Being* (Chicago: Henry Regnery Co., 1967), p. 363.

CHAPTER 4

1. See M. R. Ridley, *Keats' Craftsmanship: A Study in Poetic Development* (Lincoln: University of Nebraska Press, 1963), p. 180, for the revised ending:

> Angela went off
> Twitch'd by the palsy—and with face deform
> The Beadsman stiffen'd—'twixt a sigh and laugh
> Ta'en sudden from his beads by one weak little cough.

2. See Herbert G. Wright, "Has Keats's 'Eve of St. Agnes' a Tragic Ending?," *Modern Language Review* 40 (1945): 90-94, who argues specifically for a tragic ending. See also Jack Stillinger, "The Hoodwinking of Madeline: Scepticism in *The Eve of St. Agnes*," *Studies in Philology* 58 (1961), which suggests that a kind of irony is at work throughout the poem and culminates in the dark conclusion. See also John Bayley's brief remarks in *Keats and Reality*

(Folcroft, Pa.: Folcroft, 1962), where he suggests that at the end the lovers die ("join the vast hosts of the dead," p. 33).

3. There is a long tradition of criticism that views the poem as an optimistic romance. The following are distinguished examples: Newell F. Ford, *The Prefigurative Imagination of John Keats* (Stanford: Stanford University Press, 1951); Earl R. Wasserman, *The Finer Tone: Keats' Major Poems* (Baltimore: Johns Hopkins University Press, 1967); R. A. Foakes, *The Romantic Assertion* (New Haven: Yale University Press, 1958).

4. See Stillinger, "Hoodwinking of Madeline," pp. 533–55.

5. Stuart M. Sperry, Jr., "Romance as Wish-Fulfillment: Keats's *The Eve of St. Agnes,*" *Studies in Romanticism* 10 (1971): 27–43.

6. See Marian H. Cusac's brief article, "Keats as Enchanter: An Organizing Principle of *The Eve of St. Agnes,*" *Keats-Shelley Journal* 17 (1968): 113–19. See also Sperry, "Romance as Wish-Fulfillment," which is suggestive on this question, but neglects to distinguish Keats from the narrator and therefore never finally allows the narrator to emerge as a distinct and central force in the poem. Also, by neglecting to make this distinction, Sperry fails to see the significant limitations in the narrator's point of view, and thereby the poem's darker ironies.

7. See Freud, "Creative Writers and Day-Dreaming," in *Complete Works of Freud,* 9:141–54.

8. Sperry, "Romance as Wish-Fulfillment," p. 40.

9. See Amy Lowell, *John Keats,* 2 vols. (Boston: Houghton Mifflin Co., 1925), 2:173.

10. See John Donne, "The First Anniversary," in *The Complete Poetry of John Donne,* ed. John T. Shawcross (Garden City, N.Y.: Doubleday, 1967), l. 180.

11. Sperry speaks of the lovers' transcendence ("Romance as Wish-Fulfillment," p. 41), and Wright and Bayley of their death. See Miriam Allott, " 'Isabella,' 'The Eve of St. Agnes,' and 'Lamia,' " in *John Keats: A Reassessment,* ed. Kenneth Muir (Liverpool: Liverpool University Press, 1969), p. 56, for the suggestion that the lovers enter a world of difficulty and danger. See also Amy Lowell, who perceptively (if somewhat sentimentally) suggests that the lovers escape "not into a live-happy-ever-after kind of existence, but into the stress and storm of a future which at least they face side by side" (*John Keats,* 2:175). Earl Wasserman seems headed toward a similar conclusion when he quotes the Mansion of Many Apartments letter on man's inevitable entrance into a world full of misery and pain (*Finer Tone,* pp. 117–23). In the end, however, the lovers' love is all bliss, the storm is simply an elfin storm, and Mr. Wasserman never does show us the lovers' entrance into a world of difficulty. This is a serious problem in an otherwise excellent interpretation of the poem.

CHAPTER 5

1. See, for example, Yeats's remark about "The Cap and Bells": "The poem has always meant a great deal to me, though, as is the way with symbolic poems, it has not always meant quite the same thing" (*CPY,* 449).

2. All quotations from the two Shepherd poems and "Nineteen Hundred and Nineteen" are from W. B. Yeats, *Collected Poems of W. B. Yeats* (New York: Macmillan and Co., 1966), pp. 7–9 and 204–8, respectively.

3. William Blake, *Blake: Complete Writings,* ed. Geoffrey Keynes (Oxford: Oxford University Press, 1969), p. 210.

4. Percy Bysshe Shelley, *The Complete Poetical Works of Percy Bysshe Shelley,* ed. Thomas Hutchinson (London: Oxford University Press, 1961), p. 458.

5. Ibid., pp. 23–24.

6. See M. H. Abrams, *The Mirror and the Lamp* (New York: W. W. Norton and Co., 1958), p. 51.

7. Samuel Taylor Coleridge, *Coleridge: Poetical Works,* ed. Ernest Hartley Coleridge (London: Oxford University Press, 1967), pp. 101–2.

8. See A. Norman Jeffares, *A Commentary on the Collected Poems of W. B. Yeats* (Stanford: Stanford University Press, 1968), p. 281.

9. We must largely rethink the kind of blanket generalizations critics have made about Yeats's rage for order. See, for example, Helen Vendler's claim, "At all cost, Yeats would insist, the illusion of control must be preserved" (*Yeats' Vision and the Later Plays* [Cambridge, Mass.: Harvard University Press, 1963], p. 121). It is interesting that Vendler supports her claim with a quotation from Stevens, not Yeats. The question is not whether or not Yeats always sought order and control: the prose is plentiful enough with remarks to the contrary, not to mention the poetry's violent and destructive images and visions. It is whether or not the search for the ecstatic moment, or for the loss of control, is possible in a systematic thinker or in the orderly world of poetry. "Nineteen Hundred and Nineteen" attempts an antisystematic systematization, if you will, not unlike Nietzsche's philosophy of ironies and contradictions. Do we see "Nineteen Hundred and Nineteen" as an ironic comment on the systems of *Per Amica* and *A Vision,* or are these prose works attempts to systematize even the Vision of Evil? We will meet with a similar attempt (and perhaps an even more successful one) when we see Forster incorporate the vision of evil, and nihilistic vision in general, within the formal bounds of art.

10. Friedrich Nietzsche, *The Complete Works of Friedrich Nietzsche,* ed. Oscar Levy, 18 vols. (Edinburgh: T. N. Foulis, 1909-13), vol. 17, p. 54.

CHAPTER 6

1. See Brenda S. Webster, *Yeats: A Psychoanalytic Study* (Stanford: Stanford University Press, 1973), p. 107, for whom the passage is important, but who misreads it by claiming that the "hollow image of fulfilled desire" is the product only of happy art.

2. Daniel Albright, *The Myth Against Myth: A Study of Yeats's Imagination in Old Age* (London: Oxford University Press, 1972), p. 84; Thomas Parkinson, *W. B. Yeats: Self-Critic and The Later Poetry (Two Volumes in One)* (Berkeley and Los Angeles: University of California Press, 1971), p. 62 in *The Later Poetry;* J. R. Mulryne, "The 'Last Poems,'" in *An Honoured Guest: New Essays on W. B. Yeats,* ed. Denis Donoghue and J. R. Mulryne (New York: St. Martin's Press, 1966), p. 132 n.

3. Parkinson, *Yeats,* p. 62.

4. Sir James George Frazer, *The Golden Bough,* abridged ed. (New York: Macmillan Co., 1963), p. 389.

5. Ibid., p. 394.

6. Ibid., p. 391.

7. Shelley, *Complete Poetical Works of Shelley,* p. 434.

8. Jane Harrison, *Epilegomena to the Study of Greek Religion* and *Themis* (New York: University Books, 1966), p. xlvi.

9. Ibid., p. 447.

10. Ibid., p. 468.

11. Northrop Frye, "The Rising of the Moon: A Study of *A Vision,*" in *An Honoured Guest,* p. 9.

12. Ibid., p. 32.

13. Ibid., p. 29.

14. Ibid., p. 32.

15. See Gilbert Murray, "Excursus on the Ritual Forms preserved in Greek Tragedy," in Harrison, pp. 341-63.

16. Friedrich Nietzsche, *The Birth of Tragedy and The Genealogy of Morals,* trans. Francis Golffing (New York: Doubleday and Co., 1956), p. 65.

17. Ibid., p. 58.

18. Ibid., p. 67.

19. Ibid., p. 103.

20. Friedrich Nietzsche, *The Portable Nietzsche,* trans. Walter Kaufmann (New York: Viking Press, 1965), p. 458.

CHAPTER 7

1. The chapter "*A Passage to India* and the Critics" in June Perry Levine's *Creation and Criticism: A Passage to India* (Lincoln: University of Nebraska Press, 1971) is still the best guide (through 1971) to the wavering critical opinions on the novel in general, and offers many examples of characters serving as the model for our attention.

2. See the ending of Shelley's *The Sensitive Plant,* in *Complete Poetical Works of Shelley,* p. 596.

3. See, for example, Ferdinand de Saussure, *Course in General Linguistics,* ed. Charles Bally and Albert Sechehaye and trans. Wade Baskin (New York: McGraw-Hill, 1966), p. 120. Also see my chapter 8 on *Women in Love,* especially n. 3.

4. Francis Bacon, *Francis Bacon: Essays, Advancement of Learning, New Atlantis, and Other Pieces,* ed. Richard Foster Jones (New York: Odyssey Press, 1937), p. 279.

5. Forster, well-read in Shelley, must have in mind Shelley's use of this dramatic triad in "Epipsychidion," in *Complete Poetical Works of Shelley,* p. 424.

6. The formlessness of the Hindu ceremony, for example, disqualifies it from being beautiful: it "fling[s] down science and history . . . yes, beauty herself" (*PI,* 288). Fielding, attempting to make Aziz write poetry not of simple pathos (however beautiful), hesitantly tells him, "There is something in religion that may not be true, but has not yet been sung." It has not yet been sung, he goes on to say, because "Hindus are unable to sing" (277), or, to put it in more typical esthetic terms, Hindus are not able to articulate, or give form to, their experience. See also *AN,* 88, for the requirement of beauty in the novel or, more to the point, pp. 163-64, where Forster explains how beauty, proceeding from pattern, is liable to become rigid and untrue, and to shut the doors on life.

7. See Northrop Frye, *Anatomy of Criticism* (New York: Atheneum, 1966), pp. 303-14.

8. I have chosen to quote not Theodor W. Adorno's *Negative Dialectics,* trans. E. B. Ashton (New York: Seabury Press, 1973), but Frederic Jameson's analysis of Adorno's book in *Marxism and Form: Twentieth-Century Dialectical Theories of Literature* (Princeton: Princeton University Press, 1971), p. 56, because Adorno's work does not lend itself to short excerpts, while Jameson has brilliantly and concisely captured its meaning.

9. See, for example, Michel Foucault's *The Archaeology of Knowledge,* trans. A. M. Sheridan Smith (New York: Random House, 1972), or *The Order of Things: An Archaeology of the Human Sciences* (New York: Random House, 1970).

10. Friedrich Nietzsche, *The Will to Power,* ed. Walter Kaufmann and trans. Walter Kaufmann and R. J. Hollingdale (New York: Random House, 1968), p. 266.

CHAPTER 8

1. Colin Clarke's *River of Dissolution: D. H. Lawrence and English Romanticism* (London: Routledge and Kegan Paul, 1969) is the only notable exception here, but even his study is too tentative on the verbal techniques in the novel. His major point—"It is never safe to assume (as critics habitually do assume) that what is being said about destructiveness and corruption on the surface is *all* that is being said; almost certainly, beneath the surface, significant qualifications are being made" (p. 71)—never quite reaches a level of stylistic analysis that is precise and comprehensive. He names the verbal ambiguity he notices "the rhetoric of corruption": "The disintegrative processes are beautiful, and also obscene" (p. 84).

2. M. Merleau-Ponty, *Phenomenology of Perception*, trans. Colin Smith (London: Routledge & Kegan Paul, 1962), p. 388.

3. See, for example, the influential statement, "in language there are only differences," in Saussure, *General Linguistics*, p. 120. Nietzsche sees language as lying, precisely because it is unable to make differentiations, that is, because it is based on equality. Using equality not simply as a moral or social category but also as a linguistic one, he explains how in language "every concept originates through our equating what is unequal" (Nietzsche, *Portable Nietzsche*, p. 46). Roman Jakobson and Morris Halle, on the other hand, continue Saussure's work by showing that language originates not in equalities, or even in similarities, but in differences: all phonemes "denote nothing but mere otherness" (*Fundamentals of Language* [The Hague: Mouton, 1956], p. 11). It is interesting to note that Lawrence's use of "equal" has behind it Nietzsche's linguistic thrust, and that *Women in Love* suggests that the genuine parts of language exist not through equality but difference (even Jakobson and Halle's explanation of "otherness" reminds one of Lawrence's attempt to discover the other both linguistically and erotically).

4. Michael Riffaterre, "Interpretation and Descriptive Poetry: A Reading of Wordsworth's 'Yew-Trees,'" *New Literary History* 4 (1973): 248.

5. See the crucial third chapter ("Object of Linguistics") in Saussure's introduction, *General Linguistics*, pp. 7-17.

6. M. Merleau-Ponty, *The Prose of the World*, ed. Claude Lefort and trans. John O'Neill (Evanston: Northwestern University Press, 1973), p. 13.

7. Friedrich Nietzsche, *Twilight of the Idols* and *The Anti-Christ*, trans. R. J. Hollingdale (Middlesex, England: Penguin Books, 1974), p. 83; *The Gay Science*, trans. Walter Kaufmann (New York: Random House, 1974), pp. 298-99; *Will to Power*, p. 428.

8. Merleau-Ponty, *Prose of the World*, p. 36.

9. It is interesting to note here that Nietzsche, as late as 1888 in a retrospective glance at his work, has the same thought—"I wish I had written it [the will to power] in French so that it might not appear as a confirmation of any *reichsdeutschen* aspirations"—because he knows that the Germans know only one meaning for "power" (Walter Kaufmann, *Nietzsche: Philosopher, Psychologist, Antichrist* [Princeton: Princeton University Press, 1968], pp. 247-48).

10. Any number of New Testament passages stand behind the clearly Biblical sound of Birkin's statement. Certainly Matt. 12:34, "O generation of vipers, how can ye, being evil, speak good things," is analogous to Birkin's claim that the actions a man performs influence the words he speaks. But more to the point, countless Biblical passages alternate between God's judgment of people based on words on the one hand and on works on the other: "For by thy words thou shalt be justified, and by thy words thou shalt be condemned" (Matt. 12:37); "and then he shall reward every man according to his works" (Matt. 16:27).

11. The relationship between word and deed, which goes back as far as Homer (see the particularly fruitful Biblical version of this relationship in the connection between words and works in note 10), is central throughout Lawrence's career. After *Women in Love*, Lawrence often emphasized the deed over the word (perhaps because he claimed, "Word-perfect we may be, but Deed-demented," *SLC*, 106), and *Lady Chatterley's Lover* becomes, according to Lawrence, a call to the Deed of Life. Lawrence here may have in mind Goethe's famous reversal of the fourth Gospel, "In the beginning was the Deed": "It is no use asking for a Word to fulfill such a need. No Word, no Logos, no Utterance will ever do it. The Word is uttered, most of it; we need only pay true attention to it. But who will call us to the Deed" (*SLC*, 105). I begin Chapter 9 with a full discussion of Lawrence's view of the Word.

12. Both Freud and Lacan use images remarkably similar to Lawrence's to characterize speech. Freud, for example, describes the function of speech in hysteria with the same image used not only by Lawrence, but also by Keats: "[the psychotherapeutic procedure] . . . brings to an end the operative force of the idea which was not abreacted in the first instance, by allowing its strangulated affect to find a way out through speech" (*Complete Works of Freud*, 2:17). It is a description of what I have already characterized, in connection with Keats in my first chapter, as the strangulation of dumb insanity. The true birth of speech (the words finding a way out) occurs also in Lacan's emphasis (following Freud's notion of "durcharbeiten" and the "dream-work") on speech as labor, where, like Lawrence, he has in mind both work and child-

birth. See, for example, *Language of the Self,* p. 10, or p. 56, where the general notion of dialectic (including the dialectic of speech, or dialogue) becomes most explicitly the birth process, "the Socratic maieutics or 'art of midwifery.'"

13. The dismissal of "I" and "you" is easier to accept in the meeting-and-mingling (a criticism Lawrence always levelled against him) of Shelley: "The words *I* and *you,* and *they* are grammatical devices invented simply for arrangement, and totally devoid of the intense and exclusive sense usually attached to them. . . . We are on that verge where words abandon us" (*The Complete Works of Percy Bysshe Shelley,* ed. Roger Ingpen and Walter E. Peck, 10 vols. [New York: Gordian Press, 1965], 6:196). On this matter of the "I," Hegel is crucial, and Alexandre Kojève's influential remarks about him especially underline the Hegelian "I"'s relation to speech: "The (conscious) Desire of a being is what constitutes that being as I and reveals it as such by moving it to say 'I . . .'" (*Introduction to the Reading of Hegel,* ed. Allan Bloom and trans. James H. Nichols, Jr. [New York: Basic Books, 1969], p. 3). See also Kojève's insistence on Speech and Action (what I have been describing in my chapter and in the last three notes as word and deed or action or work) as the two crucial premises of the *Phenomenology* (p. 39). Finally, see Nietzsche, whose whole philosophy is supported by such linguistic underpinnings as his sense of the fiction that there exists an "I" (*Beyond Good and Evil,* trans. Marianne Cowan [Chicago: Henry Regnery Co., 1969], pp. 17–18).

14. See Roman Jakobson's highly influential essay, "Shifters, Verbal Categories, and the Russian Verb," in *Selected Writings,* 4 vols. (The Hague: Mouton, 1971), 2:130–47. See also Otto Jespersen, *Language: Its Nature, Development, and Origin* (New York: W. W. Norton and Co., 1964), pp. 123–24, where Jespersen explains the child's difficulty with shifters and how adults try to obviate such difficulties by speaking of themselves in the third person to children.

15. *The Logic of the Humanities,* trans. Clarence Smith Howe (New Haven: Yale University Press, 1967), pp. 112–13. For a recent essay on this passage in "Flitting," see Garrett Stewart, "Lawrence, 'Being,' and the Allotropic Style," *Novel* 9 (Spring 1976): 237–42, who argues persuasively in support of Birkin's criticism of "I" and "you."

16. See, for example, Plato's *Republic* 427a.

17. This may be something of a simplification. Lawrence does, for example, describe Ursula as childlike in passages that suggest a genuine innocence, a purity that escapes (to use her own words in "Sunday Evening") the ignominy and dirt of this world. It seems to me, however, that this kind of image is always coupled eventually with the desideratum to mature; the child must develop, move forward, and its momentary innocence may lapse (and here the sexual vision in Keats, Yeats, and Lawrence, absent in Wordsworth, is crucial) into sterility and impotence. Clearly, the overwhelming meaning of the child in the novel is one of regression. Lawrence's criticism of the Bohemians' pseudoprimitivism is made in terms of the babyish Minette (her lisp, by the way, is a particularly vivid detail that manages to link linguistic disability to immaturity and childishness); even the genuine primitivism pictured in the African statue where the woman in labor herself looks like a fetus, suggests, if not the evolutionary regression of the Bohemians, a kind of evolutionary stagnation.

18. See Freud, *Complete Works of Freud,* 20:90, where he speaks of "writing, which entails making a liquid flow out of a tube on to a piece of white paper. . . ."

19. See my last chapter for an explanation of the *logos spermatikos.*

CHAPTER 9

1. Karl Marx, *Economic and Philosophic Manuscripts of 1844,* ed. Dirk J. Struik and trans. Martin Milligan (New York: International Publishers, 1964), where he is most clearly influenced by Hegel, but still careful to distinguish between himself and Hegel: "The object of labor is, therefore, the *objectification of man's species life:* for he duplicates himself not only, as in consciousness, intellectually, but also actively, in reality, and therefore he contemplates himself in a world that he has created" (p. 114). We need, eventually, a full reading of romanticism in terms

of such a statement. In fact, T. H. Adamowski ("Being Perfect: Lawrence, Sartre, and *Women in Love,*" *Critical Inquiry* [Winter 1975], pp. 345-68) decries the lack of intellectual context in analyses of Lawrence (and I wholeheartedly agree), and is reduced to comparing him to "a peer" (350), namely, Sartre, because of a strikingly similar vocabulary. But Adamowski neglects to explain that this is a rhetoric that both Lawrence and Sartre inherit from Hegel and Marx. The terminology of desire, and desire's void, which the self seeks to fill; the dialectic of master and slave; the notions of work and valuation, and of a material Nature that needs to be transformed by man, are all crucial strands of the argument of *Women in Love,* and an early essay like "The Crown" is a youthful echoing of whole sections of the *Phenomenology of Mind.* But these delicate relations deserve a full-length essay on Lawrence's revisionism.

The reader should also consult the "Lordship and Bondage" section of Hegel's *Phenomenology* both for Hegel's and Lawrence's starting point on this idea of man's objectification of himself to himself, and for the concept of the transformation of nature through work. Cf. Nietzsche's idea, "In man there is united both *creature* and *creator*" (*Beyond Good and Evil,* p. 151), with the view of Loerke as craftsman and creature.

2. See Josephine Miles, *Wordsworth and the Vocabulary of Emotion* (New York: Octagon Books, 1965), pp. 58 and 18, respectively.

3. Ibid., p. 86, and William Empson, *The Structure of Complex Words* (London: Chatto and Windus, 1951), pp. 289-305.

4. See, for example, *The Stoics, Epicureans, and Sceptics,* ed. and trans. Oswald J. Reichel (New York: Russell and Russell, 1962), p. 172, for the use of the term in various ancient writers, or Edwyn Bevan, *Stoics and Sceptics* (New York: Barnes and Noble, 1959), p. 43, for a brief explanation of the term.

5. Quoted by the translator in his introduction to Søren Kierkegaard, *The Concept of Irony,* trans. Lee M. Capel (Bloomington: Indiana University Press, 1968), p. 23; originally from Kierkegaard's *Papirer,* vol. 1, A, para. 333.

6. Milton, *Complete Poems and Major Prose,* pp. 345-47, 361.

7. Nietzsche, *Gay Science,* p. 203.

8. Kierkegaard, *Concept of Irony,* p. 23.

Library of Congress Cataloging in Publication Data

Ragussis, Michael.
    The subterfuge of art.

    Bibliography: p.
    1. English literature—History and criticism.
2. Psychoanalysis and literature. 3. Romanticism—
England. 4. Creation (Literary, artistic, etc.)
5. Nature (Aesthetics) I. Title.
PR408.P8R3   820'.9'3   78-5845
ISBN 0-8018-2059-6